THE RECOVERY OF SELF

REGRESSION AND REDEMPTION IN RELIGIOUS EXPERIENCE

Kevin Fauteux

PAULIST PRESS

NEW YORK, N.Y. • MAHWAH, N.J.

Acknowledgments
Lines from "Among School Children" and "A Prayer for Old Age" are reprinted with permission of Macmillan Publishing Company from *Collected Poems of W. B. Yeats*, copyright 1928, 1934 by Macmillan Publishing Company, renewed 1956, 1962 by Bertha Georgie Yeats. Excerpts from "Little Gidding" and "East Coker" in *Four Quartets*, copyright 1943 by T. S. Eliot and renewed 1971 by Esme Valerie Eliot, are reprinted by permission of Harcourt Brace & Company.

Library of Congress Cataloging-in-Publication Data

Fauteux, Kevin, 1953–
    The recovery of self: regression and redemption in religious
experience/Kevin Fauteux.
       p. cm.
    Includes bibliographical references and index.
    ISBN 0-8091-3423-3 (pbk.)
    1. Experience (Religion) 2. Regression (Psychology)
3. Adjustment (Psychology)—Religious aspects. 4. Psychoanalysis
and religion. 5. Psychology, Religious. I. Title.
BL53.F27 1994
291.4'2'019—dc20   93-37488
                                                                              CIP

Published by Paulist Press
997 Macarthur Boulevard
Mahwah, New Jersey 07430

Printed and bound in the
United States of America

Man sallies forth into nature only to learn at last that what he seeks he has left behind.

Samuel Taylor Coleridge

I hear, I hear, with joy I hear!
　But there's a Tree, of many, one,
A single Field which I have looked upon,
Both of them speak of something that is
　Gone:
　The Pansy at my feet
　Doth the same tale repeat:
Whither is fled the visionary gleam?
Where is it now, the glory and the dream?
William Wordsworth

Contents

Introduction

OCEANIC EXPERIENCE

This book examines the psychological regression that takes place in religious experience. Some people will take offense at the suggestion that religious experience is a return to primitive psychological processes. Others will say it is obvious. Their differing views can be traced back in this century to the debate between Sigmund Freud and the French philosopher Romain Rolland. In response to Freud's sending him a copy of his *Future of an Illusion*, Rolland agreed that religious belief was an expression of childish needs but asked Freud to consider religious experience separately from belief. Rolland personally had experiences in India that involved a blissful submersion into what he called the "oceanic." What distinguished these experiences, he explained to Freud, from the illusion of religion is that while the latter induced infantile wish fulfillment, the former did not "in any way harm my critical faculties and my freedom to exercise them" (quoted in Fisher, 1967, p. 21).

Freud responded to Rolland by adopting his phrase "oceanic experience" to describe self-surrender and submersion into God, but he described it negatively. Freud suggested that only in the experience of love or in therapeutic transference does a person temporarily erase ego boundaries in merging with another without sacrificing personal identity. Oceanic experience, on the other hand, induces "feelings of an indissoluble bond, of being one with the external world as a whole," that represent a regressive escape from the demands of reality and a return to the selfless state of maternal unity (Freud, 1961d, p. 39).

Readers of the present book who expect allegiance either to Freud or to Rolland will be disappointed. Instead of taking sides, this

1

work examines religious experience from a dialectical perspective that synthesizes insights from these two approaches but also questions their basic assumptions. For example, while finding value in Freud's analysis of the regressive loss of ego and reactivation of primitive processes that take place in religious experience, this book asks why a dismantling of ego boundaries and restoration of archaic processes *repairs* unconscious conflicts when it takes place in therapy or creativity but not when it occurs in religious experience.

Similarly, the following pages question the naive assessment of oceanic experience held by individuals like Rolland. Their understanding of unitive experience might accurately portray people's hunger for greater wholeness but it lacks the psychological sophistication to recognize the unresolved conflicts, the hidden fears, or the childish needs that might unconsciously motivate a person to "lose herself"[1] and experience God. Hence while traditional psychological interpretations will be challenged for their blindness to oceanic experiences that can teach people to "swim," benign images of mysticism will be questioned for idealizing oceanic experiences while failing to acknowledge the unrelenting pull of their undertow.

This work relies heavily on psychoanalytic insights into unconscious processes, especially those that describe dissolution of ego boundaries and a return to undifferentiated psychological structures. To approach religious experience from this perspective will not, as one may first suspect, reduce religious experience to pathological regression. By looking at *what takes place* in the regressive return to unconscious processes—rather than assuming that regression to an oceanic experience is pathological—the reader will understand how the same kind of analysis that has been applied to regressive processes in therapy or art can be applied to regression in religious experience. Just as therapeutic transference restores archaic parental images in order to rework and resolve developmental failures, and just as creativity revives primitive processes so as to reintegrate them on a higher level, so too religious experience *can* restore maternal unity (represented in Nirvana or communion with God) and unneutralized instinctual energy (manifested in ecstasy and visions) in order to confront unresolved conflicts and to synthesize previously repressed instincts.

Religious experience *is* a regression, but a regression that can either be malignant (resulting in pathological disorders ranging from narcissism to psychosis) or "regression in service of the ego" (resulting in the integration of the unconscious processes into higher levels of ego functioning). The task of this work is to demonstrate how regression in religious experience is one or the other. The task begins with an analysis of what makes religious experience regressive. This first section is separated into three chapters examining the three major stages of religious experience. Religions generally present these three stages as (1) purging the sinful or egocentric self. This gives rise to (2) greater openness and hence divine illumination or *satori*, resulting in (3) experience of unity with God or Nirvana. These chapters will analyze, respectively, how purgative "dying to self" is a regressive renunciation of ego functioning, followed by a descent into primitive processes, resulting in a revival of infantile symbiotic structures.

The history of religious experience, especially the way cults in our day appeal to youths' desire for experience rather than institutions, is replete with examples of people who surrendered their identity to the authoritarian control of a spiritual mentor or a blissful encounter with God. Psychology has been rightly suspicious of those who in the name of becoming free of egocentricity and of submitting themselves to a "higher" consciousness instead experience the tragedy of a Jonestown or mind-altering practices leading to bondage rather than spiritual liberation.

Without making light of the dangers of losing oneself in an oceanic experience, the second section of this work describes how the loss of self and merger into God analyzed in the first section as pathological can instead be, in psychological language, reparative, and in religious language, redemptive. I will do this by reexamining the concept of regression.

Several psychologists have expanded Freud's original ideas on regression. Utilizing their insights—most notably those of Kris in his studies on creativity—the second section of this work argues that regression should no longer be presumed pathological. By comparing the three stages of religious experiences with similar processes that take place in creative experiences, we will see that potentially the former are not only *not* pathological but are indispensable to psychological growth.

The same disciplines shown to be ego-regressive in the first section therefore may become the critical means for vanquishing the defensive "false self." The primitive processes that diminish ego control, and that are represented in feelings of ecstasy or visions, have a capacity to stimulate creativity and the richer range of emotional depths that were repressed in early psychological development. And the experience of communion with God that reactivates archaic symbiotic structures has an ability to make a person feel secure enough to confront, and eventually to resolve, the unresolved conflicts that unconsciously motivated religious experience. In the process one can resume psychological development at the point where those conflicts first led to psychological arrest.

Although religious experience's reactivation of unconscious structures and repressed instincts does not have to be the pathological experience Freud presumed it to be, it does not in itself constitute healthy transformation. The final chapters of this book will suggest that only by acting on, by doing something with or expressing one's experience—as the artist elaborates on or paints that which was inspirational—does the experience regressively restore primitive structures in order to repair them rather than use them as refuge. In this way religious experience will be recognized not only for the unconscious processes it sets in motion but for what it subsequently does with them that makes the experience adaptively as opposed to malignantly regressive.

> Must we call it regression if man thus seeks again the earliest encounters of his trustful past in his efforts to reach a hoped-for eternal future? Or do religions partake of man's ability, even as he regresses, to recover creatively? At their creative best, religions retrace our earliest inner experiences, giving tangible form to vague evils and reaching back to the earliest individual sources of trust: at the same time, they keep alive the common symbols of integrity distilled by generations. If this is partial regression, it is a regression which, in retracing firmly established pathways, returns to the present amplified and clarified. (Erikson, 1963, p. 264)

PART ONE

Regression and Religious Experience

Regression and Religious Experience

RELIGIOUS EXPERIENCE

This book examines a particular type of religious experience. What makes a religious experience appropriate for consideration is that it is, first and foremost, an experience. It is not a relationship with God based on discursive reflection or theological concepts but an actual experience.

> Enclose me not in cages of matter or mind; through heavenly vastness my soul does soar, unfenced by the walls of heart or deed, by walls of ethics or logic; I thirst for truth, not concepts of truth; I ride about the heavens, wholly absorbed with the truth. (Kuk, 1951, p. 79)

Religious experiences examined in this work arise out of a personal, subjective encounter between the individual and God—or between a person and Brahma, self, Nirvana, Truth, or whatever Ultimate Being/Reality[1] is perceived to transform a person's life dramatically. Alfred, Lord Tennyson described it as

> A kind of walking trance
> I have frequently had,
> quite up from boyhood,
> when I have been all alone.
> This has generally come upon me
> thro' repeating my own name
> two or three times to myself silently,
> till all at once,
> as it were out of intensity

of the consciousness of individuality,
the individuality itself seemed to dissolve
and fade away into boundless being.

Whether the experience is of the Tao or of God, it is an *experience*. The person *feels* religious in his encounter with God; he *grasps* or is grasped by Truth, *knows* Nirvana or *intuits* Krishna's presence. The person directly engages the divine in an innermost realm of self where mind, senses, and feelings seem to come together. Some refer to this unified inner place as one's self, Atman, Christ within, or soul.

The innermost self in which God or Nirvana is experienced is not normally accessible to a person's conscious awareness. As will be described, this innermost self usually is hidden beneath a more pragmatic self. Religions traditionally offer dogma and faith to the pragmatic self as a substitute for the experience of God in the inner self. But religions also offer mystical traditions that express discontent with the religiosity of the pragmatic self. Mystics are people who are not satisfied with theological reflection and instead strive to experience God or Truth directly. Via a varied assortment of approaches and teachings, they seek to experience a higher or divine state that exists beyond the mundane threshold of the pragmatic self.

> Our normal waking consciousness, rational consciousness as we call it, is but one special type of consciousness, while all about it, parted from it by the filmiest of screens, there lies potential forms of consciousness entirely different. (James, 1961, p. 378)

The attempt to leave behind normative consciousness in order to experience God or Nirvana generally follows a three-stage process: purgative, illuminative, and unitive. The purgative stage typically begins with a confrontation of the pragmatic self. The pragmatic self is preoccupied with its own importance, and often is prideful and possessive. If the inner self is to be recovered and God is to be experienced, then the pragmatic self must be purified or purged. Through a variety of disciplined self-denying practices, a person learns to surrender his ego and to "die" to the pragmatic self.

The purposeful purgation of ego alters the normative state in which consciousness perceives and reflects on experience. An encounter with God no longer has to be filtered through preconditioned categories of the mind, nor externally mediated via priests or creedal statements. God instead can be experienced directly, immediately. Nirvana or self can be grasped intuitively by the person's inner self.

> A special tradition outside the scriptures,
> No dependence upon words and letters,
> Direct pointing at the soul of men,
> Seeing into one's own nature and the attainment of
> buddhahood.
> (Boddhidharma)

The unimpeded apprehension of Nirvana/God is the illuminative stage of religious experience. A person knows God not through external teachings or logical surmises, but from an experience in which God seems to have been directly revealed. He simply knows God. And what he knows he knows with certainty, for his mind and senses do not question the experience but know it to be self-evident.

The alteration in consciousness that allows for this direct experience oftentimes is accompanied by heightened perceptions or intensified awareness. No longer clogged by concepts or cognitive filters, the person feels as if he is seeing God, or life, for the first time. He feels awakened, enlightened, "born again." That which before was hidden—the truth or beauty that previously eluded him—suddenly is apparent. As a result he feels ecstatic or pervasively tranquil; at a minimum he is filled with awe and reverence for what he has experienced—feelings that give his experience a sense of sacredness or ultimacy.

Surrender of self and divine illumination are important stages of religious experience, but greater importance lies in their leading the way into the final stage. For not only does a person "die to self" in the experience of God but the self he loses is lost in God and the illumination he experiences is so intense as to absorb him into it. Such a person enters into the third stage of religious experience, that of merger into God or Nirvana.

Without becoming God (though some monistic traditions suggest that the person is God), the individual becomes less conscious of himself as a separate entity from God as he is consumed in the experience. He ceases to think of himself as being illuminated by God and instead *is* illuminated. He loses the dualistic mentality that distinguished between knower and known, inner and outer, self and God. The Upanishads (1926) describe this experience with the image of a river flowing into the ocean. Buddhists portray it as abandoning "maya" and sinking into Nirvana, and Christians as dying to self and experiencing unity with God. Evelyn Underhill suggested a "self-forgetting attentiveness, a profound conscientiousness, a self-merging, a real communion between seer and seen" (1911, p. 300). Abraham Maslow summarized it thus:

> It is always described as a loss of self or ego, or sometimes as a transcendence of self. There is a fusion with the reality being observed, a oneness where there was a twoness, an integration of some sort of the self with the non-self. (1971, p. 60)

The religious experience that begins with a loss of self and culminates in Nirvana or communion with God is the subject of the following pages. I examine how the stages of dying to self, of being illuminated by and united with God, are regressive phenomena—and regressive phenomena that can be reparative as well as pathological. An introductory section offers an explanation of the concept of regression.

PSYCHOLOGICAL REGRESSION

Regression is the temporary or permanent disavowal of developed behavior or mentation, in order to return to "primitive methods of expression and representations that take the place of the usual ones" (Freud, 1924b, p. 248). Psychological development normally proceeds from less complex states to more complex states. When, for instance, the relatively blissful existence of the infant is disturbed by frustration, he develops increasingly more sophisticated strengths to master the frustrations that threaten to overwhelm pleasurable feelings. Progressive development of the psychological strengths necessary to manage an increasingly complicated existence can reverse itself when, due to any number of intrapsychic or environmental factors, the child's experience of the intolerable and unavoidable creates more anxiety than the experience of the desirable and attainable creates pleasure. The child returns to an earlier stage of development, reverting to a simpler existence that does not require the psychological functions to manage pleasure and displeasure, where pleasurable experiences are immediately available and displeasurable ones easily avoidable. That is, the child regresses to earlier ways of functioning, such as wish-fulfilling fantasy and dependency, in order to overcome frustration.

A child who relies on regression to manage a particularly problematic area may grow up with acceptable strengths in other areas, but will remain fixated (or stuck) in a primitive means of managing one (or more) problematic area. He will feel drawn back, in the event of a particularly stressful situation, to these early fixated memories or feelings because they—unlike his present efforts—have already demonstrated their ease in dispelling stress. The earlier feelings of security, or of protection and unconditional love, they recreate, substitute for the anxiety generated by tasks incumbent on adult functioning.

Most people—even the apparently mature—possess these "Achilles' heels" that were never developmentally resolved: the private fears, unacknowledged weaknesses, or hidden insecurities that from time to time threaten a seemingly secure and ordered existence. A particularly stressful situation penetrates a person's normal control. It may tip the balance in a less strongly constituted individual and reveal hidden fears or insecurities. He might temporarily abandon more sophisticated strengths and regress to less complex psychological structures, where once again choices are simple, anxiety is overcome with wishes, instincts are not frustrated, and an omnipotent parental image can be relied on. As T. S. Eliot said, "Human beings cannot face too much reality." Or as Freud said,

> If reality becomes inexorable . . . the libido will finally be compelled to resort to regression, and to seek satisfaction in one of the organizations it had already surmounted or in one of the objects it had relinquished earlier. (1938, p. 268)

Freud described three categories of regression. Temporal regression implies a loss of time, a reversal of chronology to earlier psychic states so they "again become the mode of expression of the forces of the mind" (1915, p. 289). Temporal regression occurs when a situation is so excessively frustrating that the person renounces the reality-based situation where frustration arises and returns to primitive mental mechanisms that create their own reality. A useful analogy is that of a stream of water that meets with an obstacle and, dammed up, flows into previously dry channels. Earlier forgotten or repressed memories are reanimated and substituted for adult behavior or cognition. The resulting conflict between reactivated infantile experiences and reality, with the latter losing the contest, is usually observed in schizophrenics. Although religious experience can regressively result in psychosis, as we shall see, it usually is less severe and is more expressive of the other two types of regression.

Formal regression is the reactivation of archaic mental representations and a less mature means of coping. It begins when the expectations placed on higher-level ego functioning—such as control, autonomy, and logical thinking—make a person feel so anxious that he abandons them. Relieved of the stress they generate, the individual subsequently restores ego activity to earlier, less stressful expressions. This magically gratifies needs and dispels the anxiety that the adult ego was unable to handle. Hence instead of taking personal initiative or being responsible, the individual's ego becomes more childishly reliant on others' choices or more willing to let others take responsibility for him. It is a "regressive revival of the forces which protect his infancy" (Freud, 1961a, p. 164).

Furthermore, the regressive primitivization of ego strengths leads to the recovery of equally primitive instincts. Impulses that would be considered nefarious or childish, and that were repressed under the control of the ego, surge into consciousness when the ego—being "died to" or surrendered—can no longer keep them controlled. In such circumstances a person returns to pregenital expression, oral neediness, compulsion toward immediate gratification, and uncontrollable rage when frustrated.

The diminishment of attention to the external world is met proportionately with a regressive shift of attention to unconscious mental processes (e.g., to fantasy and wish fulfillment). This backward movement from the conscious system of the mind to an earlier unconscious mental organization is the third or topographical category of regression. The reactivation of primitive mental structures regressively confuses, even diffuses, the psychological boundaries between inner and outer, fantasy and reality, self and nonself. As we will see, regression of this type is what takes place in the final unitive stage of religious experience. The regressive restoration of archaic undifferentiated sensations, in the form of communion with God, reverses the way one relates to the world realistically: a process that begins with the purgation of mature ego functioning and that subsequently leads to evocation of primitive euphoria or hallucinatory images.[2] (Later chapters will discuss how these regressed stages can be reversed and become reparative.)

2

Ego Regression and Purgation

DYING TO SELF

Purgation is the first stage of religious experience, but even before purgation commences, a person generally is afflicted with some sort of discontent or malaise. Gradually or suddenly, a person begins to feel uncomfortable about himself. He might even appear "successful" but serious doubts about the goals and values that instilled success have made him dissatisfied. Religions traditionally refer to this uncomfortable state as the product of alienation from God. People's superficial pursuit of pleasure or power causes them to lose contact with a deeper "true self," and leads to greed, envy, and self-centeredness that make them feel sinful.

Religious experience begins with the acknowledgement of one's sinfulness, but religious experience involves more than merely atoning for faults and feeling forgiven. It includes the purgation of, the "emptying of" or "dying to," the alienated self. If people have fallen from grace and into sin, they have to renounce the first Adam so as to experience the New Adam. They learn any number of spiritual disciplines to overcome the wishes, thoughts, and actions that make them feel empty and separated from God. They shed the ego that veils them from a true self by going to the desert like Jesus, sitting patiently under the boddhi tree like Buddha, or entering a monastery like Thomas Merton. Less dramatically, they meditate, fast, develop a relationship with a mentor, isolate themselves periodically through spiritual retreats, deny themselves certain pleasures, and so forth. However it is done, purging the self is an attempt to surrender the limited self and to experience God. "All the mystics agree that the stripping of personal initiative, the I . . . is an im-

14

perative condition of the attainment of the unitive life" (Underhill, 1911, p. 508).

Religious traditions are replete with references to purging the self. Buddhism's Four Noble Truths, for example, emphasize egolessness (*annata*). There is, first, suffering in the world (*dukkha*). Suffering is the result of ego. It is the product of the greed and vanity that cling to the world of impermanence. People cannot be happy as long as this ego exists. Therefore suffering is eradicated through the cessation of ego. The ego is lessened through a clearly defined lifestyle known as the Eight-Fold Way. Through acts such as meditation, right-mindfulness, and right living, a person overcomes the permanent ego. No longer bound by the self-centered patterns of existence, he ultimately experiences an egoless nirvanic state.

Christian institutions do not refer as explicitly to the annihilation of the ego as Buddhism does. Yet they, too, focus on the greed, pride, self-centeredness, and other "deadly sins" that are synonymous with the ego and that need to be conquered if the Christian is to experience God. The New Testament represents Jesus' act of "emptying himself" (Phil 2:3) and abandoning his will to the will of God as the epitome of getting rid of the self. In general, it refers to these and similar acts as dying to self—"If anyone would come after me, he must deny his very self" (Lk 9:23; Mt 18:2–4, 10–37; Lk 14:25). Not unlike the Buddhist perception of *maya*, the New Testament speaks of the need to reject the insubstantially of the self: "You must lay aside your normal way of life and the old self which deteriorates through illusion and desire, and acquire a fresh, spiritual way of thinking" (Eph 4:22).

The scriptural mandate to die to self is described even more explicitly in voluminous spiritual tracts that advise a Christian on how to experience God. These works span the spectrum from John of the Cross's (1959) vivid descriptions of the "dark night" to Brother Lawrence's self-denying attentiveness to mundane activities. They include spiritual disciplines such as being obedient to a religious superior in order to become free of self-centered volition and thereby open to God's will. The *Rule of St. Benedict* states that "monks have neither free will nor free body, but must receive all they need from the abbot" (1952, p. 76).

Numerous other spiritual practices are aimed at renouncing the self. Solitude isolates a person from the external influences that origi-

nally led to the identification of self with egocentric pride and possessions. A vow of poverty not only denies material comfort but more
importantly leads one to confront the possessiveness of the self that
underlies an absorption with material possessions. Meditative practices and prolonged periods of silence still inner mental activity so as
to allow a person to "hear" God, and ascetical acts that deprive one
of sensual pleasures, such as fasting and celibacy, free a person of
single-minded lascivious cravings in order to refocus attention on
higher pursuits.

When bodily needs, independent thinking, verbalization, and
volition are purged and disappear, the self-consciousness that main-
tains a person's separateness also disappears, and he merges into the
"mystico unico." As John of the Cross declares:

> To reach satisfaction in all
> desire its possession in nothing.
> To come to possess all
> desire the possession of nothing.
> To arrive at being all
> desire to be nothing.

REGRESSION AND DYING TO SELF

Although purgative acts may reflect a sincere wish to renounce
self-centeredness, dying to self can—on an unconscious and sometimes not so unconscious level—be motivated by fear of the individuality and sexual desires that are renounced. Ridding oneself of independence and sexuality may be a response to the pain of inner
emptiness, but independence and sexuality, along with assertiveness,
responsibility, and intimacy, are also characteristics of adult maturity. They make a person feel in control of life rather than out of
control or controlled by others. They help a person to trust his own
judgment and instincts, enable him to "give" himself in an intimate
relationship without "losing" his identity, be confident in his opinions and willing to share them with others as well as to take responsibility for them.

The expectations placed on these various ego tasks make mature
adulthood a state that is constantly challenged, rather than one oper-

ating on auto-pilot. For example, people have to work at relationships, have to become vulnerable and take risks if they want relationships to grow. In a similar way independence requires belief in one's self; volition demands the courage of convictions. So, too, assertiveness implies the strength to express what one believes, while responsibility requires the willingness to stand on one's actions.

Expectations placed on adult ego functioning can make a person anxious. He might appear on the surface to be in control and confident but within himself is a sense that he is not as prepared as he should be for the tasks of adulthood. He might feel burdened, rather than confident, by the demands of autonomy. He might be nervous about taking control and be intimidated by the emotional vulnerability expected in relationships. He also could be insecure about managing certain conflicts and anxious about decisions that he sometimes wishes were not his to make.

A person can save himself from being pulled apart, from being destroyed by a society he perceives to demand too much and internally by unresolved conflicts or hidden insecurities. He can save himself by learning to confront conflicts and to develop the inner strengths to master the tasks of autonomy—or save himself from society's demands and from unconscious pressures through self-destruction. That is, in the purgative stage of religious experience he defensively destroys his ego and dies to self.

Dying to self destroys the self before society or inner pressures can destroy it. Before society completely unnerves the person with what he perceives to be excessive expectations placed on individuality; before his limited and perishable self makes him feel too anxious; before the fear of being alone can no longer be silenced; before the ego gradually weakens and completely collapses under the strain of imperious instincts—before any or all of these, the person in the purgative stage of religious experience dies to the world and to its expectations. And he dies to himself and to the autonomy, mortality, and instincts that make him anxious. This message is echoed by many spiritual teachers:

> He who pursues learning will increase everyday
> He who pursues Tao will decrease everyday.
> (*Tao Te Ching*)

I must decrease in order that he might increase.
(John the Baptist)

I must reduce myself to zero.
(Mahatma Gandhi)

The decrease in self meant as an antidote to an ego perceived to have grown too big—so bloated with its own importance as to have blocked the direct experience of God—can be a defensive escape from an ego that is not adequately developed. The ego purged in religious experience may not have formed the necessary skills to make a person comfortable with being assertive or sexual. The alienation that is assumed to be the result of an inflated ego may instead be anxiety emanating from an ego that never developed the confidence to manage inner psychological needs or external expectations. And *if* the ego is too big or self-centered, it is often the result of compensating for this lack of development: a compensation that exacerbates the intensity of inner feelings of inadequacy. As Harvard psychologist Jack Engler (who is generally receptive to much of what Eastern religions teach about the self) concluded from his studies of Buddhist students:

> The Buddhist teaching that I neither have nor am an enduring self is often misinterpreted to mean that I do not need to struggle with the tasks of identity formation or with finding out who I am, what my capabilities are, what my needs are, what my responsibilities are, how I am related to other selves, and what I should or could do with my life. The *annata* (no self) doctrine is taken to justify their premature abandonment of essential psychosocial tasks. (1984, p. 35)

Feelings of insecurity that infuse some adults' sense of self are diffused when spiritual disciplines dismantle the self. By promulgating an image of the self as illusory or sinful, and by making a spiritual value of renouncing the self in order to experience God, a person discovers a convenient vehicle for ridding the self of that which makes one anxious.

The purging of personal volition, for example, that occurs in the early stages of religious experience eliminates the need to make personal decisions and thereby face the anxiety aroused in those decision-making processes. So, too, the stressful demands placed on autonomy and on asserting that autonomy disappear when a person renounces his independence (since independence is a sign of egocentric pride) and abandons assertiveness ("turning the other cheek"). A similar psychological defense can be observed in people whose apprehension about being in control or expressing sexual longings is overcome when they abandon the control that becomes associated with resistance to God and denigrate the sexuality equated with baser instincts unworthy of their spiritual being.

Purgation of self makes the person feel secure or "holy" because it vanquishes the anxiety of being an adult, *not* because it develops the mature strengths to manage that anxiety. The self forfeits the potential for learning a healthy sense of control and sexuality when it is died to or "forgotten" (*ghafila* in Islam). "All things I then forgot/all ceased and I was not" (Dante). The experience of dying to self can thereby become an escape from the world in order to avoid the dread of interacting maturely with the world—of being autonomous, assertive, responsible, and sexual. It is what Bertrand Russell called a "disease born of fear" (1957, p. 24).

PRIMITIVIZATION OF EGO

Self-abnegation sheds anxiety not only because it vanquishes a person's insecurities and fears. Equally important with surrendering anxious ego functioning is the notion that it is being surrendered to God. The person not only renounces independence, assertiveness, and volition, but becomes passive, dependent on, and submissive to God. What began with the purgative renunciation of adult functions regresses to earlier and less demanding functions that make life more childlike and simple.

The return to the comforts of childhood is not as consciously desirable (or attainable) as the relief it offers would make it seem. Adults, like children, find themselves in a world that confronts them periodically with frustrations and limitations. Yet no matter how anxious life makes them feel, adults are no longer as free as children to turn back to less anxious modes of functioning supported by need-gratifying, godlike parents. In the real world social and physical demands eventually inhibit regressive reliance on parents, leading to increased independence and responsibility. Yet a child grows into adulthood with the repressed (albeit imperishable) memory of what it felt like to be provided for and protected. Stressful situations that make him feel overwhelmed or overly anxious elicit these unconscious memories. They revive what it was like to depend on omnipotent parental protection rather than being independent, to be passive and submissive instead of being assertive and in control. These nonconflictual aspects of childhood provide a regressed psychological realm to which one can retreat to find pleasure and counteract anxiety. "Vestiges of this phase (early maternal symbiosis) remain with us throughout the life cycle" (Mahler, 1975, p. 78).

As much as an adult might find the expectations of individuality or responsibility stressful, he cannot implore his parents to tuck him in at night or protect him as they did in childhood. While a literal return to a childlike relationship with one's parents would be unacceptably embarrassing, turning to a Supreme Being is socially and psychologically acceptable. "Kneeling before God is less an unmanly act then kneeling before a competitor or peer" (Maslow, 1971, p. 351). An individual can surrender ego functions that characterize adulthood when the God to whom he surrenders is viewed as providing a grownup type of parental protection (without consciously invoking the primitive parental relationship it represents).

> Biologically speaking, religion is to be traced to the small human child's long-drawn-out-helplessness and need of help, and when at a later date he perceives how truly forlorn and weak he is when confronted with the great forces of life, he feels his condition as he did in childhood, and attempts to deny his own despondency by a regressive revival of the forces which protected his infancy. (Freud, 1964c, p. 123)

Ego purgation restores earlier modes of functioning that make managing life's vagaries less stressful. Unlike those demanding adult functions, early functions have already been tested and proven safe. They were able to rid the self of anxiety without involving stressful autonomy or assertiveness. Later they were repressed and relegated to an unconscious realm. When an adult is faced with stressful expectations of autonomy, assertiveness, logical problem solving, or sexual relations, primitive modes of functioning regressively draw him back to where they fixated on less anxious ways of managing these tasks.

For example, a person afraid of making choices or taking responsibility for those choices may renounce volition and control as egocentric, then subsequently surrender his will to a God who makes decisions and takes responsibility for him. Instead of being accountable for his thoughts and actions, he reverts to childish modes of functioning in which he expects his parents, in the form of God, to do his thinking and take control over his actions. Like a child, he is not responsible for what he does because it is the result not of his own will but of his obedience to the will of an idealized other. Relief from life's difficulties comes not only from surrendering adult functioning but from surrendering oneself to a superior power that takes responsibility and provides the imprimatur of "God's will" to rationalize whatever one does (or fails to do).

> When my mother died, I was twelve years of age or a little less. When I began to realize what I had lost, I went in my distress to an image of our Lady and with many tears beseeched her to be a mother to me. (Teresa of Jesus, 1944, p. 12)

Instead of submitting to an image of God, a person can escape the demands of being in control by attributing responsibility to an impersonal concept like karma. Karma is the universal law of causality, an accumulation of moral and physical effects that chain the individual to the world of suffering. Karma can be overcome, but not through action; it is confronted through inaction— "letting go" of desire, possessiveness, assertiveness, and so forth. Inaction might free a person of possessiveness, but it also frees him from personal responsibility. It is a defense against the fear of taking action, a way of converting a fatalistic "I cannot do anything about it so why do anything" into a seemingly noble expression. In the process of submitting oneself to karma the person becomes detached from life's struggles, as happens by giving oneself in obeisance to Allah[1] or surrendering one's fate to God.

Surrendering personal responsibility to a divine authority further ameliorates anxiety by allowing the person to share in qualities he feared admitting within himself. Hidden longings projected onto God do not have to be acknowledged as one's own and yet can be vicariously enjoyed in the submission of oneself to a "powerful" or "righteous" God. Thus it is not the person but God who inspires him to greatness, who graces him with abilities: "Make me an instrument of your peace" (Francis of Assisi); "I do nothing of myself . . . I am not myself the source of the words I speak to you: it is the Father who dwells in me doing his own work" (Jn 8:28, 14:10); "Not me who lives but Christ within me" (Gal 2:20).

Surrendering one's self to God can result in noble feelings but can also lead to tragedy. People at Jonestown, for example, felt free from the anxiety of controlling their own lives when they surrendered personal responsibility to Rev. Jim Jones. But when their own lives became indistinguishable from the will of Jim Jones they were unable to differentiate between Jones's will that they should kill themselves and their own responsibility to themselves.

Most people's experience of abdicating responsibility to a divine authority does not result in suicide. Not far short of that, however, surrendering personal responsibility often leads to—or is an expression of—self-hatred. It, along with other acts of purgation, is a self-belittling experience. Renunciation of responsibility and autonomy makes a person feel free, but the freedom is not the mature feeling that arises from healthy adult functioning. It is a freedom that derives from making oneself small and weak in order that God becomes big and powerful. In submission to the unbounded deity the person feels specious freedom which reaches its climax when one becomes so small as to disappear into God. St. Paul summarized it by saying, "When I am weak then I am strong" (2 Cor 12:10).

Devaluing and chastising the self make a person feel acceptable before God. Purgative acts that diminish one's worth become spiritual traits credited with liberating the individual from egocentricity —"He who humbles himself shall be exalted" (Mt 23:12). Humility, however, often humiliates rather than liberates, turning the self-accusation that aims to deflate the bloated ego into the self-denigration that destroys self-esteem.

The most prominent forms of self-denigration are physically ascetical and are often undisguised acts of masochism. Martyrdom can be an extreme feat of self-abuse, a sometimes almost ecstatic drive to destroy oneself completely. More typically, purgative masochism is the punishment of one's self for feelings or needs that have become associated with being "bad." The individual turns back into himself, by various expressions of corporal mortification (fasting, denial of pleasure, sleep deprivation, etc.), the aggression and guilt derived from feeling bad about himself.[2]

Some people, for example, believe that sex, or hunger, or what St. Augustine in general called "nature's appetites," are deceitful and can too easily lead to hedonism. These appetites are, if not entirely evil, at least temptations or diversions from higher spiritual pursuits. In order to experience the incorruptibility of the spirit and the perfection of God, the individual must discipline, even deny these baser instincts.

Penitential acts (as in "suffering for Jesus") feel redemptive because they subdue natural desires and the guilt they generate, but on a deeper level they also redirect attention away from the inner psychological self that is truly suffering. They help the person escape the self and its various trepidations (becoming "beside himself with pain") by turning the self into a body, an object, and directing inner frustration and aggression at the body.[3] "All masochistic strivings are ultimately directed toward the goal of oblivion, of getting rid of self with all its conflicts and all its limitations" (Horney, 1966, p. 248).

Bodily mortification, such as flagellation or long hours of kneeling, may be the most obvious manifestation of masochistic purgative practices. It is the physical counterpart of the self-abnegation of the bowed head, of self-denigrating subservience, of blind obedience and other psychological expressions of denying the self pleasure and even existence.

> If I abase myself and reduce myself to nothing; and shrink from all self-esteem, and grind myself to the dust that I am: Thy grace will be propitious to me. (Thomas à Kempis, 1986, bk. 4, ch. 8)

> He that loves his life shall lose it, and he that hates his life in this world shall keep it into life eternal. (Jn 12:25)

Other purgative acts in addition to masochistic submission primitivize ego functions. Of these, the most notable is the dissolution of individuality. A person not only renounces his independence (having learned that it reflects egocentric self-pride) but becomes dependent on God. Relying on a deity instead of on oneself restores the primitive way that autonomy was sheltered from life's various demands. Instead those demands were facilely allayed by becoming dependent on an idealized other to manage them.

Dependence of this type is not the healthy dependence of learning from others. It arises from a fear of independence and from the fixated longing for others to provide the protection and gratification that the person cannot, or will not, produce on his own. Hence he will gladly surrender everything that reflects distinctiveness—independent thinking, idiosyncratic behavior, personal expression of emotions—and will take on the ideology of a spiritual group, its unified form of behavior, and universal expressions (such as love of humankind). He does this in order to escape having to think for himself or to express personal feelings and to make decisions on his own, even decisions as mundane as what to wear. "Then forthwith he shall, there in the oratory, be divested of his own garments with which he is clothed and to be clad in those of the monastery," commands the *Rule of St. Benedict* (1952, ch. 58). Or he is like the adolescents the psychoanalyst James Masterson described as

> giving up the struggle [adolescent development] and throwing in with an authority figure who will relieve them of the task of taking responsibility for themselves and provide them instead with an authority and a system of beliefs, including a set of guidelines to direct their lives. Their loss of self is hardly noticed in the relief at not having to continue the struggle on their own. These adolescents are a significant proportion of those who join religious sects. . . . It is not America's social values they reject as much as the need to establish and take responsibility for a self. (1981, p. viii)

A person who depends entirely on an omnipotent deity or an omniscient guru is saved from the anxiety of having to manage life's realistic demands. Surrendering of self to a God who provides the certitude that life is reluctant to provide eliminates the personal struggle of grappling with life's questions, of looking within oneself to find meaning.

Life might become safe by surrendering oneself to God, but it also becomes predictable and uninspired. The individual's deity is the epitome of Marx's critique of religion as a drug that makes people lazy, that lets them avoid taking initiative. Drugs bring up "regressive dependency needs" and have a "sedative effect," thus "serving to desensitize the ego" (Grinker, 1945, pp. 391, 436). God, like drugs, puts the person's mind and initiative to sleep when surrender to God regressively restores a previous mode of letting another do one's thinking and decision making.

Cognitive processes therefore may not expand but instead may be circumvented, even narrowed, in purgative religious practices. Meditative disciplines that induce hyperattention to a restricted focus (a spot on a wall, for example, or the Jesus Prayer), and that are confined to an ideology or practice that a person is expected to accept uncritically,[4] can diminish adult cognitive processes. They undermine analytical abilities to question and to judge for oneself or to synthesize a broad range of ideas and stimulation. With the abandonment of rational reasoning comes freedom from the fear of thinking for oneself, of making important or even mundane decisions on one's own, and of the "horror of being alone":

> Religions and nationalism, as well as any custom and any belief however absurd and degrading, if it only connects the individual with others, are refuges from what one most dreads: aloneness. (Fromm, 1941, p. 90)

Forfeiting the mature capacity to be "alone" with one's thoughts or to think independently causes a person to become susceptible to suggestion. He can be easily swayed by the noncognitive intensity of his experience, accepting whatever comes to him in that altered state and accepting it as revelation.[5] Chanting and whirling-dervish dancing are examples of religious activities that induce and allow the individual to lose himself in auto-hypnotic trances. So, too, a pervasively peaceful Nirvana or a constant immersion in feeling loved (e.g., the "love bombing" of the "Moonies") deflates cognitive processes and restores the feeling of unbounded love experienced in infancy.

An experience that offers unlimited love and security has an obvious appeal to underlying aspects of human nature that childishly resist growing up. It attracts the weaker, confused, and sometimes frightened aspects of people that welcome a less demanding and more simplistic solution to life's anxieties. The person attracted to such an experience finds in Jesus' admonition to become like little children a literal invitation to be dependent and needy rather than a metaphor for openness, as in Taoism's saying:

> The sage is shy and humble
> To the world he seems confusing
> Men look to him and listen
> He behaves like a little child. (*Tao Te Ching*, 49)

As Freud said of the person whose relationships exist primarily to allay anxiety and to gratify needs, "It therefore encourages the individual to remain in a state of childhood" (1924a, p. 167).

PRIMITIVIZATION OF EGO AND THOUGHT REFORM

Primitivization of ego functions can be manifested in purgative religious experiences as tragic as those that took place in Jonestown and as innocuous as a person praying to God for guidance. Robert Jay Lifton (1963) investigated a similar type of primitivization in his studies on "thought reform." His eight characteristics of thought reform originated from his investigation of the Chinese communists in Korea who brainwashed their prisoners (*hsi nao*). Their intention was persuasion, not coercion, with the goal of dismantling resistance and replacing previous cognitive processes with new ones. Although Lifton's work refers to the involuntary brainwashing that radically restructures cognitive/affective processes of people such as prisoners of war, a similar alteration occurs in voluntary acts of renouncing old cognitive/affective structures found in purgative "cleansing of mind" or "dying to self." The following text describes Lifton's characteristics of thought reform as they apply to the present discussion of self-abnegation in religious experience.

Milieu Control. Although milieu control is more obvious in the situation of a prisoner whose environment is forced on him, spiritual purgation often begins with a similar structuring of a person's physical environment. The implications of this type of control are profound. First, the individual's contact with the outside environment, with society at large and with normal routine, is diminished if not eradicated. The "old" self is denied and along with it the reference groups whose familiarity once reinforced the old self. Its values, ways of thinking, and even particular habits are rejected and frequently dismissed as sinful or counterproductive to the new self.

The old self is replaced with a new self that conforms to the practices and philosophy embraced in the new structure. Whether in an ashram or a personal relationship with a guru or God, the person who previously enjoyed times of solitude, for example, learns to perceive solitude as selfish or antisocial. He subsequently surrenders himself to a spiritual practice that constantly surrounds him with people and seldom gives him the opportunity to be alone. He learns to share his deepest thoughts and to reveal his most personal feelings with strangers, thereby diminishing the normal autonomous structures that define him as an individual.

The opposite can also happen. A person who once felt it was good to be gregarious learns to reject relationships as frivolous, including one's family. He then immerses himself in the solitude of an isolated environment such as a monastery. To be alone and to be surrounded by others, when chosen as a way of life, are two sides of the same coin.

Seclusion from one's normative frame of reference and adaptation to a more narrow frame of perception radically affect a person's identity (Modell, 1984). The implementation of new routines or practices, coupled with the loss of autonomous structures, induces profound changes in the manner in which a person processes thoughts and feelings.

This profound change can take place on a psychological and/or a physical level. The spiritual discipline of fasting, for example, or a sudden change in one's diet from protein-based to vegetarian, alters one's state of consciousness. It does this, first, by removing the person from a normative frame of eating and from a wider choice of culinary activities. On a more radical level it affects the way the mind and body function in tandem. The change in diet alters the intake of protein and causes a substantial increase in carbohydrates or a precipitous change in blood sugar level. The reduction in sleep that occurs in nightly vigils and early rising, and the resulting constant feeling of tiredness, affects the brain and other parts of the body. The restriction of motility in the lotus or kneeling position, like the sensory deprivation that takes place in the closing of eyes in meditation, inhibits the stimulation normally responsible for activating the brain.[6]

Mystical Manipulation and Sacred Science. Part of the reason that milieu control can induce self-sacrifice is that the projected image of God (or religious mentor) makes the person feel it is not only good to surrender oneself but an honor as well. He can renounce his old identity without fear or embarrassment because the deity or guru to whom he abdicates it possesses a mystical aura of superior power.

God, unlike a prisoner's captor, is already endowed with an image of superiority. Hence the struggle that takes place in religious experience to purge the autonomy and values that resist surrender is less pronounced than the experience of a prisoner who is pushed to acknowledge his captor's superiority. In both cases, however, once the person assents to the power of those above him, he vanquishes the objections or judgment that separated him from them. Since they possess a mystical or divine aura, the subordinate person will not question or criticize them. They transcend his human nature and are beyond the reach of his mortal understanding. When he surrenders to their wisdom or truth, he abdicates critical judgment and independent thought and returns to the primitive state where he uncritically accepts what those in authority dictate.

Demand for Purity. Self-purgation strives for a perfect state of spirituality not diluted or polluted by base physical sensations. Sexual feelings are perceived to be lust-ridden; sexual and other desires of the body are the result of greediness and have to be overcome. "By the destruction of desires, there is complete disinterest and cessation, Nirvana" (Udana Kikay, of the Buddhist Scriptures, 1959, p. 33). Celibacy thereby becomes the perfect spiritual state. It is also perfect because on an unconscious level it restores the pregenital sexuality that most perfectly hides an individual's fear of genital sexuality: "Those who restrain desire do so because their's is weak enough to be restrained, and being restrained it by degrees becomes passive, till it is only the shadow of desire" (Blake, 1975).

The celibate suppression of desire is not always the preferred choice for achieving a spiritual state free from lust. Sex can be purified of its lustful drive, as when St. Paul directed that one should be celibate but if this was not possible then at least one should marry. The married state provides the external control over sexual licentiousness that the person cannot internally summon. It provides even greater control when marriage is arranged by a spiritual teacher —Rev. Moon, for example—whose authority to dictate when and with whom to have sex saves the person from having to control his own sexuality.

Through these and other purgative practices, an individual attempts to achieve a state of purity that in reality is unattainable. Because such perfection is unattainable, the individual feels guilty and ashamed. As a result, the person's guilt prevents him from being satisfied with who he is and what he does. He sees himself as imperfect, as are all people. But unlike others he chastises himself for his imperfection. He feels embarrassed, if not sinful, because his own efforts at spiritual growth do not produce the enlightenment he believes is expected of him.

The demand for purity cannot create perfection within the person, but the sense of inferiority it engenders reinforces the person's dependence on God or God's ministers for perfection. *They* possess the truth and wisdom that the person strives to attain. Hence if he does not achieve perfection, the problem is not that the teacher or teachings are incomprehensible. The fault, he is convinced, lies within his imperfections. He is easily persuaded—through manipulation of the guilt surrounding his feelings of imperfection—that he has not grasped God's truth because he is unworthy of it, or lacks the faith to grasp it, or has not completely surrendered himself to it, or is still relating to it "out of his head" instead of "out of his heart." The result is further renunciation of autonomy or sexuality or whatever seems to contribute to his imperfection and more diligent striving to surrender himself to the perfect God or guru.—"The idealized object serves as a substitute for some unattainable ego ideal of our own. We love it on account of the perfection which we have striven to reach for within our own ego" (Freud, 1960, p. 44).

Only through the complete loss of self and unification with an idealized spiritual mentor or God (as will be examined in a later section) does the person gratify the unconscious longings he cannot gratify through autonomous strivings. As Freud said in conclusion to his statement above: "The ego becomes more and more unassuming and modest, and the object more and more sublime and precious. Until at last it gets possession of the entire self-love of the ego, whose self sacrifice thus follows a natural course" (1960, p. 44).

Cult of Confession. The public confession of one's sinfulness or imperfection is a symbolic act of self-surrender. It creates a kind of humility that deflates the hubris of the ego. Humility, however, often disguises the fear of taking greater responsibility for one's life by substituting childhood functioning. Self-accusations humiliate the person, making him feel like a child chastised before—and grateful for forgiveness from—his parents. L. Streiker describes converts to revivalism:

> The prospect is directly confronted with his sins. His physical and psychic space are invaded by these self-confident strangers. He is discomforted and thrown off balance. He becomes anxious. The group tells him that his feelings are caused by his sinfulness. He is overcome with guilt and sadness. He realizes that his life is not working. Eagerly he confesses his shortcomings . . . sexual longings, lies, petty thievery, drug abuse, and so forth. Guided by the group, he prays that God will forgive him and receive him as His child. He is urged "Ask Jesus to come into your heart." He does, and the inner turmoil subsides. The recruit senses an inner release and relief. (1984, p. 51)

Loading the Language. Dying to self primitivizes language by restoring childhood thought processes. The person learns to communicate through clichés, such as "est-talk," rather than out of personally felt and individually articulated thoughts or feelings. He similarly takes a fervent interest in global subjects, such as "humankind's suffering," thereby avoiding having to communicate feelings that arise directly out of personal experience.

Loading the language also refers to the reduction of complex thoughts into simplistic phrases and easily memorized expressions. "God is love" and "We are all brothers/sisters" appeal to the uncomplicated cognitive structures of childhood. Or, just as commonly, complicated thoughts are made so complex that a person cannot comprehend them. Clarity is replaced with obscurity. Yet the person is expected to understand a bizarre cosmology or philosophy that is logically impossible. He can understand it only when he surrenders himself to it instead of trying rationally to comprehend it.

Doctrine versus Person. Self-surrender is the sine qua non of purgation, but it can become more important than the experience it was meant to facilitate. Whether the encounter with God takes place in all its fullness becomes secondary to the pleasure secured in the ascetical processes of fasting, meditation, obedience, dependence, and so forth.[7] The person loses sight of the desire to experience God and becomes fascinated with the teachings or the derivatives of religious experience (e.g., miracles, visions, euphoria).

Dispensing of Existence. The final characteristic of thought reform is that those in control decide who has worth and who lacks worth. A person is made to feel less worthy of life than others. He is made to think of himself as a miserable sinner and to realize that the only way he will become worthy of God's love is to surrender himself to God.

RELIEF AT LOSS OF EGO

Self-surrender brings a sense of relief so great that it sometimes feels ecstatic.

> The transition from tenseness, self-responsibility, and worry, to equanimity, receptivity and peace, is the most wonderful of all those shiftings of inner equilibrium, those changes of the personal center of energy, which I have analyzed so often; and the chief wonder of it is that it so often comes about, not by doing, but by simply relaxing and throwing the burden down. (James, 1961, p. 175)

Feelings of relief for mature people come from the completion of a difficult task, but in purgation they often come from stripping away stress-creating autonomy and regressively restoring stress-free primitive feelings. The person becomes carefree, like a child from whom no one expects too much and to whom small rewards are given for being carefree. However, a more pervasive elation can arise from the explosive expression of instincts that have been purged of the ego that once controlled them. We will now examine that phenomenon.

3

Instinctual Regression
and Religious Experience

FROM SELF-SACRIFICE TO PRIMITIVE INSTINCTS

Purgative dying to self is not necessarily pathological. A person's ascetical renunciation of self can be motivated by a sincere wish to be free of egocentricity. The problem, however, is that the surrender of autonomy and control, or of assertiveness and sexuality, rends the psychological fabric of the self. An internal psychological frame grew out of, and had been relatively successful in resisting the regressive pull back to, primitive instinctual desires. In the absence of this autonomous structure (achieved via dying to self), these archaic drives cease to be regulated and their unfettered resurgence into consciousness is equated with the experience of God.

A distinct and separate sense of self is critical to a healthy psychological identity. Identity derives from a perception of self, from the senses, images, thoughts, ego functions, instincts, and physical/psychological boundaries that define the uniqueness of self. Psychological growth, at a minimum, is the maintenance of this self, and ideally is its enhancement.

A sense of self unfolds, as suggested, from less complex to more complex structures. Its least complex structure is dominated by what Freud (1915a) called "primary process." Primary process thinking is the earliest psychological activity of the infant prior to cognitive and ego development. As such, it is not subject to delay, to time or space, to realistic limitations, but is instead based on wish fulfillment, condensation (as in dreams), fluid psychological structures, and immediacy. It thereby defines a sense of unbounded libidinal gratification, referred to by Freud as the "pleasure principle."

Gradually, external expectations and internal maturation pressure the child into developing more complex psychological functions. She learns to harness instincts, to tolerate frustration, to think logically, to separate reality from fantasy as well as self from an undifferentiated relationship with the mother. These secondary functions, as Freud called them, make a person capable of managing the demands of reality while at the same time gratifying inner drives as much as possible without contradicting those demands (the reality principle).

Secondary functions grant autonomy or freedom from drive impulsivity by making a person feel in control of drives rather than controlled by them. They also give autonomy or freedom from social pressures by enabling the person to adapt to expectations and to modify expectations that are excessive or inappropriate.

If, however, a person becomes too distant from the environment, she experiences a corresponding change in control over her instincts. For example, if a person who previously conformed to social expectations by being responsible for her actions were to rescind that responsibility by isolating herself from society, she would experience a lessening of the control she once responsibly levied over her instincts. Rapaport described it succinctly: "Since reality relations guarantee autonomy from the id, excessive autonomy from the environment must impair the autonomy from the id" (1958, p. 18).[1]

Regression reverses the development of ego control over instincts by diminishing ego control and reviving the primitive processes that expect gratification regardless of reality. Hence purgation of self first regressively weakens the autonomy the ego has over the external environment. The person loses ego control normally exerted over outside influences when she is excessively bombarded with extreme stimulation—for example, being inundated with information (secular or religious "propaganda"), being incessantly surrounded by the presence of others (lack of privacy), or being overwhelmed by elaborate appeals to emotions (love-bombing). She loses secondary functioning when the opposite—cessation of stimuli —takes place, that is, sacrificing an autonomous relationship with the external environment through ascetical acts such as isolating herself from the environment, refocusing energy away from investment in daily activities and toward internal processes (meditation), or withdrawing sexual feelings from expression (celibacy).

In the first situation, the person's surrendering of self to external stimuli allows the stimuli to penetrate normal ego defenses and to appropriate control over instincts. The external environment (God, church, guru), and not the ego, structures or subdues inner psychological processes. In the second situation, the internal psychological realm becomes free of all external control and dominates the person. Sudden resurgence of primary process and primitive instincts—manifested in religious visions and euphoria—leaves the person incapable of testing reality and makes reality subservient to the unrelenting gratification of this inner realm.

PRIMITIVE INSTINCTS

Ego purgation revives need-gratifying primitive psychological functions and in the process reverts instincts to a primitive level where they too find satisfaction via infantile expression. The secondary function of the ego is critical in transforming the raw energy of instincts into constructive expressions ("neutralization"; Hartmann, 1958b). Dismantling secondary functions causes instincts to return to the untempered and unneutralized intensity of the archaic state that existed prior to realistic ego constraints. They return to a pleasure-principle orientation that is based on immediate gratification or wish fulfillment, and that abandons control and delayed gratification. This is the id, as Freud said,

> in which individual instincts have made themselves independent, pursue their aims regardless of the person as a whole and henceforth obey the laws only of the primitive psychology that rules in the depths of the id. (Freud, 1918, p. 203)

Love and work, for example, the qualities Freud often said define a healthy adult identity, are mature developments of libidinal and aggressive drives. More attention will be given to their development in a later section; it is sufficient here to note that what begins as a primal libidinal hunger for maternal attachment and an aggressive drive to overcome frustration ideally become integrated into creative expressions of intimacy and productivity. Previously unbounded libidinal drives develop into loving expressions of tenderness and mutuality, while undisciplined aggressive drives are channeled into constructive behavior and the self-assertiveness of the work place.

Instinctual regression occurs when the mature expression of

these drives is abandoned and a more primitive or childish expression is restored. Libidinal regression is marked by a shift from healthy expressions of love to its degeneration into narcissistic gratification or tenacious neediness. Regression similarly takes place in aggressive drives when healthy expressions of assertiveness are replaced with passivity, or when mastery is replaced with a primitive compulsion toward immediate discharge, as well as by the infantile rage that results when discharge is blocked.

Religious experience regressively restores these primitive libidinal and aggressive drives. When the autonomous ego functions that were instrumental in binding instincts into loving and constructive expressions are purged, instincts return to their unbounded and un-neutralized primitive mode. The experience of a perfectly loving God, for instance, "condenses"[2] or brings back from infancy the unbounded libidinal feelings of being unconditionally nurtured by the mother. The all-loving deity makes the person once again feel what it was like in infancy to be so unequivocally loved as never to have libidinal longings frustrated. She does not have to manage the tasks incumbent on mature expressions of love, reconcile unbounded libidinal instincts with reality's restraints, or expose herself to the vulnerabilities of intimacy when the unconditional love she experiences from God gratifies unconscious attachment needs and archaic instinctual cravings.

Aggressive drives similarly revert in religious experience to a childish impulsivity and magical conquest of obstacles. The person retreats from a world that expects her to be logical about her actions and to be in control of her emotions, and, in the experience of a God who vanquishes frustration, returns to a primitive instinctual level where she does not have to be assertive, master tasks, or tolerate frustration—because God does it all for her. However, since she forfeits the ego functions to manage these aggressive drives in a healthy manner, when the world intrudes on her blissful experience of God—as will happen—she lacks the maturity to express aggression in a healthy way and resorts to affect-laden and explosively impulsive expressions of aggression.

ELATION

Instincts that are gratified on this primitive infantile level generate a sense of euphoria. A person already feels elated due to the ego purgation that relieves her of the anxiety-arousing task of being responsible or autonomous. She feels further elated in the release of tension that accompanies the actual surrendering or letting go of the stressful effort to be responsible. But her elation intensifies most dramatically when the dissolution of self restores instincts to their unconstrained primitive expression. "He who knows God is freed from all fetters" (Upanishads, 13).

The immediate and unmediated apprehension of God regressively returns instincts to an unharnessed level of functioning that existed prior to ego "fetters." The hidden drives and primitive processes that had been pressing imperiously on consciousness since the ego first developed to contain them are suddenly, and rapturously, set free. Once again they are expressed on an archaic level where the mother, in the form of God, immediately gratifies longings and seems to anticipate every need.

> He knows the thoughts within the breasts. God is all-hearing, all-seeing. (The Koran, quoted in Arberry, 1955, p. 109)

> You know when I sit and when I rise,
> You perceive my thoughts from afar. (Ps 139:2)

The direct appeal of this type of immediacy to childhood thinking is revealed in childhood thinking:

> He knows when you are sleeping
> He knows when you're awake
> He knows when you've been bad or good
> So be good for heaven's sake.

The omnipotence of this magical type of thinking represents a regression to infancy's omnipotent equation of wish with gratification and thought with action. It thus frees people of the constraints normally placed on instincts and behavior. They feel cleansed of the old self (of the limitations of that old self) and experience *mokṣa* (liberation in Hinduism) or being "carried out of themselves" in a divine frenzy of God's redemptive love.

Religious experience *is* ecstatic. That is, religious experience is *ex-statio*—literally "out of self." It is an experience that seems to take place out of self not only because its restored primitive instincts transcend the limitations of self-boundaries but because these primitive instincts and processes come from such a deeply repressed and inaccessible unconscious realm that they are not experienced as belonging to the person. They are too powerful to have been derived from a self that, from the time of the development of an ego that controlled them, has associated itself with control and limitations. They are too mysterious and unknown to belong to an adulthood that has learned to make logic and mastery the sine qua non of its existence. Hence their recovery is endowed with a sacred nature.

The tendency not to recognize rapturously released instincts as one's own, and instead to attribute them to God, allows the person to express particularly pernicious pent-up feelings with impunity. And the act of expressing those feelings frees the person of some of their unconscious pressure without her having to acknowledge their original intent.

For example, a person who is intimidated by sexual instincts renounces sex and blissfully surrenders herself to God. The experience not only defends her from the powerful instincts she fears and from the guilt they might engender but also allows repressed sexual passion to be gratified indirectly in the rapturous intensity of surrender to God. And it does so without leading to or expecting direct action on those passions.

A sublime religious experience might not be directly associated with sexual longings but it sometimes barely veils the underlying sexual motivation. The angel in St. Theresa of Avila's vision, for example, "held in his hand a long golden dart," which by "plunging" it into her heart "wounded" her and set her aflame with divine love. So too St. Catherine of Siena, after having apparently purged herself of sexual feelings, instead found herself "tormented by visions of fiends, who filled her cell and with obscene words and gestures invited her to lust" (Underhill, 1911, p. 392).

The experience of unity with God, which will be examined later on, similarly expresses intense sexual desires—longings that seek an orgasmic oneness but that are denied due to an individual's fear of sexual vulnerability or bonding (where two bodies become joined as one in the act of intercourse).

At the height of being in love the boundary between the ego and object threatens to melt away. Against all evidence of his senses, a man who is in love declares that "I" and "you" are one, and is prepared to behave as if it were a fact. (Freud, 1961b, p. 66)

An experience of oneness with God or Nirvana vicariously gratifies the longing for sexual union without activating the anxiety surrounding sexual intimacy. Hence John of the Cross could say to God, "For today you shall be my wife," and indirectly experience the excitement of becoming a newlywed without having to take on the responsibility of being a husband or experiencing the trepidation of the first night's sexual encounter. Others safely channel repressed sexual energy away from the love of a single person and toward a "love of all people," thereby avoiding the erotic instincts of love elicited in the former but dissipated in the latter.

They protect themselves against the loss of the object by directing their love, not to the single objects but to all men alike; and they avoid the uncertainty and disappointments of genital love by turning away from its sexual aim and transforming the instinct into an impulse with an inhibited aim. (Freud, 1961b, p. 41)

Anna Freud elaborated on her father's idea of escaping sexual urges through spiritual love when she suggested that many people's love of others is an "altruistic surrender" (1946, p. 123). A person gives up the instinctual gratification she truly seeks because she is afraid of it. Then, in a type of reaction formation, she does the opposite. Instead of acting on sexual feelings she becomes celibate. Instead of acting on her needs she seeks to gratify other peoples' needs. Her love and compassion appear commendable but they are motivated less by an authentic wish to serve others than by the compulsion to escape urges she cannot control. "The surrender of her instinctual impulses in favor of other people had thus an egoistic significance, but in her efforts to gratify the impulse of others her behavior could be called altruistic" (A. Freud, 1946, p. 126). Christians' "agape" love typifies an emphasis on a so-called spiritual love that excludes eros, a phenomenon Anna's father observed in celibate love:

The Catholic church had the best of motives for recommending its followers to remain unmarried and for imposing celibacy upon its priests; but falling in love has often driven even priests to leave the church. In the same way love for women breaks through the group tie of race, of national divisions, and of the social class system, and it thus produces important effects as a factor in civilization. It seems certain that homosexual love is far more compatible with group ties. (Freud, 1960, p. 73)

Religious experience induces feelings of elation through released pent-up sexual instincts as well as other primitive processes. The "eternal now" of the divine encounter, for example, or the spiritual anthem of the sixties, "Be here now," manifests the euphoric timelessness of religious experience. Its euphoric transcendence of time is a regressive return to the unconscious processes that are "in themselves timeless" (Freud, 1920b, p. 168). Primary process and primitive instincts functioned before there was conscious awareness of time. They operated in a period dominated by wish fulfillment. The infant's wish for comfort and the mother's seemingly immediate gratification of that wish were experienced as the same by the infant, thereby precluding the existence of time between wish and gratification of wish. Later, when the mother becomes less immediately available for gratification, time enters into consciousness. The infant becomes aware of past gratification and present frustration. She learns through a loving mother who in time gratifies needs that time is acceptable, benign. She then develops trust in, even anticipation of, future experiences.

If the infant's experience of the mother is one of inconsistency or absence, however, the infant learns not to trust in the future. Time becomes frustrating, depriving. The limitations imposed by time—including the ultimate limitation, death, and its attending anxieties—evaporate in the religious revival of primitive processes that are not subject to time. Experiences that are blissfully eternal, such as the timelessness of Zen meditation (*muji*), make time seem to slow to a crawl, accelerate, or be suspended. A person can even be in two places at once in an experience that generally ignores temporal categories (astral projection). Or feelings that arise from one's psychological past are reinterpreted as meaning that the person had a historical past (reincarnation). The mystic Eckhart wrote that an individual in the unitive experience "is unaware of yesterday or the day before and of tomorrow and the day after, for in eternity there is no yesterday, nor any tomorrow but only Now" (quoted in Blackney, 1941, p. 153).

Another example of how elation arises out of regressively restored primary process is the experience that is so perfectly euphoric as to defy communication. Human language is inadequate to describe the divine ecstasy, which, since it transcends mortal comprehension, is beyond human discourse. Words cannot do justice to the experience; it is ineffable, sublimely beyond words.[3] Not only does it defy explanation; talking about the experience would itself separate an individual from the experience and reveal that she never truly had it.

> The Tao that can be spoken
> Is not the Tao. (Lao Tzu)

> Those who know
> Don't say,
> Those who say
> Don't know. (*Tao Te Ching*)

The immediacy of religious experience transcends talking about God because it regressively takes place in the preverbal state that precedes the language skills or logical reasoning to communicate experience. The inexpressible love and indescribable mystery are a return to this early state in which an infant's experience came through intense feelings rather than through thought processes. She knew her mother, as the adult knows God, by feeling her presence and love instead of by reflecting on or analyzing it (and especially not by talking about it[4]). So too she communicated with her mother not through words, but through wishes—wishes that magically seemed to be answered without being voiced, as when longing for the breast and the appearance of the breast seemed to coincide.[5]

> My confession is made both silently in your sight, my God, and aloud as well, because even though my tongue utters no sound, my heart cries to you. (St. Augustine, 1961, p. 28)

> When you fully absorb yourself into Mu [nothingness], the external and internal merge into a single unity. But, unable to speak

about it, you will be like "a mute who has had a dream." One who is dumb is unable to talk about his dream of the night before. In the same way, you will relish the task of samadhi yourself but be unable to tell others about it. (Kapleau, 1967, p. 80)

The ineffable experience of God not only resists logical interpretation but comes about only after logical interpretation is eliminated. Through spiritual exercises such as struggling with a Zen koan—"What is the sound of one hand clapping"—the person abandons logical constructs. The attempt to think about or rationally analyze the sound of one hand clapping is fruitless.[6] But in surrendering logic the person appears to "grasp" the truth of the conundrum. By abandoning secondary functions she regressively restores primary process thinking, which exists prior to logic and does not operate by rational rules, by an ordered sequence of time, or by connections that are comprehensible. Instead, in the regressive restoration in religious experience, primary process allows for the irrational, the noncommunicable, and even the coexistence (condensation) of contradictory thoughts—like one hand clapping.

> The governing rule of logic carries no weight in the unconscious; it might be called the Realm of the Illogical. Urges with contrary aims exist side by side in the unconscious. (Freud, 1940, p. 168)

Religious experience induces a form of elation that arises not from psychological regression to the pervasive pleasure of instinctual immediacy or unbounded primary process but from psychosomatic alteration in consciousness due to spiritual discipline. For example, the subtle elation experienced in meditation can be caused by lowered heart rate and blood pressure. Controlled breathing can induce a mild euphoria due to altered carbon monoxide intake to the brain (anoxia). In a similar way, a slowing of physical activity, as in sedentary prayer, lessens the body's energy needs, and so blood flow decreases to the muscles and instead moves to the brain, producing a warm and peaceful sensation.

A spiritual "high" can also arise from a release of endorphins (chemical transmitters in the brain that attack pain, serving as a type of analgesia), induced by actions no less disparate than jogging and the frenetic dancing of whirling dervishes. The latter, along with

rhythmic chanting, also can lull the brain into a quiescent autohyp-
notic state (equated with a divine trance).[7]

The problem with physically or psychologically induced elation
is that a person can become dependent on it. Just as a drug-induced
high can replace the psychophysiological self-care actions of the
body, and thereby create addiction, the religious individual's high can
become a substitute for the natural strengths of the person's body and
mind. She becomes addicted to elation as her body shuts down its
own operation in the reliance on elation to maintain positive feelings.

ELATION AND SUPEREGO REGRESSION

An ecstatic release of instincts does not mean that the person
directly indulges these previously repressed instincts, for along with
the regressive loss of ego that permitted their euphoric recovery is a
regressive return to a primitive superego structure. The reactivation
of this archaic superego elicits another type of elation when, instead
of directly expressing formerly forbidden feelings, the person discovers in the experience of God the simultaneous release of and
control over them. That is, she finds that the instincts she cannot
control can be controlled in an experience of God that imposes authority over those instincts while at the same time allowing some
unconscious gratification of them.

The authority restored in religious experience is the primitive
superego. Originally, parental reward and punishment provided a
framework in which the child learned to distinguish acceptable and
unacceptable behavior. Gradually she internalized parental reward
and punishment into an inner structure that henceforth served as her
superego or conscience. This internal voice of moral judgment and
propriety helps her determine what is right and wrong, and guides
her ego, as she matures, to limit instincts to acceptable expressions
and to chastise deviations from the acceptable.

However, ego control over instincts can be inadequate. The ego
can feel overwhelmed by instinctual pressure or by external expectations to be in control. Either situation can reactivate the archaic
internal image of parental prohibitions and rewards. The person
turns to this inner image, or to its external manifestation in society's
various authority structures, to dominate the instincts her ego cannot
control.

Religious experience regressively restores this archaic superego in order to defend against the anxiety elicited when the purgation of ego leaves the person unprotected against primitive instincts. Although religious experience euphorically recovers repressed primary process, it also frighteningly reactivates undesirable feelings such as unresolved oedipal guilt toward one's father and unresolved sexual feelings toward one's mother (for the male, and vice versa for the female). The arousal of these conflicts brings fears of castration, rejection, or loss of approval.

The child overcame castration anxiety and fear of rejection by submitting herself to the parent, but the adult is inhibited from directly submitting herself to parental punishment and reward in order to restrain instinctual behavior. Hence she experiences an unbearable tension in religious experience when these unconscious drives are revived. She learns to minimize some of the conflict between the recovered unacceptable instincts and the narrow avenue of socially approved means of expressing and gratifying them by complementing the purgative loss of control over them with spiritual disciplines that reinforce their repression (e.g., celibacy). "The task which asceticism sets itself is to keep the id within limits by simply imposing prohibitions" (A. Freud, 1946, p. 165).

The regressive reconstruction of an outgrown childhood superego—in the form of strict spiritual practices that replace ego control over instincts, coupled with an equally watchful omnipotent deity—has a dual effect. On the one hand, the implied punishment/reward of the superego God reasserts the parental authority that guards against unacceptable behavior. At the same time, it restores the ecstatic freedom of not having personally to restrict instincts or to be responsible for them, since the archaic superego—and not an internal conscience—assumes authority over them.

Consider, for example, the experiment in which students were told to administer shocks to other students (Milgram, 1974). When the tester told the subjects that he would take full responsibility for the shocks delivered to the subject on his command, students delivered the shocks. By submitting themselves to the authority figure, the students isolated themselves from social responsibility and from the fear of reprisal for normally proscribed actions ("deindividuation"). They thereby were able to lessen ego control and to discharge normally repressed or antisocial impulses as they relinquished the role and responsibility of their own superego and relegated them to the tester. Obedience to the dictates of his external authority reinforced an archaic constraint on their instincts but at the same time offered a nefarious thrill when the external superego gave them permission to act on forbidden instincts and to do so with impunity.

Religious experience similarly reactivates an archaic superego, in the form of a powerful God whose authority places strict prohibitions on instincts and at the same time euphorically allows their indirect expression. Society has endowed God with the power to issue rules that must be obeyed and to wield threats of hell-fire for disobedience of them. God's power is sufficient to produce enough fear and guilt to inhibit people from even thinking about unacceptable impulses. The God who "knows your thoughts even before you voice them" takes on the role of the superego, which "calls the ego to account not only for its deeds, but for its thoughts and unexecuted actions, of which the superego seems to have knowledge" (Freud, 1940, p. 205).

As the child trembled at the thought of rebelling against her parents and experienced great relief in the oedipal competition by surrendering herself to them, so too the omnipotence and perfection of God so decisively demand submission that the adult surrenders herself to the religious experience. As a result of submitting herself once again to the authority of her parents—this time in the form of God—the person blissfully "lets go" of the struggle she previously experienced between faulty superego constraints and imperious unconscious desires, and replaces imperfect control over instincts with omnipotent divine control.

Take, for example, sexual feelings that are repressed in the purgative stage of religious experience. They are returned to a primitive instinctual level where they are vicariously gratified in the thinly disguised erotic passion of the divine encounter. But along with their passion they bring the hidden guilt and fear of punishment that first motivated their repression.[8] To defend against this, the passionate experience of God not only partially gratifies repressed sexual longings (by indirectly and anonymously indulging them). It also allows the person, via submission to God, to replace her own faulty superego with the archaic/divine superego that vitiates consciously acknowledging those sexual feelings (as well as their derivatives of guilt and anxiety). St. Augustine is a frequently cited case study in which the surrender of self to God ecstatically releases unconscious conflicts (unresolved oedipal feelings toward his mother) that are then kept controlled by a God whose strict moral authority substitutes for Augustine's own besieged superego.

Freud (1964c) cited a patient's religious experience as an example of a superego regression that not only restored oedipal sexual feelings but cathartically released repressed aggressive drives. In his analysis of an American physician, Freud described the doctor's experience of seeing the body of an old woman who was to be dissected. The physician suddenly felt that no God would allow the woman's death, and so abandoned his religious belief. Later, God directly spoke to him and told him to believe.

Freud suggested the old woman evoked memories of the doctor's own mother, the result of intense unresolved oedipal longings. The hostility and aggression he felt toward his father were manifested in trying to vanquish the father's authority through the expulsion of his belief in God. But the guilt of his oedipal rebellion, coupled with the unacceptable incestuous feelings toward his mother, regressively reactivated the powerful oedipal father in the form of God's command to believe. Because the revival of competitive oedipal feelings toward his father elicited anxious feelings of inevitable defeat (the oedipal father/God being obviously stronger), salvation was in "complete submission to the will of God the father. . . . He had a religious experience and had undergone a conversion" (Freud, 1961c, p. 170).

RETREAT FROM REALITY AND FLIGHT INTO FANTASY

The ego, with help from the superego, imposes constraints on instincts so as to make their expression acceptable in civilized society. When primary process is expressed with little direction from the ego—the ego having been purged—and when religious experience does not restore an ordered superego and instead allows primitive instincts to be expressed with minimal regard to the sanctions of the external environment, reality is often sacrificed. Wish-fulfilling drive gratification and the denial of anxiety define the person's interpretation of what is real and what is not.

Freud labeled God an illusion because the image of God is a product of this unconscious wish-fulfilling defining of reality. God is an illusion not because an absolute does not exist but because it is primarily related to unconscious needs rather than conscious ego functions. Religious experience shapes reality to avoid the latter and to accommodate the former.

> The hermit turns his back on the world and will have no truck with it. But one can do more than that; one can try to recreate the world, to build in its stead another world in which its most unbearable features are eliminated and replaced by others that are in conformity with ones' own wishes. But whoever, in desperate defiance, sets upon this path to happiness will, as a rule, obtain nothing. Reality is too strong for him. He becomes a madman. (Freud, 1961d, p. 28)

Reality in religious experience is defined by the primitive primary process it regressively restores. The revival of primary process reverses normative development away from a reality determined by constraints and expectations, toward one based on fantasy and wishes. This regression to primitive processes is most notably manifested in religious visions.

Mystical literature is replete with references to men and women who talked with God or who saw the Supreme Being "face to face." Hindu and Buddhist sacred texts describe peoples' vision of Krishna or of Buddha. Christian scriptures record situations in which disciples saw Jesus after he died and heard God's voice in thunder. So too Judaism presents Moses talking to God, and "the word of the Lord came to Abraham in a vision." Mohandas Gandhi heard a voice say, "You are on the right track, move neither to your left, nor right, but keep to the straight and narrow" (quoted in Chatterjee, 1987, p. 99).

Religious visions or voices usually are preceded by ascetical practices that purge autonomous cognitive processes. St. Anthony of the Desert, for instance, saw demons and naked women after having withdrawn from the world and having endured self-flagellation. Moses heard God after an extensive time of solitude and fasting. Long hours of meditation lead to "meeting Buddha on the road." Ecstatic visions are experienced after the overstimulation of the whirling dervishes' dance, and, just the opposite, after long hours of sensory deprivation (note, for example, John Lilly's [1956] research in sensory deprivation tanks).

Religious experience displaces autonomous psychological structures and in the form of supernatural visions reverses mental processes based on realistic thinking to those based on perception—and not just any perception, but the primitive perception of precognitive wish-fulfilling hallucinations.

Hallucinations are the property of primary process thinking. They first occur, according to psychoanalytic thought, in the infant's earliest experience of hunger and satiation of hunger. Because an early undifferentiated state with the mother means that the infant does not experience a delay between the sensation of hunger and the appearance of the mother's breast to satisfy that hunger, gratification of the wish to be sated is experienced as the same as the wish itself. When at times the mother's breast does not immediately appear, the infant—unable at this early age to tolerate or to understand drive tension—cannot comprehend why frustration of instincts occurs or how to resolve it.[9]

These instincts are, as explained, directed by primitive processes. They are unbound, seek immediate gratification, are not subject to constraints of reality (such as temporal considerations). Hence, when hunger drives the infant toward the object that gratifies hunger (the mother's breast) but the mother is absent and the infant cannot yet tolerate the buildup of drive tension or gratify the drive on her own, she temporarily gratifies that drive by remembering the breast that in the past gratified it. The infant's primitive cognitive processes form "a mental image of mother's breast so as to reestablish the situation of the original satisfaction" (Freud, 1915b, p. 163). The image or hallucination of the mother's breast provides the temporary relief from drive tension and the gratification of needs as did the physical breast.[10]

Adults sometimes gratify instinctual needs by regressing to these primitive precognitive processes. They respond to life's occasionally unmanageable vicissitudes by reverting to fantasy and even hallucinations. In some situations this leads to creativity. Usually, however, hallucinations are regressive means of escaping the limitations placed on instinctual gratification in the real world. Drives that cannot be satisfied through healthy secondary functions are freed of adult constraints and return to the early instinctual level in which the intensity of wishes creates hallucinatory gratification.

The most common and universal means by which a person

abandons, temporarily, developmentally mature cognitive processes, and restores precognitive hallucinatory processes, is in dreams. The condensation, displacement, and symbolism of dreams most perfectly represent primary process hallucinatory activity. The wishes and instinctual cravings that the daytime ego cannot gratify can, in dreams—when the daytime control of the ego vanishes and repressed unconscious activity surfaces—be gratified. In dreams, as in the hallucinated breast, wishes can come true; needs can be immediately satisfied and are not bound by time or delay; thoughts can be entirely irrational and yet still make sense; people can merge and separate and remerge, and in the process gratify unconscious longings.

Dreams have always been a significant source of religious experience. Most societies find spiritual meaning in dreams. The mystic who hears God's voice while sleeping attributes it to a divinely inspired dream. When the same experience takes place in an awakened state, she attributes it to a celestial vision. While the former and the latter are frequently found to coexist in religious experience —"Dreams are indeed often regarded as the portal to the world of the mystic" (Freud, 1961a, p. 77)—dreams usually are not equated with reality while visions are hallucinations that are equated with reality.

Hallucinations, like dreams, gratify instinctual desires that could not be gratified by the conscious working of the ego. Also like dreams, hallucinations occur when the ego's monitoring function is set aside and unconscious processes arise in the form of images. Unlike dreams, however, hallucinations do not occur in sleep. They take place when the reality-testing ego, having been diminished, allows for a regressive return to primary process thinking in which needs are magically gratified, contradictory images coexist, symbols predominate, boundaries are erased, and time or place has no bearing.

Hallucinations are not common occurrences. A daytime retreat into fantasy as a way of managing stress is not uncommon but a hallucination, an actual return to primitive images that are interpreted as real, occurs primarily when the drive for gratification is so strong—and the ability of the ego to manage it so weak—that frustration of the drive is intolerable.

The vision of God or of supernatural beings is a hallucinatory response to this frustration. Through various spiritual disciplines, such as isolation and sensory deprivation, the person abandons autonomous cognitive functioning. In the place of relying on secondary functioning to gratify needs in a realistic manner—on logic, control, and mastery to overcome frustration—the person restores precognitive wish-fulfilling images and fantasy to gratify needs and to vanquish frustration. She hallucinates a divine image to gratify internal longings that, as in infancy, not only could not consciously be gratified but possess a drive tension so strong as to be insufferable if frustrated.

To "see Buddha on the road," or to have a vision of God, completes the regressive retreat from maturely developed thought processes to primitive cognition based on perception.[11] A normative perceptual system takes in perceptions in an orderly fashion. It records what was received in memory and analyzes, thinks about, and acts on it. Visions or hallucinations are a regressive return to a primitive process of perception that precedes cognitive development. Lacking the secondary functions to think about or to verbalize perceptions (the ego having been renounced and restored to a nondiscursive or preverbal state), an individual does not act on perceptions according to how they have in the past gratified or failed to gratify needs. She instead is driven by unbounded primitive processes that find in a percept the immediate discharge of drive, regardless of whether the percept is based in reality or in the intensity of drives that create need-gratifying images. The latter is a hallucination derived from precognitive interpretation of those images and the inner excitation that creates them as coming from outside. They are projected onto an external screen where they are vividly portrayed and taken literally.

Take, for example, St. Anthony of the Desert, who withdrew from society's temptations and purged himself of desires. In spite of this deprivation, previously banished sexual longings returned—and returned with a vengeance. Instead of dealing maturely with them, he re-repressed and relegated sexual urges to an unconscious realm, then reexperienced them in the form of precognitive images, images projected outside of himself as hallucinatory visions of seductive women.

> An internal perception is suppressed, and instead, its content, after undergoing a certain degree of distortion, enters consciousness in the form of an external perception. In delusions of perse-

cution the distortion consists in a transformation of affect; what should have been felt internally as love is perceived externally as hate. (Freud, 1911a, p. 442)

Sexual feelings that St. Anthony should have learned to "love," or at least to become comfortable with, instead are distorted into uncontrollable urges and projected onto a hallucinated hostile object. Although the image of naked women was experienced as persecutory, and therefore unwelcome, it also represented a primitive form of indulging sexual instincts vicariously. Images of seductive women might be only hallucinations but they are no less sexual in nature. Their encounter is a sexual encounter and, because it takes place "out there," is a *safe* sexual encounter that is not directly acknowledged as originating within oneself.

Furthermore, by distorting the wish "If only I had conquered those sexual feelings" into a hallucinated image of women whose temptations he could resist, St. Anthony felt he had reconquered his sexuality and thereby reinforced repression of sexual longings. Freud's famous analysis of Schreber reveals a similar disdain for sexual urges and a projection of them onto an experience of God where, in spite of their persecutory elements, they are at least capable of being vicarioulsy gratified.

> "From the beginning of my contact with God up to the present day my body has continuously been the object of divine miracles. . . . Hardly a single limb or organ in my body escaped being temporarily dominated by miracles." (Quoted in Freud, 1911a, p. 448)

Jesus had a vision of an angel in Gethsemane. Feeling abandoned and misunderstood, Jesus experienced intense longing for comfort—"If this cup can pass away"—which was gratified in the apotheosis of a hallucination. An angelic image arose out of a regressively restored unconscious to replace the object of gratification whose absence, like that of the mother in infancy, causes unbearable tension. As a mother's hallucinated breast offers comfort, so too the angel who offers Jesus a cup of comfort temporarily gratifies the longing he can satisfy neither on his own nor through those who have become absent.

Whether through visions or rapturous gratification of drives, the regressive recovery of primary process and primitive instincts usually does not occur in isolation. It is inseparable from the regressive sacrifice of ego functioning that allows their reactivation, and so too from a deeper descent into unconscious mental structures that gratify even more profound primitive needs: a regression Freud called topographical, and which I will now address as the regressive symbiotic experience of communion with God.

4

Symbiotic Regression:
The Experience of Unity

Although religious experience begins with purgation and leads to illumination, it is not merely the surrendering of self or a feeling of euphoria. It is not only becoming obedient to God or meditating. These and other spiritual practices are necessary disciplines for the divine encounter but they are primarily preparatory; they are rarely promulgated as ends in themselves. Religious experience is not only "losing self" but "finding self." It is not simply surrendering self in order to be rid of self but surrendering it to God in the attempt to merge selflessly into communion with God.

UNITIVE EXPERIENCE

The experience of unity with God is the goal of spiritual discipline. People adhere to strenuous self-denying practices in order to free themselves of a self whose egocentric needs and preconceived notions of God impede that unity. When the empirical ego disappears, the distance, and even distinctions, between self and God disappear, resulting in the unitive experience. Abraham Maslow summarized it thus: "There is a fusion with the reality being observed, a oneness where there was a twoness, an integration of some sort of the self with the non-self" (1971, p. 60).

The aim of Buddhism, for example, is the oneness of Nirvana. Nirvana literally means extinction, as in the extinguishing of a limited ego and the dissolution of the self into *satori* or formlessness. Hinduism emphasizes *Tat tvam asi* (Thou art That; Upanishads, 1926, 6.11). That is, you are everything and everything is you. Taoism refers to an integration into the harmony of nature, of life, whereby the person's energy and the energy of life fuse into the one energy the Chinese call *chi*. In yoga, the aspirant works at uncovering self or Atman, so as to merge seamlessly with the unbounded consciousness of Brahma. Sufis speak of *fana*, or disintegrating the self, so as to experience *Baqa*, or unity. Christian mystics refer to the experience as achieving God-consciousness. So too their scriptures, and not just their mystical literature, have references to unitive experience: "The Father is in me and I am in the Father" (Jn 10:39); "I live now not with my own life but with the life of Christ within me" (Gal 2:30); "Let that mind be in you which was in Christ Jesus" (Phil 2:5).

Unity is not confined to sacred encounters with God. Zaehner (1961) wrote extensively about animistic identification with nature, while the early American Transcendentalists spoke about a pantheistic type of oneness with the earth (e.g., Emerson's "Nature," 1936). So too humanistic and transpersonal psychologists stress peak experiences or unitive consciousnesses that do not necessarily involve a concept of God. Romantic poetry portrays images of individuals whose love for each other defies logical self-boundaries and forges a single whole where once two existed.

> Bound up with love together in one volume,
> The scattered leaves of all the universe.
> Substance and accidents, and their relations
> Together fused in such a way
> That what I speak of is a single flame.
> (Dante)

Other poets speak of becoming momentarily "lost" or absorbed in an aesthetic experience whereby a person feels indistinguishable from the experience.

> Music heard so deeply
> That it is not heard at all, but you are the music
> While the music lasts.
> (Eliot, 1943, p. 46)

> O body swayed to music, O brightening glance,
> How can we know the dancer from the dance? (Yeats, 1966)

Unity that is experienced with God or Nirvana is the achievement of spiritual perfection. Psychologically, however, the experience indicates the regressive completion of ego dissolution and a reactivation of archaic internal objects. Infantile omnipotence is recovered, and is confused with enlightenment, while early unity with the mother is recapitulated and reinterpreted as the unitive state. That is, the experience of Nirvana or communion with God is a symbiotic regression. It is a backward movement from the development of a separate and conscious system of the mind to a more primitive, undifferentiated, and unconscious mental organization. Before examining how this experience of communion with God represents a reversion to the earliest symbiotic unity with the mother, a few words are needed to clarify the previous discussion of Freud's analysis of religious experience as a regressive return to the developmental stage of superego formation, and thereby to distinguish the unity experienced in superego regression from that of symbiotic regression.

SUPEREGO REGRESSION AND UNITIVE EXPERIENCE

Freud wrote only sparingly of religious experience as a regressive return to the earliest relationship with the mother. He instead focused on the religious experience that regressively reactivates a stage of mental functioning developmentally more sophisticated. He perceived in the experience of God a type of superego regression motivated by unresolved oedipal tension. But superego regression involves more than the elation that arises from overcoming instinctual tension. It also elicits a type of unity, for in the experience of God a person momentarily feels an alignment between the imposing constraints of God and the archaic restraints of the superego. No dissension, or even distance, exists between the person's will and the will of God. Needs are denied and instincts repressed so as to maintain the conflict-free supremacy of an archaic superego restored in becoming submissive to the omnipotent God. "No longer my will but your will be done" (Lk 22:42). "By thy grace, I remember my light, and now gone is my delusion. My doubts are no more, my faith is firm and now I can say 'Thy will be done' " (Bhagavad Gita).

Freud (1960) analyzed the regressive alignment of one's superego with the superego of another, or of an Other, in his study of group psychology. A person is able to renounce the inadequate attempts of his superego to regulate instincts when he abandons himself to the dictates of the group, which embodies the superego constraints that effectively rule him. The group leader in particular is invested with the authority and sometimes omnipotence that, in the child, were attributed to the powerful parents.

The Roman Catholic Church is an example of a highly organized and hierarchical group that elicits the obedience and respect due to the superego (Freud, 1960, p. 32). Its power has a superego control over its adherents similar to that of the army. Each provides the unquestioned authority to dominate individual wishes; into one or the other a person can abandon the fragility of his superego until he merges into the authoritarian structure that replaces his superego. The difference between the two is that the army's superego ability to command obedience is not translated into sacred feelings of awe and devotion (though nationalism elicits feelings of loyalty not entirely different from religious reverence).

Religious experience involves the surrender of self to the authority of God (or to a particular representative of God). That authority becomes the external superego that helps the person to restrict unacceptable instinctual activity. The result is twofold. First, identification with the church or with its leaders, as identification with any group, enlarges the person's sense of self. To become obedient to and to identify with the majesty of church/God is to reject a limited definition of self. The person feels absorbed into a larger identity, a new whole, and in the process euphorically feels expanded beyond his old psychological boundaries. The strengths issuing from that divine identification, however, are not one's own but arise from a primitive superego reactivated in the form of God. Erich Fromm suggested that a person escapes himself and merges into a group in order "to acquire the strengths which the individual self is lacking . . . a more or less complete surrender of individuality and the integrity of the self . . . to fuse one's self with somebody or something outside of oneself" (1941, p. 148).

Outside the unity experienced in aligning oneself with a particular religious group or with God, the superego constraints that were instilled through identification with that group disappear. This is a common complaint among people whose experience of personal transformation was in encounter groups like "est" or whose experience of God was that of being "saved" by itinerant preachers such as Billy Graham. Feelings of salvation often disappear with the departure of the evangelist/group whose charismatic authority revived archaic superego constraints and subsequent feelings of salvation.

The second effect of aligning one's superego with the archaic superego projectively experienced in God is that when strength is found primarily in the experience of God, and not from within the person, then even with an inflated image of superego control the individual internally denigrates himself for what little strength he authentically possesses. "The members [of a group] perceive the leader as omnipotent and omniscient, while they consider themselves inadequate, immature and incompetent" (Kernberg, 1966, p. 250). Because the person who finds his worth in an externally deified superego feels worthless without that superego's constraints, his identity tends to center on the deified superego. His sense of self becomes based less on his uniqueness or on an ability to balance inner needs with external demands, and more on how he conforms to the group or the unitive experience.

> Every man is, in a certain sense, unconsciously a worse man when he is in society than when alone, for he is carried by society and to that extent relieved of his individual responsibility. (Jung, 1970, p. 165)

EGO IDEAL AND GROUP UNITY

In addition to experiences in which divine prohibitions and superego restraints are felt as one, unity occurs when a person idealizes God and encounters in that idealization the embodiment of his own ego ideal.

The ego ideal is a counterpart to the superego. It is not, however, motivated by guilt and the avoidance of punishment; rather, it is based on a nostalgic longing for all that the person once wished to be but realistically never could attain.

The ego ideal forms during the oedipal stage when the child internalizes parental values and goals. While the oedipal drama is resolved through the withdrawal of libido from the opposite-sex parent and the development of a stable although constrained inner self, an internal mental organization—the ego ideal—is invested with the narcissistic libido that makes it the replacement for the feelings of perfection that were sacrificed in the oedipal development of the more realistic self.

Just as the child once preferred the secure feelings of unconditional love and bonding to the anxious feelings of individuality, so too the adult sometimes experiences the realistic limitations of his individuality severely restricting intense libidinal feelings and inhibiting a greater sense of unity. Several avenues are available to recreate these feelings of bonding and wholeness. He can take refuge in unconscious flights of fantasy or perfection, but since he is no longer a child he feels uncomfortable or self-conscious about this. He can instead find refuge from the constraints of reality by submerging himself in one of various group situations that satisfy regressive idealized longings as well as superego constraints (Freud, 1960, p. 78). Without necessarily abandoning all his healthy secondary ego functions, he allows the dynamics of the group to pull from within him the regressive wish to rely more profusely on the idealized image of what the group—or God—represents.

The group into which a person submerges himself is not simply an environment in which libidinal feelings are exchanged and interaction with others (or with God) affords a greater sense of togetherness. Instead, group membership induces heightened libidinal feelings that are generated by intense unconscious wishes to believe in the group or to believe as those in the group believe, as well as by the tenacious need to be accepted and loved by the group.

The idealized divine image, like the group, represents this regressive reactivation of uncomplicated parental love and unimpeded parental bonding. Feelings such as these are the stuff of which fantasy and the unconscious ego ideal are made. They have not been realistically experienced since childhood's innocence was sacrificed in accepting the struggles with imperfection and the responsibilities of individuality. Hence God becomes the unconditionally loving and highly libidinized Perfect Being that the person's ego ideal unconsciously wishes for itself but cannot consciously attain due to realistic constraints.

> The object serves as a substitute for some unattained ego ideal of one's own. We love it on account of the perfection which we have striven to reach for within our own ego. (Freud, 1960, p. 44)

When the unconscious longings of a person's ego ideal are fulfilled by God, then that individual's realistic ego becomes less distinct from the fantasy of the ego ideal. For instance, most people make demands on themselves that they cannot meet. They might feel sinful, as a result, because they cannot live up to the ego ideal of perfection. But sinfulness and limitations seem to disappear in an experience of an all-loving God's acceptance of them, which causes them to forget the disparity of the weaknesses that once distinguished a conscious self (sinful) from an idealized self (holy). They thereby not only project unconscious ego longings onto God but, once they experience being loved by this perfect God, they feel the fulfillment of unconscious longings. In psychological language they introject—take back into self—the unconscious longings displaced onto God. To surrender oneself to an all-loving God therefore is to feel reunited or "in touch" with the unconditional love a person's ego ideal unconsciously seeks, has deified, and into which it has become absorbed.

> The ego becomes more and more unassuming, until at last it [the idealized object] gets possession of the entire self love of the ego, whose self sacrifice thus follows a natural consequence [until] object love, so to speak, consumes the ego. (Freud, 1959, p. 44)

SYMBIOTIC UNITY

Freud relegated religious experience to an unconscious longing to resolve conflicting oedipal feelings, but he also acknowledged the religious experience that was a regression to a more primitive "oceanic" unity.[1] He suggested that the latter experience was the submersion of ego into the undifferentiated maternal unity from which it first emerged. While Freud described the resulting uninterrupted and pleasurable unity with the mother as "restoration of limitless narcissism" (1960, p. 89), I refer to it as a return to symbiotic unity.[2]

Symbiosis is the infant's earliest postnatal experience of life. At this tender age he does not yet differentiate between mother and self, between inner needs and external object-satisfying needs. If the infant is hungry, a breast appears to sate that hunger. A unitary system appears to exist between hunger and breast, between desire and fulfillment of desire, that makes them magically and omnipotently experienced as the same. The infant identifies the mother as inseparable from either the hunger or the gratifying sensations; he is a symbiotic part of the mother, an organism within an organism. Margaret Mahler described symbiosis[3] as:

> that state of undifferentiation, of fusion with mother in which the "I" is not yet differentiated from the "not-I" . . . the essential feature being hallucinatory or delusional somatopsychic omnipotent fusion with the representation of mother and, in particular, the delusion of a common boundary of the two actually and physically separate individuals. (1968, p. 9)

A nondifferentiated, boundless identification with the mother is not destined to last more than the minimal amount of time in which the newly exposed infant must be shielded from the harsh demands of the environment. With time, and through experience of periodic satiation and frustration, the infant becomes aware of the difference between inner needs and gratification of needs, and thereby between inner sensations and external reality. This experience of sensations arising from different internal and external sources is the beginning conscious awareness of an "I" in contrast to a "not-I."

When the symbiotic relationship with the mother provides a stable and consistent satisfaction of the infant's needs—what Winnicott called "good-enough mothering" (1965)—the infant's I gradually develops a critical twofold sense of confidence. First, he becomes confident about the dependability of the external world—that it is not a hostile environment that should be avoided rather than engaged. Second, he eventually internalizes this confidence into an ability to manage the responsibilities of individuality. This confidence facilitates the child's willingness to leave behind the security of the symbiotic relationship and to form an interiorly secure and distinct personal identity.

Although maternal unity and magical feelings of immediate gratification are abandoned in the development of a separate identity, they are never entirely forgotten. Vestiges of symbiosis last "throughout the life cycle"[4] (Mahler, 1975, p. 42).

Symbiosis is not only not left behind in the development of a separate identity but continues unconsciously and regressively to press for reactivation. Its longing for the "good old days," for the time of unequivocal acceptance and unbounded love, is normally kept hidden beneath the mature development of qualities such as autonomy and control. Sometimes, however, a person feels insecure about these strengths, or feels that excessive expectations are placed on them. This causes him regressively to remember—and possibly to reactivate—the underlying comfortable feelings of a time when there was no individuality or responsibility and instead only a selfless symbiotic attachment to the omnipotent mother.

Mahler suggested that the early symbiotic state was a perfect haven for those who altogether abandon their autonomy, who "in cases of the more severe disturbance of individuality" renounce personal initiative and responsibility (1968, p. 9). People who reject their individuality and regress to a selfless symbiotic unity usually are not comfortable with—and more likely are intimidated by—the expectations of autonomy and the pressures of responsibility. As discussed in the section on ego regression, they are people who have not developed the necessary ego strengths to feel in control; they never became truly secure in themselves, confident in their abilities to think independently, to adapt to their environment, to express their own will, or to engage in mature intimate relationships.

An experience that allows—even encourages—these people to surrender self and its attending anxieties would be (at least unconsciously) a welcome experience. Instead of exhibiting personal qualities such as volition and assertiveness, these people could merge selflessly into a greater whole: the symbiotic unity that does not expect individuality and responsibility.

If the men and women who escape autonomy by merging selflessly into a larger whole could be compared to pieces in a jigsaw puzzle, they would be pieces that do not organize a completed picture by recognizing the uniqueness of their own (or each other's) jagged edges and distinct curves. Instead, they attempt to throw all the pieces together, ignoring whether they properly fit. They bend unique corners of their identity in order to fit into the whole, or wear away the particular curves of their personality so as to fabricate a unity.

These men and women are afraid of their singular qualities and may even destroy them in the attempt to achieve perfect unity. The unity they achieve, however, is that of a jigsaw puzzle that creates a whole but ignores the uniqueness of individual pieces. "The discrepancy between the 'I' and the world disappears and with it the conscious fear of aloneness and powerlessness" (Fromm, 1941, p. 185).

Religious experience is a prime example of fulfilling the unconscious (and sometimes not so unconscious) longing to undo separateness and the anxiety attendant on it, and to return to a selfless symbiotic state represented in communion with God or Nirvana.[5] Spiritual traditions that teach that individuality is an impediment to unity with God conveniently provide the rationalization to reject the autonomous attributes a person fears, and subsequently to succumb to the symbiotic urges that offer refuge from them. One of the tasks of a stable psychological self-structure is to provide the internal fortitude (especially in times of stress, when demands placed on individuality are most keenly felt) to resist this underlying regressive "wish for reunion with the 'love object' " (Mahler, 1975, p. 77). Hence along with the ascetical dissolution of the ego functions that normally define a separate sense of self there is, first, the dissolution of the psychological resolve that maintained the boundaries between inner and outer, between I and not-I. Second, repressed merger wishes or unconscious desires for symbiotic-like gratification are awakened, and gratified, in the resulting unitive experience.

The surrender of ego or the submersion of a single drop of water into the ocean (Upanishad metaphor for unitive consciousness) recapitulates the earliest oceanic state out of which the ego originally struggled to distinguish itself. Like the earlier example of the seamless puzzle, a person uses self-denying spiritual disciplines, such as obedience, to contemplatively smooth over the edges of autonomy. Or he adopts celibacy to round out angles of sexuality until he sheds everything that defines him as distinct and, becoming indistinguishable from others—to the point of extinction as a separate self—merges into the "oceanic feelings of complete fusion and oneness with mother" (Mahler, 1968, p. 66.) Erikson stated that the person rejects the "aloneness" of a limited self and succumbs to the regressive urges beneath it: the "deep nostalgia for fusion with another, and this in an exclusive and lasting fashion, be that 'Other' a mentor or a God, the universe or the innermost self" (Erikson, 1969, p. 41).

For Christians, symbiotic regression takes place when the psychological boundaries that separate them from God are dissolved and they merge into divine communion. "If therefore I am changed into God and He makes me one with Himself, then, by the living God, there is no distinction between us" (Eckhart). Nirvana dedifferentiates the boundaries that distinguish separateness and restores the state of selflessness (*annata*) or being "unborn" (*sunyata*). Islam's *fan-f'allah* expresses a similar extinguishing of self, though into Allah, and Hindu practices create a womblike environment in which individuality is suppressed and the person regressively merges into an archaic selfless unity.[6]

> As the bees, my son, make honey by collecting the juices of distant trees, and reduce the juice into one form, and as these juices have no discrimination, so that they might say, I am the juice of this tree or that, in the same manner, my son, all these creatures, when they have become merged in the True, know not that they are merged in the True. (Madhyamaka-karida, 10, line 7; quoted in Nakamura, 1964, p. 68)

Dedifferentiation of the psychological boundaries between self and God does not mean that the mystic thinks he is God. Although some monistic systems speak of becoming God—"He, verily, who knows Supreme Brahma becomes Brahma himself" (Upanishads, 1926, 111, 2.9)—the religious individual generally does not become like the psychotic who says "I am Jesus Christ" (Rokeach, 1964).

Instead, the mystic ceases to experience a deity who exists "out there." As the infant did not experience the symbiotic mother as being out there, and did not distinguish between sensations arising inside and those from outside—and instead in experiencing mother experienced self, and in experiencing self experienced mother—so too the adult's experience of unity dissolves the boundaries between self and God and creates a sense of shared boundaries and thoughts. The infant's "delusion of a common boundary of the two actually and physically separate individuals" (Mahler, 1968, p. 9) is reexperienced through the regressive submersion into communion with God: "We behold that which we are, and are that which we behold" (Rhenish mystic Ruysbroek). The fluidity in the boundary between God and self allows the mystic this immediate sense of participation in God. He feels himself to be an intimate and inseparable part of God, and God to be the innermost part of himself—a symbiotic organism within an organism: "No longer I but Christ who lives within me (Gal 2:20). "God is nearer to me then I am to myself" (Eckhart).

An indissoluble unity creates in the mystic the impression that everything—not only God but nature, others, the universe—exists within the unity, and outside the unity nothing exists. Just as the infant takes in everything he can get hold of or can mentally imagine (oral incorporation), and thereby feels that everything is a part of him and he is a part of everything, so too the mystic feels as if a unitive state has consumed him or has been absorbed by him, and subsequently feels that he and the whole are one.

The Hindu *Tat tvam asi* (Thou art That) represents this omnipotent and symbiotic type of thinking. Everything is connected in this unitive state as everything was connected in the infant's mind. All actions are interrelated (karma); nothing takes place that does not have some connection with everything else (synchronicity) or that cannot be ascertained as to what invisible force makes that connection (I Ching). "All that a man has here externally in multiplicity is intrinsically One. Hence all blades of grass, wood, and stone, are all one" (Eckhart). Prayers have the power to effect change (miracles) and without separateness between self and God do not even have to be voiced to be heard and answered.[7]

> In this state the soul is like a little child still at the breast whose mother, to caress him while he is still in her arms, makes her milk distill into his mouth without ever moving his lips. (St. Francis de Sales)

PARADISE RESTORED AND LOST

Unitive experience redemptively restores an earlier innocence and wholeness. Buddhism, for example, refers to the "original mind" that was lost in the development of egoistic attachments. Christianity and Judaism promulgate a paradisiacal garden of Eden that was forfeited through disobedience. Unitive experience recreates this harmony; it does so, however, by dissolving the separateness that is feared and indulging the unconscious wish for the anxiety-free state, or what Erikson called the "universal nostalgia for a lost paradise" (1963, p. 80).

Feelings of bliss, of boundless well-being and ecstatic whole-ness, permeate unitive experience. However, the same regressive processes that revive this pleasurable paradise also eventually revive unconscious forbidden impulses and unmanageable negative feelings. Communion with God is not perfectly harmonious. With the renunciation of a personal ego and the reactivation of symbiotic one-ness comes susceptibility to deeply disturbing ambivalent feelings that threaten the unitive state.

The neonatal paradise restored in the experience of God is not always perfect. In spite of the presence of a symbiotic mother who magically makes frustrations disappear, frustrations inevitably intrude into the infant's idyllic realm. Their intrusion makes him aware that his mother does not immediately and always gratify needs. At this tender age the infant's embryonic ego cannot comprehend a mother who loves and nurtures but also disciplines and does not automatically ameliorate pain. In his mind she loves and nurtures or else withholds love and punishes. The prospect of losing the secure symbiosis elicits abandonment anxiety in the infant.

The ambivalent feelings surrounding the mother's nurturance and seeming withdrawal of nurturance are compounded when the infant begins to experience the pressure (internal and external) to become autonomous. He experiences a drive toward autonomy in order to learn to manage, on his own, the times when his mother does not gratify needs. Hence he feels on the one hand secure with and affectionate toward his mother, but on the other hand afraid of her abandonment and defiantly compelled to develop autonomous strengths.

The renunciation of adult ego functions and submersion into a unitive state restore these conflicting feelings. Purgation blissfully gets rid of anxiety surrounding autonomy but purgation becomes its own nemesis when, without an ego to maintain control over repressed unconscious processes, the unresolved conflicts and forbidden impulses buried therein are released.

Freud, for example, suggested that ascetical practices of solitude and silence rid the self of the normative psychological structures that keep a person distant from childhood fears and so elicit the "infantile anxiety from which the majority of human beings have never become guilt free" (1963, p. 252). Hidden fantasies may be fulfilled in the regressive restoration of unconscious symbiotic structures but they can elicit intense anxiety when they also bring back to consciousness what could be called the "shadow" or dystonic side of a person's unconscious: nefarious drives, unresolved conflicts and abandonment/separation anxiety. Anxiety is also aroused in the wish for unity because of fear of that very unity, the fear of being swallowed and consumed (Jonah and the whale), of becoming faceless and nameless.

For instance, St. Anthony of the Desert's ascetical struggle to free himself of sexual longings appeared successful until its regressed state restored even greater anxiety in the hallucinated form of voluptuous women. "Those elements of character which were unaffected by the first purification of self . . . are here aroused from their sleep, purged of illusion" (Underhill, 1911, p. 388).[8] The psychoanalyst Groddeck metaphorically described such an experience:

> The miner, like Faust, is driven into the kingdom of the mother, his calling is this eternal, never-ceasing longing for the body of the mother, into whose depths the shaft leads him with unholy magic, in whose depths rest all joy and the delight of life and all loves, which blessedness is dimly and unconsciously remembered in the idea of lost paradise and the hope of a heavenly kingdom and eternal happiness, as well as the fear of the unceasing fires of hell. (1937, p. 151)

Just as the mine represents the recovery of fear as well as hope, so too the ecstatic encounter of God, and the blissful symbiosis it represents, gives way to the darker side of God and the reexperience of unconscious conflicts and forbidden impulses. "I am Yahweh, unrivaled, I form the light and create the dark. I make good fortune and create calamity, it is I, Yahweh, who do all this" (Is 45:7).

Feelings that presumably were vanquished in the unitive state but that insidiously manage to sneak back into consciousness make the person believe he has jeopardized, if not destroyed, the unitive state. God, like the symbiotic mother, has been perfect and omnipotent, always loving and never frustrating; therefore to reexperience frustration and forbidden impulses makes the person helplessly[9] feel that the all-loving and omnipotent deity is withholding love or is no longer present. These frustrations and forbidden feelings were originally experienced by the infant as being cast out from secure maternal symbiosis; they then became symbolized in Adam and Eve's expulsion from Eden; their reappearance in religious experience presents the dreaded possibility once again of the individual's being cast out of paradisiacal unity.

In spite of heroic efforts to surrender the self to God, the resurrection of unconscious desires and unresolved conflicts makes one anxiously feel alienated from, unworthy of, and in the end rejected or abandoned by God. The dread that ensues, the pervasive sense of emptiness, privation, restlessness, and depression over loss of the loved object (or the loved object's love), has been called in Hinduism the experience of Kali and by Zen Buddhists "the great Doubt." It has been addressed by those who experience cosmic consciousness as the awareness of insignificance, and by Buddhists as the *viadhimagga* or sense of fear/weariness that remains after a meditative state is dispelled. Buddha himself experienced it:

> Scorched, frozen, and alone,
> In fearsome forest dwelling,
> Naked, on fire worn,
> Bent on the quest is the sage.
> (Magjhimn Nikaya, I, 166)

Dante describe a similar experience:

> How shall I say
> What wood that was! I never saw so drear,
> so rank, so arduous a wilderness!
> Its very memory gives shape to fear.

Christians call this encounter the "cloud of unknowing," the nadir experience, or more generally the "dark night of the soul."

"Thou hast been a child at the breast, a spoiled child," said the Eternal Wisdom to Suso. "Now I will withdraw all this."

Whatever form the "dark night" assumes, it must entail bitter suffering: far worse than that endured in the Purgative Way. Then the self was forcibly detached from the imperfect. Now the Perfect is withdrawn, leaving behind an overwhelming yet impotent conviction of something supremely wrong, some final Treasure lost. (Underhill, 1911, pp. 386, 389)

The Bhagavad-gita expresses a similar dark night in Arjuna's experience of extreme doubt on the eve before battle, in which he prays to Lord Krishna, "In the dark night of my soul I feel desolation. In my self-pity I see not the way of righteousness" (1962, p. 48).

The dark night occurs when forbidden impulses and feelings of frustration, once banished in the unitive experience of God, return and burst the blissful bubble of paradise. After a long and sometimes arduous struggle to experience God, the individual feels frightened and fragmented, left alone to peer hopelessly and helplessly into the vast expanses of inner emptiness. He might be tempted to overcome the frustration and helplessness by striving to master it. He also might, like the biblical character Job, who finally could not tolerate more of tribulations sent by God, lash out in anger at the deity, whom he blames for his helplessness. To be angry at God, however, or to aggressively attempt to overcome feelings of helplessness, does not extricate one from the dreaded bowels of the dark night. It only exacerbates the experience.

AGGRESSION THREATENS UNITY

In spite of the best effort to surrender self and to experience God, a dreaded dark night resurrects the unresolved conflicts or forbidden impulses that exist beneath the surface calm of unity.

> At the beginning of the night's third watch,
>   before there is moonlight,
> Don't be surprised to meet yet not recognize
> What is surely a familiar face from the past.
> (Tung-tiang Cheh)

In the midst of recognizing hidden aspects of the self that alienate

God, the person still clings to hope. In spite of feeling unworthy of the deity's presence, he longs to be pulled from the darkness of the "inferno" and to ascend into the glory of "paradisio." The mystic believes the darkness is a necessary time of privation, a trial of fire, an opportunity to burn away the last remnants of self-will that separate him from a perfect union with God or Nirvana.

The mystic must be patient, and passive, humbly awaiting the final moment in which the residues of self-pride are seared off and the "fire and rose become one" (Eliot, 1943, p. 59). Impatience in the dark night, or the willful desire to move through it facilely and by means of one's own strengths—rather than through unequivocally surrendering to the will of God—makes manifest the intransigent qualities of an ego that resists surrender.

Ego purgation does not completely get rid of the ego. It renounces the active efforts of the ego but the ego continues, albeit in a primitive state of passivity and dependency, to master conflicts. Becoming obedient and receptive to God is spiritually praiseworthy but is still motivated by one's volition, the latter being what impedes the direct experience of God, and so even the desire to become obedient must be purged in order to submit unreservedly to God.

The primitive ego's effort to remaster the helplessness and anxiety elicited in the dark night is destined to fail. It simply repeats earlier ego attempts at becoming passive and dependent in order to master a stressful situation.[10] The fruitless effort to overcome the anxiety elicited in the dark night intensifies feelings of being abandoned by God. The person feels further deprived of the paradise he worked diligently to experience and becomes angry at the absent God.

Anger at God for withholding love, as well as expressions of aggression in general—assertiveness, self-will, mastery of tasks— threatens communion with God as it threatened the maternal symbiosis that is restored in the experience. Early aggressive feelings endanger symbiotic security in two interconnecting ways. First, the wish-fulfilling relationship with the mother is disturbed when the mother, no longer able to shield the growing infant from reality, exposes him to the frustrations that bring an end to paradise. The infant's resulting anger makes him aware of the separateness of the object of his anger; hence anger brings up dreaded separation anxiety from maternal unity (or later in life from objects with which the adult has merged) (Kegan, 1982, p. 97). At the same time, innate aggressive urges stimulate a surge toward separateness and thereby reaffirm the end of blissful unity and reinforce the association of aggression with the loss of symbiotic security.

For instance, an early expression of infant aggression is biting the mother's breast while suckling. Because the result of this aggression is withdrawal of the nurturing breast, the infant experiences his aggression as hurting his mother. This causes her not only to deprive him of gratification but to reject him (push him away). Since the infant still needs the mother's protection and nurturance, he equates aggression with danger, "leaving the impression that once upon a time one destroyed one's unity with a maternal matrix" (Erikson, 1963, p. 74).

Aggression is particularly pernicious to the infant because it not only disturbs the symbiotic state but is experienced with a raw intensity that the infant cannot manage. Early aggression is an uninhibited drive that has not yet been "neutralized" (Hartmann, 1958b). That is, in their primitive state libidinal and aggressive drives seek goal gratification independent of each other. Libido seeks only bonding, attachment, and nurturance, without respect for individuality or assertiveness. Aggressive attempts to overcome deprivation similarly are pursued single-mindedly, regardless of libidinal feelings that crave closeness and bonding. Hence unintegrated aggression is experienced by the infant as rage; because his fledgling ego is too fragile to contain it and because the drive itself is too uninhibited to be contained, the infant fears its raw intensity will overwhelm or destroy the good graces of the loving mother.

Only later in development, with a strong ego, will the child be able to synthesize aggression and libido—"the fusion of both instinctual drives" (Hartmann, 1945, p. 19). Aggression that is synthesized with libido will be "softened," making it more an expression of self-assertiveness and less one of hostility.[11] In this way the child gradually recognizes that libidinal feelings are not lessened when he expresses frustration or anger, and that the mother's temporary absence—and especially the anger he feels toward the mother as a

result—does not destroy his love for the mother. Before this integration of a cohesive identity takes place, however, and before drives are
neutralized so as to fall under the management of the ego, the infant's
embryonic ego will not be able to endure the raw intensity of aggression without fearing that libidinal feelings have been destroyed (and
the internal image of a loving mother along with them):

> The aggressive urges are not brought into fusion and thereby
> bound and partially neutralized, but remain free and seek expres-
> sion in life in the form of pure, unadulterated, independent de-
> struction. (A. Freud, 1949, p. 496)

The aggression and anger that threaten to rupture symbiotic
bliss arise in the adult's unitive experience with a similar destructive
capacity, and the same tandem tendency—the first part being an
inability to express aggression.

Adults usually express aggression by means of sublimation.
Their egos channel aggressive drives through work, competition,
assertiveness, and conflict mastery. Hence ascetical purgation of assertiveness and control means renunciation of the various functions
normally necessary for the safe and satisfactory expression of aggression. For example, an individual forfeits satisfactory channels to
release anger elicited in the dark night when he believes anger is a
sign of possessiveness and that he is supposed to "turn the other
cheek" (Christian) or transcend all aggression (*dosa*, in Buddhism).

> No one who loves true prayer and yet gives way to anger and
> resentment can be absolved from the imputation of madness. For
> he resembles a man who wishes to see clearly and for this purpose
> he scratches his eyes. (Evagrius Ponticus)

Dark-night disillusionment turns to despair when a person
seeks to extricate himself from the experience in which he feels
angry and abandoned, and to master the aggression and unresolved
conflicts that put him there, but cannot because he no longer possesses the ego functions to do so. The aggression and anger are
further experienced as dangerous to the unitive state since the now
defunct ego can neither express nor manage them.

> An id in which individual instincts have made themselves inde-
> pendent, pursue their aims regardless of the person as a whole
> and henceforth obey the laws only of the primitive psychology
> that rules in the depths of the id. (Freud, 1918, p. 203)

Because communion with God expresses primitive libidinal
drives that serve entirely to bind the anxiety-free symbiotic unity
into which the person has submerged his identity, any arousal of
aggression in this libidinal state is experienced as uncomfortably un-
familiar (ego dystonic) and threatening. And because aggressive
drives that arise in the dark night are devoid of libidinal integration,
the person not only is angry at being deserted by God but experiences that anger as unbridled passion or orally voracious rage. The
resurgence of primitive aggression in the dark night thereby negates
unconscious merger tendencies and endangers the libidinal bonds of
communion with God. As Freud said, "Libido is to establish ever
greater unities and to preserve them thus—in short, to bind them
together; the aim of aggression is, on the contrary, to undo connections (so to destroy them)" (1940, p. 148). Margaret Mahler similarly
spoke of this type of aggression as being "unleashed in such a way as
to inundate or sweep away the 'good' object, and with it the 'good'
self representation" (1979, p. 78).

As in infancy, the religious person blames his aggression and
frustration for costing him paradisiacal bliss (for "biting" the bounti-
ful breast of paradise).[12] He also fears that his rebelliousness will be
punished by the Other's annihilating rage, or at least by withdrawal
of previously unlimited nurturance and ejection from paradise.
When angels with fiery swords stand outside Eden to ensure permanent expulsion, the person's dark-night despair slips deeper into an
inexorable depression over the loss of paradise.

> That which this anguished soul feels most deeply is the convic-
> tion that God has abandoned it, of which it has no doubt; that He
> has cast it away into darkness as an abominable thing. (John of the
> Cross, quoted in Underhill, 1911, p. 389)

SPLITTING OF AGGRESSION AS DEFENSE
AGAINST LOSS OF UNITY

The dark-night experience of abandonment and the failure to
overcome it expose the person to a final fragmentation of self. When

the attempt to overcome dark-night frustration and to experience God (by becoming even more obedient and determined) instead meets with silence from God, an individual is confronted with the futility of his actions. "If the soul desires or tries to experience it [Unity], it cannot" (John of the Cross, 1959, 1.9.7). The only way to penetrate the dark night and to experience God fully, the mystic discovers, is to "let go" of even the most praiseworthy intentions to experience God. It is to give up the active drive to reach Nirvana, the determined will to know God, because this is motivated by an entrenched separateness and personal volition that distinguishes the person from (and hence prevents the absolute submersion into) the unitive experience.

The anonymous writer of the *Cloud of Unknowing* (1961) distinguished the fullness of the latter submission to God from the former by describing two types of purgation. The first is an active pursuit of God in which the individual consciously purges the self that separates him from divine communion. (John of the Cross [1959] called it the dark night of the senses, in which some light of reason and action are necessary to ascetical practices.) The second, and more radical, purgation is the passive dark-night experience in which the individual so unequivocally surrenders himself to God that God— and no longer the individual—purges the self: the final fragment of self that clung to its own effort to experience God. (John of the Cross [1959] called it the purification of the soul, in which only darkness and no self exists.) Rather than work at experiencing God —"work" still being the product of personal volition—the person abandons all pretense of being able to grasp God and allows God to take control: "Until a soul is placed by God in the passive purgation of that dark night . . . it cannot purify itself. God must take over and purge them in that fire that is dark for them" (John of the Cross, 1959, 1.3.3).

The mystic yields himself completely to the God who alone can initiate a truly unitive experience (infused contemplation, or in Buddhism *arupa* or formless meditation as opposed to *rupa* or form meditation). He does this when, exhausted by Herculean efforts to experience God and exasperated by their futile efforts to bring him to the absolute unity he seeks, he confronts his limited, finite, impotent self and gives up. In the giving up, in what Nietzsche called the "weariness" that comes after the struggle, he lets go of the final fragments of self and experiences God.

> Weariness that wants to reach the ultimate
> with one leap, with one fatal leap, a
> poor ignorant weariness that does not
> want to want anymore: this created
> all gods and afterworlds.
> (1954, p. 143)

T. S. Eliot expresses it thus:

> I said to my soul be still and
> let the dark come upon you. (1943, p. 66)

Only complete submission to God ends the experience of unfulfilled expectations over which one becomes angry or which causes one to feel rejected. "Total surrender, the absolute leap in the dark, is demanded" (Lewis, 1975, p. 182). Hence only when Jesus cries out in dark-night doubt and despair—"My God, my God, why have you forsaken me"—and then resigns himself to God—"yet no longer my will but your will be done" (Lk 22:42)—does he completely surrender his will to the will of God. And only when Arjuna, "In the dark night of my soul," surrenders himself to that experience instead of trying to resolve it does he experience enlightenment: "By thy grace I remember my light, and now gone is my delusion. My doubts are no more, my faith is found; and now I say 'Thy will be done'" (Bhagavad-gita, 1962, p. 122).

What spiritual traditions label the passive surrender in the dark night—"ceasing all conscious, anxious striving and pushing to experience God" (Underhill, 1911, p. 123)—is, from a psychological perspective, a regressive return to symbiotic passivity in order to be saved from the pernicious aggression and frustration of the dark night. Having discovered that God, like the mother God represents, is an "unattackable authority" (Freud, 1930, p. 122), and having discovered this when the anger and aggression experienced in the dark night threatened to destroy the authority of the unitive state, the person gives up final active efforts to overcome obstacles to God.

Giving up, he sinks passively into the symbiotic unity that existed prior to self-assertiveness. He returns to the early infancy state of not *thinking* about abandonment, but viscerally feeling it. By restoring this passive condition[13] he rids himself of, and subsequently defends against the return of, the last vestiges of aggression.

Freud suggested that religious experience gets rids of aggression —aggression being dangerous because it elicits castration anxiety— by repressing it and becoming submissive to the father, represented by a powerful superego God. The aggression and anger elicited in the dark night, however, are deeper and more profound than oedipal aggression. They result from feelings of helplessness—but not the helplessness encountered in a competitive struggle with a powerful father. Instead, it is the helplessness that arises when reality bursts the bubble of symbiotic oneness and leaves the infant—as well as the adult in relationship with God—feeling abandoned.

Dark-night abandonment anxiety revives the rage and aggression first felt in response to the original loss of symbiotic security. To become passive and submissive to God, therefore, in the attempt to shed the aggression that threatens libidinal bonding, is an earlier psychological defense than the repression of aggression in the relationship to the powerful superego God.[14] It is a regressive reactivation of the earlier psychological defense of splitting.

Splitting is a defense mechanism that first arises during a kind of dark night of the infant. The infant feels angry when the hitherto omnipotent mother ceases to gratify needs immediately. Because the infant's embryonic ego cannot reconcile a mother who simultaneously loves and disciplines, the anger that results from the latter appears to destroy the gratifying maternal image and causes the infant to feel abandoned. In order to defend himself against being abandoned, the infant gets rid of the pernicious aggressive feelings by splitting mother into separate images of "good" and "bad" (Freud, 1915c, p. 170; Kernberg, 1979; Mahler, 1975).

The good mother is the unending source of love and need gratification. She is the personification of the infant's libidinal feelings. The bad mother appears to withhold love and disciplines the infant. She is the personification of the infant's frustrations. By separating the image of the bad mother from that of the good mother, the infant is able to express negative aggressive feelings toward the frustrating mother without affecting—and thereby endangering or contaminating—the loving feelings elicited from the separately held good mother. "The ego in varying degrees fragments its objects, and in this way achieves a dispersal of the destructive impulses" (Klein, 1957, p. 58). By investing solely libidinal qualities in a split-off image of mother, the infant makes her so unfailingly loving that he would never have reason to be frustrated or angry with her.

The unitive experience restores the primitive mechanism of splitting to ward off pernicious feelings. "In this fusion between the self and the object the operation of aggression has been eliminated" (Bak, 1954, p. 132). Unity recreates a psychological paradise characterized by the exclusive presence of good libidinal feelings and images, and the conspicuous absence of the aggression and anxiety that is split off as bad. It emerges out of the dark night when the all-good mother is restored in the form of the all-good God or Nirvana, and when the perfectly libidinal deity is isolated from the image of the bad God who seemingly withholds love and causes abandonment anxiety. The latter is successfully defended against when the person separates those aspects of God that elicit pernicious aggressive feelings and isolates them from the aspects that nurture and love (more on this later).

What remains in the unitive experience after splitting off aggression is an impeccably loving God or an unequivocally anxiety-free Nirvana. The individual experiences a God who not only nurtures but is so unfailingly nurturing that, like the all-good mother's breast that never ceases to flow with milk, communion with God makes the person always feel satisfied. As a result of never being frustrated, the person never has to be angry or assertively overcome obstacles to gratification. Hence the experience restores the early psychological state that is free of frustration and aggression: "A tendency arises to separate from the ego everything that can become a source of unpleasure, to throw it outside and to create a pure pleasure ego" (Freud, 1960, p. 67).

The restoration of the all-good mother or purified pleasure ego strips aggressive feelings of their pernicious power. "The lion shall dwell with the lamb and the leopard shall lie down with the kid, and a little boy shall lead them" (Is 11:6). The experience of a peaceable kingdom in which lamb and lion lie together, and God and self are in communion, creates a defense against the normal hostility between lamb and lion or the expectable frustrations of any relationship.

Anger, confrontation, assertiveness, and other expressions of aggression are a sign that some need has not been gratified; in the idealized kingdom of communion with God, however, all needs are gratified and aggressive feelings thereby are warded off. "The unmodified aggressive impulse threatens the existence of the object and the investment of the object with libido acts as its protection" (Hartmann, 1945, p. 19).[15]

Aggression and anger do not exist in the unitive state because the aggressive "bite" has been taken out of the lion's mouth—the same bite of aggression that lost Adam and Eve paradise and cost the mystic the regained paradise of communion with God. The person surrenders the last vestiges of his bite, the final fragments of aggression that tenaciously remain buried beneath his various ascetical attempts at dying to self, and sinks selflessly into the blissful maternal/ divine symbiosis that precedes the fateful bite of the infant's first and formidable experience of aggression (biting the mother's breast).

PROJECTION OF SPLIT-OFF AGGRESSION

Unitive experience regressively restores a nondifferentiated pleasure ego that puts the label *God* on that which in the person's experience makes him feel unequivocally loved and secure. He experiences only libidinal gratification in this relationship with God because those aspects of it that in the dark night elicited aggression have been split off and projected elsewhere.

> For the pleasure ego the external world is divided into a part that is pleasurable, which it has incorporated into itself, and a remainder that is extraneous to it. It has separated off a part of its own self, which it projects into the external world and feels as hostile. (Freud, 1915c, p. 136)

The regressive wish for reunification with the all-good mother is gratified when communion with the all-good God splits off final fragments of aggression and projects them onto a "bad" entity that exists outside it. The "out-group" onto which aggression is projected is an individual or group of individuals who exist outside the boundaries of the person's communion with God. They do not belong to the immediate experience, or to the group, nation, or family that are included within the person's libidinal boundaries. The outsider usually does not conform to or hold sacred the values that the person and his group revere. The out-group thereby provides a suitably different and often contradictory environment onto which to project the split-off primitive aggression that arose in the dark night.[16]

The out-group serves as a scapegoat for the feared split-off aggressive feelings and images. It enables the person to project onto an "enemy," and thereby to rid himself of, the aggression that is not appropriate to libidinal communion with God. The most common out-group onto which the religious person projects split-off aggressive feelings is the all-good God's counterpart: the all-bad devil.

> If the benevolent and righteous God is a substitute for his father, it is not to be wondered at that this hostile attitude to this father, too, which is one of hating and fearing him and of making complaints against him, should have come to expression in the creation of Satan. (Freud, 1923, p. 86)

God, like the infant's mother and like what the ancient Greeks created in the two-faced deity Janus, is split into separate images of good and bad. The person projects onto the bad devil the dark-night feelings of the withholding bad mother.[17]

The aggression that cannot directly be defended against inside oneself can be defended against directly when it is projected onto the other outside of oneself. Since the other embodies the aggression projected onto it, it is perceived as being aggressive and dangerous. Its aggression, and not one's own, threatens to destabilize the "all-good." Therefore when the aggression the person projects onto others comes back to him in the form of their aggression, it is only natural and acceptable—and even a duty—to protect the all-good by defending against it, and in the process the person vicariously feels as if he successfully defends against his own unacknowledged aggression.

To defend oneself against the other involves aggression, but people rationalize it by suggesting that it is simply a defense against the aggression of others.[18] The psychoanalyst Kernberg described it in therapy:

> The main consequence of this need [projection of bad] is the
> development of dangerous, retaliatory objects against which the
> patient has to defend himself. . . . They have to control the object
> in order to prevent it from attacking them under the influence of
> the [projected] aggressive impulse. (1979, pp. 30, 31)

The religious individual is "righteously" aggressive—not because he is malicious but because others' aggression or immorality requires it. Sadistic aggression as a result is transformed into sanctimonious aggression, and continues to be vicariously gratified—with impunity, and even with the erotic pleasure associated with sadistic acts—via the direct expression of aggression against the out-group.[19]

Acceptable aggression expressed in judging or subduing others is also a safety valve for discharging remaining pent-up aggression. For instance, Jesus' admonishment of aggression (turn the other cheek, blessed are the meek) provides the rationalization for a person to suppress aggression, but before this aggression builds up internally and explodes, some of it can be released by expressing righteous indignation at the out-group (as Jesus did toward the moneychangers in the temple). Aggression similarly is intensely released in the zealousness of a person who channels split-off aggression in the "fire and brimstone" preaching that imposes beliefs on others or aggressively converts them from their evil ways.[20]

Mostly, aggression can be expressed toward an out-group because its expression does not affect the "good." The out-group is endowed with an image that is split off from the all-good image of God and so, when a person aggressively defends himself or expresses anger against the out-group, it is expressed directly but without affecting the separately held image of the all-good deity.

For example, a person cannot express the anger he feels toward an all-good God for the inexplicable suffering that God seemingly inflicts on the world. To do so would be to destroy the illusion that an all-good God never withholds love or causes the frustration that gives reason to be angry. He can, however, express anger at suffering when he expresses it toward an impersonal other such as the cruel capriciousness of fate, or as did Adam and Eve by becoming angry at the "bad" serpent they blamed for making Eve eat of the forbidden fruit ("The devil made me do it"). In this way, the all-good God is granted immunity from life's realistic conflicts, while at the same time the person's expression of aggression does not incriminate him in an act against libidinal communion with God.

Rather than endangering communion, the expression of aggression toward the bad out-group has the opposite effect. When one projects aggression and defends against it, the experience of God or Nirvana is solidified. The absence of aggression reinforces Eros (Freud, 1960, p. 114), and so "projection of destructive unneutralized aggressive energy beyond the body-self boundaries" keeps the unitive state free of the aggression that could weaken the libidinal bonds that hold it together (Mahler, 1968, p. 11). Furthermore, by expelling aggression from within their ranks, the various elements of the in-group are free of the aggression that otherwise might divide them, and are more bonded in their aggressive opposition to the out-group.

Aggression expressed toward others, however, sometimes insidiously seeps through the psychological defenses that forbid the personal acknowledgment of aggression. The guilt an individual feels for these forbidden feelings (guilt for the fantasized aggressive attack against the "good breast"; Klein, 1937) can cause him to intensify aggressive behavior. Doing so makes the other appear more evil and thereby makes him feel less guilty for his aggressive actions.

A person also can take projected guilt and aggression back into himself. He discovers a further solidification of libidinal bonds when, instead of projecting aggression entirely onto an out-group, he "confesses" the aggressive behavior (or even thoughts of aggressive behavior) that caused him to feel alienated from communion with God. Confession of sinful aggression partially mends painful separation by relieving the person of some of the guilt surrounding his "omissions." Mostly, it causes him to feel catharticly cleansed from the aggression that threatened the loss of unity, especially as he contritely resubmits himself to the authority and libidinal bonds of his God. Not only is the rift in that relationship thereby repaired but its libidinal bonds are reforged with greater tenacity in the gratefulness of being forgiven and welcomed back as a prodigal son.

Confession of aggression, unfortunately, is not always as libidinally rewarding as it appears. When a person defends himself against the aggression he has projected onto an invidious out-group, he not only protects himself against others but unconsciously defends himself against his own forbidden impulses. He vicariously chastises and conquers his own hidden aggression when he chastises and conquers it in the "evil" other onto whom he projected it. But when he does not project aggression onto others and instead confesses it, he comes face to face with that aggression. He might feel forgiven by God for his sinful acts but the reconciliation often is not complete until an implacable conscience, or more primitively a voracious oral need, extracts some type of harsh penance.

Repentance serves to cleanse the person of sin and so to make him worthy—that is, filled only with libidinal bonds and free of all aggression—of reunion with God. But since aggression instigates a guilt he cannot ignore, and since the all-good deity cannot punish him for that guilt and still be all-good, the person punishes himself for his aggression. He repeats the experience of infancy when, in the frustrating absence of the mother's love, he took back into himself the "bad" feelings he could not express toward or attribute to the all-good mother (Fairbain, 1986), as in "I am bad, not mother, and that is why she punishes me." The mystic defends the all-good God against his rage at the dark-night experience by taking back into himself the bad feelings he cannot attribute to the God who has cast him into darkness—"I am bad, not God, and that is why God has abandoned me"—and then penitentially redirects that aggression at himself for being bad.

Adler explains it thus: "When the aggressive drive turns in upon the subject, we find traits of humility, submission and devotion, subordination, flagellantism and masochism" (Ansbacher 1956, p. 35).

ABSENCE OF AGGRESSION DIMINISHES UNITIVE EXPERIENCE

Aggression that is split off and projected out of the unitive experience is critical for psychological growth. When aggression is developed alongside libidinal drives, as mentioned, it does not lead to hostility or domination. Instead it gives the stimulus to manage the demands of daily living and the confidence to master frustration. But when a person "dies" to the ego necessary to manage aggression, he forfeits the synthesizing function of the ego to integrate aggression alongside libidinal feelings. The result is twofold.

First, splitting off bad aggressive feelings from the good libidinal feelings experienced in communion with God strips the latter of any real strength or conviction. The person expresses libidinal feelings and emotional attachment but, because they lack the fortitude that would preserve the person's autonomous psychological structure (i.e., integrated aggression), he experiences them as symbiotic cravings or spineless sentimentality.

> When the aim is to be only guided by love, assertion and aggression are obviously ruled out as being too tainted with power. There results a clinging to one another, an absorption in each other. Missing are the firmness of assertion, the structure and sense of dignity that guard the rights of the partners. (May, 1969, p. 115)

The love and intimate closeness experienced with an all-good God are illusory. This is not real love, marked by mutuality, nor is it real closeness, characterized by sharing that is so profound that two seem to merge into one. This is not to suggest that the experience of God does not generate loving feelings but when that experience is motivated, at least in part, by a need for an all-good God to defend against dangerous aggressive feelings, then that love is the love of a child who equates love with the absence of frustration. The person might truly wish to do good and so share with others the love he experiences in communion with God, but he loves less to initiate intimacy and more to defend himself (and his God and others) against the deeply embedded aggression surrounding repressed feelings of helplessness and anger.[21]

Second, the lack of aggression integrated into libidinal bonds of communion with God also means that the world is facilely divided into the good—that which nurtures communion and gratifies needs —and the bad—that which disrupts communion and demands personal responsibility. Bifurcation of the world creates a childishly uncomplicated environment. Instead of being comprised of uncertainties, ambiguities, and shadows, life is either good or bad, nurturing or withholding, us or them.

The perception of God divided into all-good and all-bad produces an internal split in the person's identity. In the attempt to prevent dreaded aggressive feelings or images from intruding on his idyllic unitive experience, he splits aggression away from his idealized self and becomes a Dr. Jekyll and Mr. Hyde. "The basis of optimism," Oscar Wilde wrote, "is sheer terror."

Stories from our culture warn of the dangerous results of splitting the human psyche. When the libidinal good is not integrated with the aggressive bad, an unconscious fear of the bad persists beneath the image of good. Dr. Jekyll appears to be the epitome of control and logic because he splits off—and his conscious refinement defends against—the hostile and destructive side of himself—until the "shadow" or beast that lurks beneath consciousness (or is projected outside the unitive state) violently erupts into consciousness in the form of Mr. Hyde. As Pascal observed: "If you try to become an angel, you become a beast." The experience of Nirvana or communion with God that defensively splits off aggression as bad, and regressively keeps it separate from the all-good, makes the person appear outwardly to be blissfully one with God but inwardly he has become the beast that the experience projects "out there."

> He remains ready to expect from some enemy, force, or event in the outer world that which, in fact, endangers him from within: from his own angry drives, from his own sense of smallness, and from his own split inner world. (Erikson, 1963, p. 361)

PART TWO

Religious Experience and Regression in Service of the Ego

5

Regression and Adaptation

INTRODUCTION

> We are never far from two conflicting tendencies: one to emerge from the womb, from bonding to freedom; another to return to the womb, to nature, to certainty and security. (Fromm, 1955, p. 27)

Psychology, at least in the West, suggests that maturity is marked by the submission of the latter tendency—the regressive wish to re-create comfortable maternal symbiosis—to the first tendency—the drive to separate from this infantile security and to become autonomous and responsible. Hence when religious experience, first, primitivizes ego functioning, turning autonomy and control into dependence and helplessness; second, infantalizes instinctual behavior, transforming libidinal drives into childish expressions of attachment while repressing aggressive drives as counterproductive to bonding; and third, elicits feelings of communion with God that restore an anxiety-free symbiotic unity—then religious experience is a regressive reversal of development toward maturity.

Freud led the psychological assault that relegated religious experience to a pathologically defensive regression. Some conflict is necessary, according to Freud, if psychological growth is to take place. The ego develops not in a vacuum but out of resolving the tension between drives and environmental restrictions. Religious experience therefore is not intended for growth because it either escapes the conflicts of living in the real world by retreating to divinized parental protection, or escapes unconscious conflicts through restoring a wish-fulfilling symbiotic unity.

Freud may have correctly diagnosed religious experience as a regressive retreat to an earlier nonconflictual state but he failed to examine the potential for that nonconflictual regressed state to induce psychological growth. He did not possess the insights of later ego psychologists, such as Heinz Hartmann, who, developing Freud's original theory, described how certain qualities of the ego develop not out of the resolution of intrapsychic conflict but independent of conflict resolution (e.g., memory and perception). Nor did he possess the even later insights of object relation theorists who suggested that personal identity is determined as much by the nature of the infant's earliest nondefensive attachment to the mother as by the drive to resolve the conflicts that arise in separating from that relationship.[1]

Freud's suggestion that religious experience was a return to an anxiety-free maternal unity did not consider what could take place in this regressed unitive state beyond a defensive escape from the demands of reality. His relegation of religious experience to a final psychological resting place, a no-return realm of infantile fixation and anxiety-free fantasy, did not take into account the experience of those for whom the encounter of God *did* create feelings of security, of selfless nondifferentiated unity, but for whom that experience did *not* remain fixated in selfless utopia or infantile attachment. If religious experience is a regressive return to unconscious processes, then religious experience—like art and psychotherapy, which will be shown to regressively restore *and* repair unconscious processes—can also be shown to be a regression that can be redemptively reparative rather than pathological. It can, as the philosopher Rolland said to Freud, not only not "in any way harm my critical faculties," but can be "a source of vital renewal."

The religious experience that regressively revives symbiotic unity can become, under the right circumstances, the fertile psychological ground in which new and healthy life is conceived. What constitutes those conditions is the subject of the second half of this work. Its chapters reexamine the regressive processes that were analyzed in Part One and demonstrate their potential for reparation and regeneration. First it shows how religious experience regressively purges ego functions but needs to purge them if the person is to become free of their defensive nature. Second, once free of superficial ego functioning, a person can restore repressed instincts and undeveloped primary process so as to induce creativity rather than childish behavior. Third, the experience of unity can restore symbiotic security that can be reparative instead of palliative, confront primitive fears, restore "basic trust," and stimulate psychological growth. Finally, a fourth chapter is added to explain how religious experience is healthy only when the person "acts on" what was encountered in the regressed unitive state, thereby returning the person, transformed by the experience, to the world. That is, these chapters examine how the regression in religious experience can be a regression that recovers unconscious structures and moves forward with them because of—not in spite of—having moved backward to recover them.

> The path to health is via turning into the fantasies, the dreams, the preconscious and conscious, the archaic, the unrealistic, the primary processes, that is, the recovery of the intrapsychic in general. (Maslow, 1968, p. 77)

REGRESSION IN SERVICE OF THE EGO

The mere presence of psychological regression should not automatically merit a presumption of pathology. The manner in which the regression takes place, and not the fact of its taking place, determines whether the particular regressive phenomenon is healthy or pathological.

Freud (1912, p. 106) first saw regression as a form of resistance to therapy but when he later recognized its value in fostering the transference relationship he bestowed on it the accolade of being an "ally in analytic treatment." In spite of this and other references to adaptive regression (e.g., in art), Freud was primarily concerned with the pathological nature of regression. It would take the analytical work of some of his followers, beginning most notably with Ernst Kris, to investigate systematically how ego diminishment could result not in pathology but in an increase in psychological health. Regression of this type would recover a person's psychological past not to flee the present but to make the psychological past more meaningful to the present, and in the process make the present more integrated with and animated by (rather than defensive about) the psychological past. Kris called such a process "regression in the service of the ego" (1952, p. 60). The psychoanalyst Schafer described it as a temporary "detour through regression toward adaptation (1958, p. 125).

Regression is in service of the ego when it temporarily diminishes ego functions in order to enhance psychological development. Kris (1952) first observed this phenomenon in his pioneering investigation into the regressive nature of artistic creativity. He concurred with Freud that artistic experiences often involve a regressive diminishment of ego functioning, followed by a return to more primitive areas of one's psyche. Whereas Freud abandoned the possibility of understanding how creativity could be healthy—"Before the problem of the creative artist analysis must, alas, lay down its arms" (1928, p. 177)—Kris examined what took place in creativity to make it healthy. Unlike Freud, he found in the artist's "dip" into the unconscious a potentially creative recovery of untapped inner resources, rather than the pathology of a weakened ego or a defense against repressed unconscious processes. As Proust wrote,

> I had to recapture from the shadow that which I had felt, to reconvert it into its psychic equivalent. But the way to do it, the only way I could see, what was it but to create a work of art. (Quoted in Shattuck, 1963, p. 149)

CREATIVITY

Kris (1952) distinguished two stages in creativity. These stages—inspiration and elaboration[2]—will be useful in understanding a similar regressive and progressive process in religious experience.

The inspirational stage of creativity can be divided further into a preparatory stage and the inspirational stage proper. The earlier stage expresses the period of ego regression. Normal day-to-day processes and the ego functions that support them are, in spite of apparent strengths, found to be rigid, dry, stereotyped, or limiting. Motivated to transcend a constricted approach to life or to see beyond the surface of things, the creative person momentarily relaxes or suspends normative ego functions. She redirects attention away from what she has been doing and prepares herself, through a particular discipline (dance, music, etc.), for a deeper and richer experience. "The preparation stage consists of observing, listening, asking, reading, collecting, comparing, analyzing" (Rhodes, 1961, p. 308).

Once free of the filters through which she learned to perceive reality, the artist refocuses perception according to an inner inspirational gaze: a less controllable realm of unfettered energy through which life is perceived more intuitively, spontaneously, directly, imaginatively, and uninhibitedly. Psychology traditionally has labeled this dip into unconscious processes regressive because the experience undoes mature logic and restores archaic structures. But as I shall explain, neither secondary functions of logic and control nor unconscious primary processes are as they appear to be. Autonomy and control are as unconsciously defensive as they are consciously constructive, just as primary process is not always the infantile and even nefarious realm Freud described as being the opposite of reality. They instead can express the spontaneity or openness that were lost in the formation of ego control, and the imagination or intuition suppressed in developing rational thinking. Regression, rather than being pathological, can be a necessary undoing of original ego development in order to recover and creatively express the psychological processes lying fallow beneath it (Arieti, 1976; Hartmann, 1934; Koestler, 1959; Maslow, 1959).

Regression to this intrapsychic world is not in itself creative. Suspension of normative ego function might be pleasurable but the pleasure—easily confused with creativity—is in part the result of a shift in mental energy away from secondary functions (which require effort and responsibility) to primary processes (immediate gratification). The artist can be seduced by this inner wish-fulfilling and fantasized world, preferring it and its freedom from constraints to life's realistic limitations. She also can be overwhelmed by the dip into her unconscious, for she encounters therein not only the idealized fantasy of infancy but the unresolved conflicts that were repressed and relegated there.

The inspiration stage of creativity is prevented from disintegrating into childish fixation or fear through the artist's expression of that which was inspirational. Kris called this the "elaboration" stage of creativity (1952, p. 60).[3] Through expressing or elaborating what inspired her, the artist lifts what she experienced out of the precarious unconscious and away from fixation or psychosis. She expresses her experience in a particular medium, and in the process gives shape to or "grabs hold of"—rather than feeling overwhelmed by—the possibly disturbing or uncontrollable unconscious processes.[4]

RELIGIOUS EXPERIENCE: FROM REGRESSION TO PROGRESSION

The description of how regression in creativity leads to recovery and elaboration of unconscious processes expands psychology's perception of human adaptability. It also contributes to the analysis of religious experience as a redemptive regressive act, an act that in the form of illumination and direct encounter with God can penetrate defensive ego functions and liberate creative unconscious processes.[5] When religious experience resolves and expresses the unconscious processes it restores, it follows the same path of inspiration and elaboration found in creative experience.

> Every creative act—in science, art or religion—involves a regression to a more primitive level, a new innocence of perception liberated from the cataract of accepted beliefs. It is a process of *reculer pour mieux sauter*, of disintegration preceding the new synthesis comparable to the dark night of the soul through which the mystic must pass. (Koestler, 1959, p. 519)

Stages of regression in religious experience might be labeled differently from stages found in artistic regression. However, when religious experience begins with a dissatisfaction with life and a disciplined dismantling of a narrow ego, leads to reactivation of primitive instincts that are experienced as illuminative, subsequently submerges the person into a symbiotic communion that potentially resolves developmental failures and resumes psychological growth, then the stages of religious experience generally parallel the creative stages of dissatisfaction with present perception of reality, lead to suspension of normative ego functioning, and turn perception inward toward unconscious processes—with the result being emergence out of the regressed state with a new perspective.

So far in this book we've been looking at the regressive stages of religious experience. It's time to turn our attention to the ways regression can be reparative and redemptive rather than pathological. We'll begin by considering how self-surrender can be an adaptive renunciation of the "false self" that formed as a defense against lost unity.

> To love a painting, one must first have drunk deeply of it in long droughts. Lose consciousness. Descend with the painter into the dim tangled roots of things, and rise again from them in colors, be steeped in their light. (William Blake, quoted in Milner, 1950, p. 25)

6

Adaptation in Ego-Regressive "Dying to Self"

INTRODUCTION

The first chapter of this book explained how spiritual disciplines aimed at self-renunciation represent ego regression. This chapter examines how "dying to self," while regressive, is not necessarily pathological. It demonstrates that regression can be a critical factor in the dismantling of what only appears to be healthy ego functioning, in order to restore unconscious processes left unfulfilled. Rather than being malignant, self-denying experiences of this type can induce an "egolessness" that is "the highest state of identity" (Maslow, 1968, p. 276).

EARLY UNCONSCIOUS PROCESS AND THE DEVELOPMENT OF A SEPARATE SELF

Symbiotic attachment to the mother is meant to last only as long as it takes the infant to feel secure enough to manage the tasks of forming a separate identity. Sometimes he accomplishes these tasks with relatively little anxiety. At other times he feels inadequate. During these latter experiences the infant regressively abandons some of the individuality and control he acquired, and momentarily returns to the security of maternal attachment. In this regressed state the child rekindles (or, in pathological conditions, fails to rekindle) the security needed to face once again the demands of new developmental tasks—this time with greater confidence and determination.

The child gradually learns that turning back to the mother is unacceptable. He learns this from internal drives that push him to separate from the mother, and from society's rewards for greater independence and control. In spite of such motivation, the child feels ambivalent about leaving the secure symbiotic relationship. To become autonomous he is encouraged to disidentify himself from previously cherished libidinal feelings of attachment (and from its derivatives of openness, spontaneity, and closeness). He learns that they inhibit separation: Bonding prevents autonomy, spontaneity vitiates control, passivity obstructs assertiveness, and so forth. The child thereby learns that the way to grow out of the libidinally fused relationship with the mother is to develop secondary ego functions, such as independence and control, that can be trusted to master the tasks of living outside symbiotic security. (Bakan, 1966, p. 204) referred to these ego functions as "agency.") But he develops these qualities only after having learned to distrust and hence omit from an expanding conscious identity the equally important libidinal qualities of receptivity, openness, intuition, cooperation, spontaneity, and feelings of connection or bonding (what Bakan called "communion").[1]

In an ideal world the child would not exclusively develop autonomy and control. Instead, he would learn a healthy balance between the drive toward autonomy and control and the longing to maintain some sense of communion and instinctual spontaneity. He would integrate communion feelings into his expanding personal identity and as a result would grow to become equally comfortable with traditionally defined ego strengths—such as autonomy and control—and feelings of communion and openness.

The child, however, does not grow up in an ideal world. He learns instead, especially in the West, the importance of developing autonomy and control while repressing—rather than integrating—feelings of communion and openness. Because the child grows into adulthood having developed autonomy and control at the expense of communion feelings, autonomy and control (as well as assertiveness, logic, responsibility, etc.) are not as maturely developed as they appear. In fact, the opposite is true. The overemphasis on autonomy and control to the detriment of communion feelings marks a premature closure of psychological development.

What should have formed alongside the separation of an autonomous self (i.e., integrated communion feelings) instead is repressed and left behind. Without communion feelings integrated into it, an individual's sense of self is impoverished. He does not form a more fully developed identity, one marked by a healthy balance between control and openness, separateness and closeness, aggression and receptivity. Instead, he relies on independence and logic to master tasks that at times could have been more effectively managed through the receptivity and openness he repressed. Furthermore, he not only values ego functions such as reason over intuition, making reason superior to intuition instead of coexisting with it; he devalues intuition, replacing it with logical reasoning and making the latter the standard of psychological health. As a result the adult characterizes himself by potent ego skills that effectively manage life's tasks but that do so at the expense of greater instinctual spontaneity and imagination, having "repressed the communion from which the ego has separated itself" (Bakan, 1966, p. 15).

THE "FALSE SELF"

Identification of oneself with ego functions that compensate for repressed communion feelings creates what the psychoanalyst Winnicott called the "false self" (1975, p. 280). The "true self" is the earliest openness and instinctual freedom of the infant, awaiting the benevolent guidance of parents to direct its development. The false self unfolds when the infant learns to repress instincts and communion feelings rather than to trust and creatively express them.

Children often learn to express themselves according to what is punished and what is rewarded—and in the West this is dependence and independence, respectively[2]—and not by the creative expression of instincts. A false self forms on the basis of autonomy and control, which are overemphasized and leave undeveloped the communion feelings that were an integral part of the true self.[3] Whatever wide-eyed openness the child might have possessed is brought to an end, and whatever awe he experienced is neutered, if not destroyed, and replaced with logic and reason.[4] Carl Rogers summarized the experience:

> The infant learns a basic distrust for his own experiences as a guide to his behavior. He learns from others a large number of conceived values, and adopts them as his own, even though he

may be distancing himself from what he is experiencing. (1964, p. 162)

The false self is built on a shell of a self, not on an integrated core identity. As the child grows he learns to relate to the world out of this shell—"the false self gradually becomes a care-taker self" (Winnicott, 1975, p. 281)—and not out of inner communion feelings and instincts that have been repressed. The latter are kept buried beneath the layers of ego function that form to compensate for their neglect.

The false self that first formed in childhood is reinforced in an adult world that rewards conformity rather than creativity. By rewarding people for external signs of success, such as power, prestige, and possessions, and by punishing them—or at least withholding rewards and recognition—for more introspective or substantive pursuits, the inner desires and frustrations of the true self are effectively silenced. As the poet e. e. cummings once declared: "Society does its best to turn us into everything other than what we are." Or as Emerson said, "Nothing is more rare in any man than an act of his own." Without the spirit of communion feelings or the true self breathed into what people do, what they do becomes mechanical, uninspired. As a result they feel like objects, sometimes efficient and highly specialized objects but nonetheless objects, who identify themselves by their machinelike output and by the oftentimes hostile competitiveness in the materialistic consumption thereof.

In spite of (or because of) the relegation of "what we are" to an external image of what we do (and do in conformity with what is expected of us), people feel false. Even if, and especially if, the person is successful in his social aspirations and control, he frequently feels himself a fraud because of unfulfilled inner needs that make a mockery of his successful appearance. He feels anxious and guilty about becoming successful and what it takes to maintain that status. Hence while Freud suggested that the external self of autonomy and control was the real, the sane self, and that the inner self of communion and primary process was the self of fantasy or illusion, Winnicott proposed that the external self was the defensive false self. He suggested that "we are all suffering from Freud's flight to sanity" (quoted in Dinnage, 1978, p. 367).

THE DEFENSIVE SELF

If the first result of ego functions that develop at the expense of communion is the alienating impoverishment of the adult's identity, the second result is that the apparently healthy aspects of a person's identity are designed in great part not only to leave behind communion feelings but to guard against their possible return. Feelings of communion and primary process might have been repressed in childhood but they dictate who the person is as much by their conspicuous absence as by their unconscious drive and the resulting pressure to defend against them.

When communion feelings are repressed rather than allowed to develop alongside agentic ego functions, they remain arrested at an infantile developmental level. Needs or wishes that have been repressed are intensified, "as is the case of any phase specific need or wish" (Kohut, 1977, p. 197). Should the adult experience these underlying communion feelings he experiences them as raw, unrelenting, needy, and driven toward clinging attachment. Even though a part of him wants to indulge their longing for communion, a more deeply entrenched part of him that fears their imperious pressure for gratification keeps them silenced. It knows that his conscious ego strengths are capable of managing autonomy and control but are inadequate to manage ego-dystonic communion urges. And it knows that if these unmanageable and unintegrated drives were to be expressed they would be experienced as if they would devour him or devour those from whom they seek gratification.

This entrenched part of the person is the defensive ego that guards against what Mahler called the "fear of reengulfment" (1975, p. 77). Deep within the psyche is the seductive wish to cling to the security of symbiosis, a wish first fervently experienced when the original separation from the mother was anxiety-arousing and thus there arose the temptation to return to her. Eventually one learns that surrender to this temptation is unacceptable, and its subsequent repression is reinforced in the formation of unconscious aspects of ego functioning that guard against it. Hence an autonomy and assertiveness develop that not only consciously separate the child from the mother but, on an unconscious level, defensively prevent underlying communion qualities from being expressed. "The essential role of the ego is to mask from consciousness its very spontaneity" (Sartre,

1957, p. 100). Freud called it "splitting of the ego in the process of defense" (1937, p. 204).

Only those aspects of the person's ego that are autonomous, assertive, and in control function on a conscious level. The remainder of the ego is split off into an unconscious function that reinforces the seclusion from consciousness of repressed communion feelings. The result is that the adult's secondary ego qualities define his conscious identity while also defining his unconscious need to defend against repressed communion longings.

Ego control, for example, suggests a conscious ability to master life's expectations, but on an unconscious level it can express a regimentation that leaves no room for (and defends against) openness and spontaneity. The ego function that constructively directs aggressive drives in the mastery of tasks can also be motivated by a compulsion always to be doing and thereby warding off inner longings to be more receptive. "A little thoughtful exploration of aggression reveals that what masquerades for aggression is a cover for passive wishes or a defense against them" (Hart, 1955, p. 595). And the ego strengths that establish solid psychological boundaries can also keep dependency needs and other unintegrated communion wishes hidden.

The splitting of ego results in conscious expressions of assertiveness and control that make the person confident managing life's tasks, and unconscious defensive aspects that free him of communion longings so as not to compromise assertiveness and independence. However, as long as a person's ego is split between conscious and unconscious functions, he is fragmented, in spite of the appearance of control. His ego is preoccupied with maintaining the repression of instincts and the expression of rigid control, and in keeping the two apart. He is pressured to avoid their conflicting and oftentimes competing goals (autonomy versus attachment, for example, or control versus spontaneity) and fails to develop the mature strengths necessary to balance them.

When much of a person's ego is concerned—if not obsessed—with repression, projection, splitting, or other defensive efforts to expel anxiety-arousing communion feelings, the energy or attention that would otherwise be available for the more healthy development of the ego is depleted. In order to be in control and independent, the ego utilizes half its attention repressing inner needs and insecurities. It expends much of its other half creating a rugged individuality and

rigid control so as not to have to acknowledge dependency needs or
to be more instinctually spontaneous.

DISMANTLING THE DEFENSIVE EGO

Secondary ego functions are important in that they "transform
freely mobile energy into bound energy" and help expand the area of
control in which a person feels confident (Freud, 1961a, p. 104). But
the ego's defensive function causes it to bind that energy too tightly
and to extend control too rigidly. It sacrifices the spontaneity of
primary process and forfeits the freedom of greater openness. People
might feel independent and successful but they cannot escape the
underlying emptiness, or the insatiable hunger of unfulfilled longings, that makes them never feel independent or successful enough.
They might turn to the plethora of palliatives provided by society to
fill in this inner emptiness or to anesthetize feelings of discontent-
ment. However, the vicarious pleasures derived from societal rewards provide only a temporary relief from underlying emptiness.

Some people reject societal palliatives and redouble the efforts
at control and independence that promise to abate inner uneasiness.
Nietzsche, for instance, suggested that people must reclaim the
strengths, the mastery and authority, that by having been projected
onto God made them feel protected but also timid and narrow-
minded. They have to reassert the volition and "will to power" that
would rid them of their fears and establish the "superman": "Every
strengthening and increase of power opens up new perspectives and
means believing in new horizons" (1967, p. 330).

The problem with Nietzsche's thesis, however, is that the new
horizons of the superman are limited by their ability to expand only
in the direction of will and control. That is, they do not expand the
inner horizons of intuition or spontaneity and instead, by making a
God of reason and volition, once again reassert external strengths at
the expense of—and as defense against—communion feelings. The
individual reappropriates the strengths he has projected onto God
and so does not need to look outside himself to find the answers he
can find in himself, but in this self-sufficiency he forfeits the openness to look outside himself, to others' wisdom or to nature and the
sense of communion with it that could be inspirational.

When society's emphasis on the development of agentic ego

qualities causes those qualities to become synonymous with identity and to preclude the development of equally dynamic communion qualities, the former need to be diminished if not expunged. "In order to integrate the agency and communion features within himself, it was necessary for the agentic to be reduced and allow the repression of communion to be overcome" (Bakan, 1966, p. 204). A return to the true self and to greater instinctual freedom cannot take place without first confronting, and overcoming, the false self that keeps the true self repressed and the tenacious ego that resists greater instinctual freedom.

Since autonomy and control had to develop in order to establish a sense of self separate from maternal symbiosis, their elimination is ego-regressive. But a regression that dismantles the defensive ego is not motivated by an escapist flight from reality—just the opposite. "The theory is being put forward of regression as part of a healing process" (Winnicott, 1975, p. 281). Ego regression can begin the healing of an autonomy and assertiveness, control and logic, that are not as healthy as they appear and instead are superficial and defensive. "Regression can be seen as the relinquishing of rigid, crippling defenses, thus making possible the beginning of progress in the development of the personality" (Bettelheim, 1972, p. 199).

DISMANTLING OF EGO IN ART

Early stages of artistic creativity offer an insight into how dismantling the false self is an adaptive regression. Most people originally learn a particular perception of reality, and by conforming to that perception are able to "fit" in society. Unlike most people, however, the artist becomes uncomfortable with—feels limited by—the normative perception of the world. The way others see life is not fulfilling, does not "grab" the artist.

The creative individual seeks another way to look at life besides that of a superficial vision, another means of expressing what he perceives besides reasonable representation. He needs to recapture the wonderment and openness of primary process, the unimpeded responsiveness to stimuli lost in the development of bounded ego functions. To do this, he first purposively suspends stereotypical perceptions, disobeys conventions, frees himself of linear thinking, and eliminates habitual ways in which the brain takes in and processes stimuli (see the discussion on deautomatization, below). In order to gain fresh and innovative perspectives on life, the creative person discards the "blindness" of seeing only that which he has been taught to see: "To make the familiar strange is to distort, invert or transpose the everyday ways of looking and responding which render the world a secure and familiar place" (Gordon, 1961, p. 35).

The artist does not move from discontent with the way things are to creativity in one easy motion. In the preparatory stage of creativity, he sets upon a particular discipline—dance, music, art— that helps to free him from a rigid perception of life. The rigors of a discipline create a resistance to laziness (i.e., living according to pre-conceived notions rather than doing innovative thinking) and refocus attention away from external pursuits and toward inner processes. Only then, after developing new skills—such as the pianist's learning to concentrate—is he adequately free of external distractions. And only then is he technically prepared—as the pianist becomes skilled in musical scales—to relax control or to "let go" of himself and to be inspired (more on this in the next chapter). The choreographer/dancer Martha Graham suggested that the artist must "destroy himself if he is to be creative" (quoted in Morgan, 1941, p. 142).[5]

RELIGIOUS EXPERIENCE AND PURGATION OF THE DEFENSIVE EGO

When the self that religious experience regressively purges is a self that excels exclusively at agentic ego control and does so in part to defend against repressed communion feelings, then the dismantling of self can be a similar dismantling of the rigid self expressed in creativity. A person "dies to" the secondary functions he fears or feels inadequate to manage without realizing that the inadequacy occurs not because *he* is unhealthy but because *they* are unhealthy. Clinging to defensive ego functions is what is unhealthy, as the artist knows, not the purgative surrender of them. "It is possible to mistake for soundness what is actually rigidity based on a sort of paralysis of affect by a fear of instinctual drives" (Barron, 1968, p. 64). Anna Freud similarly wrote that inhibition in creativity can be

> ascribed to a fear of regression to an undifferentiated state in which the boundaries between id and ego, self and object, become blurred. . . . There is the same unwillingness to transgress

beyond the reassuring limits of the secondary process and "to accept chaos as a temporary state" (A. Freud, quoted in Milner, 1958, pp. xiii, xv)

The false self that forms out of a compulsion to escape communion feelings has been labeled by Christians the sinful self, the prideful and materialistic self that alienates people from God. The Trappist monk Thomas Merton called it a "mask and fabrication" that hides the true self (1969, p. 70). Buddhism and Hinduism describe the false self as *maya*—as that which is driven to seek gratification instead of truth, and in the process separates the person from his true self.

> The Modern Man believes himself adult, a finished product, with nothing to do for the rest of his life but alternately earn and spend material things (money, vital forces, skills), without those exchanges having the slightest effect on the thing called "I." The Hindu regards himself as something still to be formed, a false vision to be corrected, a composite of substances to be transmuted, a multitude to be unified. (Rene Daumal, quoted in Shattuck, 1963, p. 152)

Whatever approach is used, the first stage of religious experience—like that of creativity—begins with acknowledging the false self that causes internal emptiness and general dissatisfaction with life.[6] Hence the Prodigal Son, unlike his brother, acknowledged the discontent in his life and rejected that life in the process of "finding himself." So too the mariner in Coleridge's "Rime of the Ancient Mariner" killed the albatross (which represents unity), thereby alienating himself from unity and requiring that he recognize his alienation before beginning the journey back to unity.

> Alone, alone, all, all alone,
> Alone on a wide wide sea.

The experience in which a person acknowledges disenchantment can happen suddenly, or over a long period of time. Maybe a crisis erupts, or an emptiness that always seemed to gnaw at one's inner self grows intolerable, or previous successful ways of managing life inexplicably cease to be operative. Robert Browning expressed the experience in these words:

> Just when we're safest, there's a sunset touch
> A fragrance from a flower-bell, someone's death,
> A chorus ending from Euripides—
> And that's enough for fifty hopes and fears
> As old and new at once as Nature's self,
> To rap and knock and enter in our soul.

However it happens, the acknowledgement of discontent with "the way things are" begins the process of purging the false self. Once awakened to his dissatisfaction with superficial values and especially with feelings of emptiness, the person begins to confront and to overcome the false self that causes alienation. "Those who fail in their once-bornness want to have another chance at being born" (Erikson, 1958, p. 117). To create a new birth, as for the artist to find the inner inspirational "voice," requires shedding the first birth, which was incomplete and in its incompleteness became a psychological block against completeness. This can be described as dismantling the agentic in order to recover communion; from a religious perspective, Eckhart elaborated on Jesus' "seed that must die" when he wrote: "The shell must be broken and what is contained in it must come out; for if you want the kernel, you must break the shell." From another tradition a similar message:

> The seed that is to grow
>   must lose itself as seed;
> And they that creep
>   may graduate through
> Chrysalis to wings.
>
> Wilt thou then, O mortal
>   cling to husks which
> falsely seem to you
>   the self?
> (Wu Ming Fu, quoted in Phillips, 1977, p. 43)

The purgative stage of religious experience provides the opportunity for the person who fails at "once-bornness" to learn to purge the product of that first birth. Such a lesson requires preparation. Particular steps and disciplines are followed for the person to initiate the reversal of the ill-fated first birth's consequences. It does not happen automatically in the awakening to one's impoverished identity. "Man's tendency to actualize himself, to become his potentialities . . . may become buried under layer after layer of encrusted psychological defense" (Rogers, 1961, p. 351). The chance at a second birth requires working through those encrusted defenses. Like the initial stages of creativity, the dismantling of the defensive ego or of the self's constricted perception of life involves disciplined work. Compare the teachings of various spiritual traditions—from the Rule of St. Benedict to Buddha's Eight-Fold Path—that expect discipline and sustained effort with that of the preparatory stage of creativity.

> In order that he should be able to give expression to the inspiration that visits him he must work constantly, keeping himself in readiness, preparing his faculties, sharpening his vision and his understanding. (Caudwell, 1951, p. 64)

Religious experience begins with similar disciplined preparation. Concentration, meditation, scriptural reading, prayer, chanting, physical labor, obedience to a superior, bhakti yoga, and so forth, are like the scales a musician must learn or the choreographed steps a dancer must practice.[7] These are the disciplined means of refocusing attention away from the world and its stereotyped perceptions, the trained skills to resist the urge toward conformity and preconceived notions. They forge an attention to detail or a meditative awareness that can deliver the individual from distractions and can help penetrate the armor of the false self. "When I eat I eat, when I sleep I sleep" (Zen saying).

The religious person, like the artist, surrenders himself to a discipline—to the practice of a particular tradition or a spiritual teacher—that helps him develop these skills to overcome the false self. "No matter what the subject may be, there is only one course for the beginner; he must at first accept a discipline imposed from without" (Stravinsky, 1962, p. 20). Submission to an externally imposed discipline is a regressive act that might not be dangerous for the pianist but can make the religious person susceptible to manipulation (the extreme being Jonestown). The defensive ego or false self, however, is intransigently opposed to change, at least to substantive change. Its unconscious defense function is tenaciously opposed to acknowledging the true self. To get rid of the false self and its resistance to the true self, therefore, is an extremely difficult task on one's own. An individual might truly wish it, and even follow a prescribed course of action to achieve it, but the tenacity with which the unconscious aspects of his ego resist being dismantled prevents the desired purgation of self. That is where surrendering the will to a teacher comes in, a teacher who has gone through the experience himself and who is learned about the ego's resistance to change (even when one sincerely seeks change.)

Freud first observed this type of resistance in patients who voluntarily came to therapy for help yet simultaneously fought that help. "Only think of it! The patient who is suffering so much from his symptoms, who is ready to undertake so many sacrifices in time and money, effort and self-discipline in order to be freed from the symptoms" will resist the therapy he engages to help him (1961a, p. 287). One of the critical tasks in therapy is to recognize and interpret this resistance, for in the resistance is the clue to the fears the person resists. To help the person confront the false self and its resistances, the therapist elicits a transference trust in which the patient surrenders resistance to the therapist (this will be discussed later). "If we can induce him to take our view of it [resistance] and to reckon with its existence, that already counts as a great success" (Freud, 1961a, p. 286).

When gurus or spiritual teachers make such statements in reference to a disciple surrendering self-will and accepting their view, our psychological warning lights go on. But they too are confronted with people who voluntarily come to them seeking help but, in spite their desire to open up to their teachers, find themselves resisting this open communication.[8] People seek their wisdom in the way of overcoming the false self and experiencing the "Christ within" or Atman, but the false self they seek to discard tenaciously resists the recovery of the true self and its own demise. Hence it is no less their task to help these people learn to surrender resistance to overcoming the false self than it is the task of therapist.

A person can come face to face with this false self, an encounter he might not have been able to achieve on his own, when its presence is brought to his attention through the spiritual teacher's interpreting his resistance to "letting go" of it.

> What we need to do is bring the director into contact with our real self, as best we can, and not fear to let him see what is false in our false self. Now this right way implies a relaxed, humble attitude in which we let go of ourselves, and renounce our unconscious efforts to maintain a facade. (Merton, 1960, p. 24)

ADAPTIVE SPIRITUAL DISCIPLINES

Some of the spiritual disciplines examined earlier as examples of ego regression can now be seen to possess the adaptive potential for getting rid of the false self. That which regressively rids a person of ego "fetters" can be shown to be a discipline that frees a defensively restricted ego: "The creative process allows man to liberate himself from the fetters of secondary processes" (Arieti, 1964, p. 52).

A vow of silence or periodic states of refraining from talking, for instance, was described as a regressive renunciation of secondary functions and a restoration of a primitive preverbal state. Talking, however, can be a gossipy expression of oral fixation or a defensive habit that keeps a person from having to be alone with the inner self—"The silent spaces terrify me," Pascal said.[9]

Silence can rid the person of a compulsion to talk, and in the process evoke the anxiety that is muted by talking (in order then to be able to repair it, and to repair other regressively reactivated conflicts, as I will discuss in the next chapter.) So too silence cultivates a greater openness to hearing others' wisdom, or receptivity to the inner inspirational "voice" that was not heard due to the noise of one's voice and to a faulty hearing learned by conforming to what the world taught one should hear. Hegel said the task in teaching philosophy was to help students to realize that they "must first die to sight and hearing, must be torn away from concrete representations, must be withdrawn into the night of the soul and so learn to see on this new level" (1984, p. 280).

Another ego-regressive discipline that can purge the defensive self is the disavowal of aggression. "Turning the other cheek" or becoming passive ("The meek shall inherit the earth")—regressively defends against aggressive impulses and against the separation anxiety they generate. But renunciation of aggression is an adaptive regression when it frees the person of an aggressive need *always* to be assertive, to accomplish, to do and to compete. (Herbert Marcuse called it the "performance principle.") It grants greater access to the communion feelings previously repressed beneath aggression, allowing the person to become receptive rather than always doing and patient instead of constantly striving. Taoism refers to it as *wu-wei*, or non-doing.

The vow of obedience to a religious superior is one of the more prominent examples of a regressive loss of self that can be a disciplined dismantling of the false self. It was indirectly discussed in the examination of surrendering oneself to a teacher in order to overcome the unconscious resistance to the true self. Furthermore, while obedience abandons adult ego functions such as personal volition, it also abandons what Buddhism calls *dittha:* the prejudicial perspective of the false self. Independent decision making and personal opinion can arise out of an egocentric self, and can create an image of the world that is based less on what the world is and more on the illusion created by what the false self wants or has learned the world to be, exaggerated by the conscious and especially unconscious needs projected onto the world. According to Lao Tzu:

> People through finding something
>   beautiful
> Think something else unbeautiful,
> Through finding one man fit
> find other men unfit.

Obedience to a spiritual master puts a person outside his limited and egocentric self in order to learn from the other just how limited and egocentric his false self is. He willingly "decreases" so as to overcome the resistance to learning from God or Tao. "Blind obedience is the only chance for radical transformation to a human being" (Beauvoir, 1979, p. 324). The religious person sacrifices autonomy in the relationship with a guru or God so as to conquer the rugged individuality that never could rely on another's help or wisdom. In doing so, he learns to acknowledge the communion feelings and dependency needs repressed beneath overcompensatory individuality.

Even seemingly mundane activities, such as wearing the same clothing as other members of one's community, can be an adaptive regression. Wearing a religious habit is regressive. It is a surrendering of even the simplest decision-making processes, while the similarity it forges with others merges the person into the undifferentiated group. But the person might learn in the process to become less attached to his ego, to an infatuation with appearances and with what externally makes him "special" or different from others. This discipline can be combined with a vow of poverty, whereby the person regressively becomes dependent on others' providing for his basic needs but in doing so rids himself of material possessiveness. He also learns through poverty that his "self" is not to be identified with the possessions and success society has taught him to identity with self. Voluntary poverty teaches him to disidentify himself from worldly goods in order to be free to seek what is essential, such as Beauty, Truth, God. As a result, he learns to "be" instead of to define himself by what he owns.[10]

Voluntary poverty can be an object of attachment as tenaciously grasped as material possessions. A person who frees himself of clinging to possessions only to cling to his vow of poverty has exchanged one set of chains for another. Hence Buddhism focuses on the meaning *behind* voluntary poverty; it emphasizes nonattachment. The person renounces not only material possessions but all psychological forms of attachment. Remaining psychologically at a distance from whatever one does, such as attributing all actions to karma or to the will of God, can be a rationalization for escaping personal responsibility, but letting go or "abandoning responsibility," as William James suggested, can also initiate the confrontation with an obsessive self (1961, p. 102). It can rid one of an egocentric compulsion to cling to everything one does or to take responsibility for everyone and everything. Through nonattachment, a person might learn to relate to others, and to life in general, not on the basis of whether they fulfill one's needs (including the need to be responsible) but rather like the Buddhist image of the mirror that reflects what is received without distorting it (unlike the ego, which distorts it for its own needs).

Another regressive and adaptive act that will be discussed in more detail later is the denigration of rational thinking. Let it suffice for the moment to be reminded that analytical and logical thinking were presented as healthy cognitive processes. The person who learns he is "too much in the head" and so has to reject logical thinking in order to "get in touch with his feelings" regressively renounces cognitive skills and returns to raw affects. Yet the diminishment of rational thinking can be necessary when the person truly is too much in his head and does have to become more aware of his feelings. Analytic thinking has developed at the expense of, and as a defense against, intuitive and less rational thinking. Sometimes the only way to restore repressed intuitive thinking is to banish the neatly ordered rational thought processes.

Coleridge, for example, distinguished logical secondary imagination in poetry from "the living power" of primary imagination. He suggested that secondary functions need to be "dissolved, diffused and dissipated" in order to recreate primary imagination (1907, p. 144). The artist experiences the everyday and rational mind as inadequate to the experience of deeper feelings and more penetrating perception. He rejects limited cognitive categories and returns to global perceptions that were left behind in the earliest drive to become analytical (Ehrenzweig, 1967). Erich Neumann similarly wrote about the "recession of the individual's tendency to wholeness in favor of ego development that is guided by the cultural canon and the collective consciousness"; the creative person, on the other hand, does not forget wholeness, unity, and instead

> slays the father, dethrones the conventional world of the traditional canon, and seeks an unknown directing authority . . . namely the self that is so hard to experience, the unknown Heavenly Father. (Neumann, 1954, p. 185)

Order and logic are necessary in life but when too much order and logic stifle life the artist and the mystic break free of their Apollonian structure and liberate the Dionysian impulses repressed beneath them. A religious individual might reject the knowledge that seems reasonable to everyone else, knowledge that is an accumulation of facts and oftentimes "fills a person's head" so as to leave no room for playing with ideas and being imaginative. He renounces a rational analysis of the world in order to regain the ability to "grasp" life; he works at "unknowing" what he was taught so as once again to know with the openness and inquisitiveness that were replaced with logical certainty.

A Zen roshi, for example, helps a student break through constricted logical reasoning by upsetting normative cognitive processes. He might insist on finding an unmediated and nondiscursive answer to an irrational koan ("What is the sound of one hand clapping?"). The answer cannot be found in logical thinking, but only by rejecting secondary (cognitive) process and dipping into the inner self. Wittgenstein advised his students: "Don't think, but look," in order to see beyond the ubiquity of analytical reasoning (1953, p. 31). Even Freud wrote:

> When there is a creative mind, Reason—so it seems to me— relaxes its watch upon the gates, and the ideas rush in pell-mell, and only then does it look them through and examine them. . . . You complain of your unfruitfulness because you reject too soon and discriminate too severely. (1939, p. 135)

Two other self-denying spiritual practices that renounce defensive ego functions are worth brief mention. Celibacy regressively excuses one from acting on sexual impulses and restores pregenital sexuality. But it also can be the initial stage in confronting and overcoming the identification of one's sexuality with society's superficial image of sexuality, and the internalization of that image.

So too entrance into a monastery or isolating oneself for a period of time can be a regressive flight from the demands of the world but it also can remove the person from social influences that, as e. e. cummings noted, turn him into something other than what he is. An individual inextricably absorbed in the seductive allure of society's specious values cannot become aware of his entanglement in it, and of the longing of his inner true self, until he isolates himself from that environment. "No progress in the inner life is possible without detachment from all that is worldly" (Zaehner, 1961, p. 172). Just as the artist secludes himself in order to get rid of all that is irrelevant and to experience only the essential, and just as the scientist withdraws to his laboratory to focus entirely on the work at hand, so too the religious individual isolates himself from the effects of society and concentrates exclusively on experiencing God. Through this isolation he gains the perspective to recognize and to reject the influence society had in shaping (or misshaping) his identity.

Disciplined practices aimed at purging the self—"the deliberate regression . . . the willingness to let the ego die" (Erikson, 1968, p. 213)—might appear extreme. Rejecting reality and renouncing autonomy are extreme and certainly are regressive but they are no more so than what Maritain said of the artist's discipline: "His first duty is to forget himself" (1966, p. 110).[11] In order to get rid of the false self and its unconscious defenses, the religious person must annihilate the ego (Buddhism), vanquish the maya of the separate self (Hinduism), and experience metanoia or a radical dying to self: "Whoever wishes to be my follower must deny his very self" (Lk 9:23). Or as Goethe said,

> And so long as you haven't experienced
> This: to die and so to grow,
> You are only a troubled guest
> On this dark earth.

MEDITATION

Meditation is an excellent example of how purgating ego functions can be adaptive rather than pathological. Meditative practices include, among others, Christian contemplation, Zen focus on breathing or on a koan, yoga, repetition of a mantra, whirling-dervish dancing, and chanting. These practices have several features in common. First, they involve at least a temporary withdrawal of attention from the external environment (closing one's eyes in meditation, for example). Psychoanalysis refers to it as the decathexis of perceptual apparatus (more on this later). Second, the attention that is withdrawn from the external environment is reinvested internally. The focus is on breathing, on inner images and the internal working of the mind. Finally, the result of isolation and concentration is an altered state of consciousness.

Meditation's isolation of the senses and blocking of external stimuli is ego-regressive. Too much autonomy or detachment from the environment, as I have explained, means the ego loses contact with reality. By withdrawing the energy usually given to the ego to master the expectations of reality, meditation diminishes the ego and causes it to become passive and to forfeit active involvement with reality. Too much autonomy makes the instinctual forces that the ego should be controlling revert to less controllable and more primitive expression. The resulting intensification of drive pressure elicits the archaic instincts (euphoric feelings) or hallucinations (visions) sometimes associated with meditation.

The regressive nature of meditation makes it analyzable as a pathological escape from reality and a return to infantile wish fulfillment. From this perspective, meditation is, at best, a type of autohypnosis that allows "archaic mechanisms to come to the surface" (Arieti, 1961, p. 20). Or chanting and controlled breathing are merely physiological processes, radically affecting the subcortical nervous system or the flow of oxygen to the brain and thereby causing a regressive confusion in interpreting inner and outer sources of sensation. Some have even suggested that meditation is a type of trance similar in origin to the immobility observed in animals who "freeze" in response to dread (Hart, 1955, p. 490). At worst, meditation is a regression the psychoanalyst Alexander called a "narcissistic masochistic affair":

> Buddhist self-absorption is a libidinal, narcissistic turning of the urge for knowing inward, a sort of artificial schizophrenia with complete withdrawal of libidinal interest from the outside world. (1931, p. 130)

Meditation might be a regressive diminishment of ego and return to primitive instincts but it can also be regression in service of the ego. This induced regression can overcome an ego that has formed an automatic and confining way of perceiving the world. Such a mode of perception is called automatization, which is a process of selecting and interpreting stimuli. The infant's first way of acquiring knowledge is through the senses. A neonatal body receives all stimuli on this deep sensory level until the later development of a diacritic means of taking in stimuli—that is, cognitive function develops. The mind learns to receive sensory input, make an image of it, store it in long-term memory, and form a concept of it. In this way one develops an orderly intake of stimuli and organizes these isolated bits of information into mental categories.

The limited capacity of a child's mind makes processing the incessant bombardment of stimuli impossible. Sleep is an often chosen, albeit temporary, escape from that burden. With the development of cognitive capacity to store information in memory, the child feels less overwhelmed by the need to process and to analyze every stimulus that enters his brain. He simply learns to check new stimuli against the data already stored in memory, thereby forming a mental chain that connects new data with old. His mind then can explain the significance of the new data on the basis of how it is relevant (or irrelevant) to previous categories. If a new stimulus does not make sense or does not fit with the old, he either alters his mind to make room for it or discards it.

The ability to focus on practical stimuli while ignoring that which is useless or illogical is a tremendous cognitive advance for the child. His brain develops a type of receptor or filter that, by allowing only certain information into consciousness, helps the child to avoid the bombardment of stimuli constantly impinging on his senses. His cognitive processes take in stimuli and automatically, sort, screen, interpret, and categorize them into schemata, retaining the useful while filtering out the rest. Hence cognitive process replaces perception as the main instrument of receiving stimulus. This frees the child from wasting energy processing useless information and prevents large amounts of data from overwhelming the information-processing capacity of his mind.

Meditation reverses this development. Its shift away from cognitive analysis of stimulus to a focus on and subsequent alteration in internal psychological processes is a regression from developed cognition to primitive nonselective functioning of the perceptual apparatus. It suspends accustomed rational mentation so that instead of thinking about what is experienced, about what stimulus is received, or organizing it into recognizable mental categories, the person uncritically receives stimuli as he did in infancy. The ego, in this regressed state, simply takes in what is perceived; it does not question or analyze it. The ego thereby surrenders its synthesizing function to interpret what is perceived and to integrate it into a meaningful part of the person's identity.

Furthermore, meditation lulls the ego to sleep. The brain needs input to be stimulated, to be kept aroused. Sensory deprivation relaxes the brain and suspends its normal functions. The person feels or senses as he did in his primitive coenesthetic body, taking in stimulus through muscles, vibrations, skin, rhythm, and so forth—but not through analytical cognitive processes.

The shift in meditation from cognitive to precognitive processes has been described by some as "snapping": "It seriously affects the brain's ability to process information and may result in impaired awareness, irrationality, disorientation, delusion, and violent destructive acts" (Conway, 1978, p. 135). Snapping of the mind or the sudden change in normal cognition can lead to thought disorder, or to the narrowing of awareness in meditation that makes a person oblivious to what is going on around him. While meditation does disorganize the brain's information-processing capacity, regressively restoring primitive cognition, the regressive change in the way the brain processes information can be in service of the ego.

The psychoanalyst Hartmann suggested that the brain's seemingly sophisticated capacity for automatic processing makes "the concept of a thoughtfully flexible ego an illusion" (1958b, p. 89). A discriminating mind frees the person from being bogged down with processing irrelevant input but the automatic processing also forms a regimented or inflexible perception of life. Only that which is familiar, which falls into preconceived and logical categories, warrants attention. That which is intuitive or inspirational, spontaneous or surprising, mysterious and especially mystical, is rejected from this processing system and not accorded consciousness. Even the familiar is by-passed as the brain automatically stores stimuli in long-term memory. The result is stereotypical and programmed thinking, with a narrow range of awareness, followed by an even narrower range of behavior based on unimaginative cognition. Instead of acting out of an open and animated inner self, the person acts out of predetermined mental categories and limited, habitual patterns of behavior. He becomes a prisoner of his mind. As Kipling once observed: "What does he of England know, who only England knows."

If the ego can learn to select and reject, then, as Hartmann further suggested (and as others recently reaffirmed, most notably Deikman [1966] and Ornstein [1977]), automatization of ego can be "deautomatized." Deautomatization is the undoing of the automatic way of perceiving and interpreting reality. It pierces habitual acts of the ego, dismantles rational and linear ways of thinking. It accomplishes this through experiences such as love, drugs, inspiration, or any of the various ways in which a person disrupts the internal structure that had been organizing and interpreting life according to automatic and preconceived categories. The result is that the person can experience new stimuli—whether originating externally or internally—with a freshness and vitality that were lacking when all stimuli were filtered through cognitive processes.

Meditation is one of the ways in which a person deautomatizes stereotypical or categorized ways of perceiving life. Meditation disrupts the normal ego function of taking in stimuli and interpreting them according to preconceived categories. It suspends habitual patterns of perception and cognition by radically altering perception and subsequently altering the cognitive processing of what is perceived.

In terms of perception, meditation changes the means by which stimuli are received. Instead of looking at the world, for instance, the meditator might block it out by closing his eyes. Rather than viewing a great variety of actions and stimuli, the person in prayer might focus on one particular object, becoming oblivious to everything else.

So too different physical postures can reorient one's way of thinking. Sitting crossed-legged in a Zen or lotus position, or kneeling for long hours on the floor, or following prescribed yogic postures can induce a change in perception from that provided by typical body movement or sitting relaxed on a chair.

Some practices, such as the whirling-dervish dance, intensify stimuli. Others dull stimuli through concentration on sound repeated internally (like a mantra) or on monotonous external sound such as the banging of drums in Tibetan Buddhism or in Native American practices.

The alteration of perception in meditation changes the accustomed way of receiving stimuli. They are blocked off altogether, intensified, or refocused; as a result, internal cognitive processes that normally automatically select and filter input are drastically affected. They cease to function automatically, and instead require new and focused attention in order to respond to the change in the way stimuli are being received. Hence meditative deautomatization of cognitive processes, like other purgative disciplines, is a regressive retreat from organized mental structures to disorganized mental structures —but with the purpose of leaving behind the rigidity of the former in order to experience the creative openness of the latter.

If the doors of perception were cleansed, everything would appear to man as it is, infinite. For man has closed himself up, til he sees all things through the narrow dinks of his cavern. (Blake, 1975, p. 5)

For now we see through a glass darkly; but then face to face: now I know in part; but then shall I know even as also I am known. (1 Cor 13:12)

ADAPTIVE DARK-NIGHT PURGATION OF EGO

Ego-purgative disciplines are taken to their logical conclusion in the dark-night experience. The dark night, as discussed previously, is a dreaded return of unconscious conflicts that dispel the illusion of paradise. It is resolved when the person splits off the final fragments of aggression that burst that bubble, thereby dissolving the remaining psychological boundaries that distinguish self from God. Resolution of the dark night *is* ego regressive but does not have to be pathological. The dark-night dismissal of the entrenched self that separated one from God can be the final dissolution of the egocentric, superficial, and false self that alienates the person from his true self.

The final remnant of self that is purged in the dark night is the defensive part of the ego that unconsciously resists surrender. When, for example, a person clings in the dark night to the vanishing image of God, the tenacity with which he clings manifests the entrenched ego's insidious attempt to prevent purgation. It is an idealized image of himself that the person clings to, dredged up from the unconscious by this primitive ego. A Buddhist might be told, "If you meet the Buddha on the road, kill him." That is, if you meet Buddha you have only encountered your innermost intransigent attachment to a particular concept or image of Buddha. Meister Eckhart suggested a similar attitude from the Christian perspective: "True poverty of spirit requires that man shall be emptied of God and all his works. . . . Therefore I pray God that he may quit me of God."

The defensive ego collapses in despair when it is confronted with the futility of its efforts to experience God. That despair, according to Harvard psychologist Kohlberg (1973), is preliminary to experiencing a new and transcendent fullness. Kohlberg described six stages of moral development, beginning with primitive preconventional mentation and concluding with a maturely integrated identity. Kohlberg later speculated on a seventh stage, a stage of nonegoistic unity. This stage does not result from logical development of the strengths developed in the previous stages. Instead, it is introduced with the dark-night despairing recognition that the greatest strengths one possesses—including moral and rational—fall short of an integrated fullness.

Jesus' dark-night cry on the cross, "My God, My God, why have you forsaken me," typifies this transformative despair. His experience of dark-night despair at being forsaken by God is transcended when Jesus, declaring "No longer my will but your will be done," purges himself of the final remnant of self that separated him from God (or from his true self). Jesus, like the great mystics, finally realizes he cannot achieve unity of will with God through his own efforts. He *can* struggle to renounce his ego, and become obedient and dependent on God. These self-denying acts are critically important in delivering him to the threshold of an experience of God but, in the end, Jesus has to renounce even his striving to experience God for such striving is motivated by the deeply defensive self.

> It is when we begin to see our lives as finite from some more infinite perspective that we feel despair. The meaninglessness of our lives in the face of death is the meaninglessness of the finite from the perspective of the infinite. The resolution of the despair which we call stage seven represents a continuation of the process of taking a more cosmic perspective whose first phase is despair. (Kohlberg, 1973, p. 501)

7

Illumination and Adaptive Regression in the Service of the Ego

INTRODUCTION

Although dark-night surrendering of ego marks the apparently successful purgation of false self, it does not imply the completion of religious experience. It means only that the self that had impeded a direct experience of God has been surrendered and that with its surrender comes a new beginning. As T. S. Eliot said,

> We shall not cease from exploration
> And the end of all our exploring
> Will be to arrive where we started
> And know the place for the first time. (1943, p. 59)

The experience that begins with the demise of the old self does not necessarily lead to the ascendance of the true self or the Christ within, as if they would automatically arise with the purging of the false self. The opposite can happen, as in Jesus' parable about the man who worked strenuously to clean his house of demons only to have his newly cleaned house filled with even greater demons (Lk 11:24). When the false self is purged, the previously repressed primitive instincts and unconscious structures are set free. Their dramatic ascent from the netherworld is represented in the experience of God, of visions and ecstasy—experiences sometimes felt as demonic but more typically as cathartic release from tension or escape from reality. Although regressive, such experiences can be reparative (rather than pathological). They can revive a symbiotic unity that brings with it the communion feelings that were lost in the overestimation of autonomy (this will be examined in the next chapter). And they can resurrect primitive processes that were left behind in conforming to social pressures and that can lead to creativity and illumination.

RECOVERY OF PRIMARY PROCESS CREATIVITY

If discontent over rigid ego functions begins the purgation process, then the actual surrender of ego leads to illumination, enlightenment, or at the very minimum the relief described by Wordsworth:

> When struggling against a stubborn obstacle,
> We sometime feel an impulse to give up, and
> giving up brings relief (Quoted in Wells, 1935, p. 878)

Relief that comes from abandoning a difficult task derives, on a conscious level, from the surrender of personal initiative and the anxious pressure that once accompanied it (ego regression). On an unconscious level, relief comes from indulging the inner impulse to operate on a more primitive level—a level of fantasy, for example, where effort is not necessary and obstacles are magically overcome. This inner world of fantasy and immediate gratification belongs to primary process thinking.

Primary process, it will be remembered, is based on wish fulfillment and unbounded energy, while secondary functions satisfy desires in realistic ways and bind instinctual energy into constructive expressions. Regression is the diminishment of secondary functions and a return to primary process, but just as secondary functions are not as healthy as they appear (and instead can be defensive), so too primary process is not as undesirable and primitive as one learned to regard it in the drive to form secondary functions. Primary process might originally represent wish fulfillment and immediate drive gratification but it is also an expression of the openness and lack of inhibition that make a child receptive to new experiences. "The drive to seek out and to explore the new is the strongest in childhood of animals and men, in the period of exploratory play" (Schactel, 1959, p. 184).

The repression of primary process thinking is not essential to growth. The adult ability to bind psychological energy and to direct drives could have been developed by leaving behind the infantile aspects of primary process without sacrificing enthusiasm and freedom. For example, if the fantasy life of childhood were allowed to be integrated into—rather than being repressed in deference to—reality, the child would become an adult who might along the way have transformed fantasy from an escapist phenomenon to expression of a fertile imagination. Openness and immediacy of experience could have been allowed to develop alongside control and logic.

Primitive processes were not integrated, however, but were repressed, as secondary functions developed. The child's spontaneity and openness to experience gradually faded, and was relegated to an unconscious realm of unfulfilled longings, as she learned the exclusive importance of autonomy and control.

> As they mature we see in the higher mammals and in most men a slackening or ceasing of curiosity, fascination, playful exploration, excitement, enthusiasm: the "open" world having now turned into a variety of objects with significant qualities. (Schactel, 1959, p. 184)

The result is a sense of self that is preoccupied with external qualities while having lost or severely limited access to feelings of playfulness, instinctual spontaneity, and the creativity that could have arisen from such access. Trust in instincts is replaced with trust in social acceptance.

A chorus of voices from different perspectives has stated the need to become free of constricted secondary functions and to experience the primary process creativity that potentially exists beneath them. The psychoanalyst Bakan called this inner realm of playfulness and spontaneity "communion" and said that "it was necessary for the agentic, masculine qualities to be reduced to allow the repression of communion to be overcome" (1935, p. 60). Jesus' familiar exhortation that heaven was available only to those who "become like little children" warned adults that their authority and control often inhibited unbridled experiences. Jung suggested that early repressed drives and affect are a potential source of wisdom to the adult and "can only be found if the conscious mind will suffer itself to be led back to the 'children's land', there to receive guidance from the unconscious as before" (1970, p. 337). So too Freud (1917) recognized that sometimes a loss of ego control and the resulting greater "flexibility of repression" can be therapeutically reparative, while Hartmann wrote that the ego needs at times "to be able to abandon itself to the id" (1964, p. 177).

ARTISTIC INSPIRATION

The artist's experience represents a regressive recovery of primary process that can be creative rather than pathological. The repressed instincts into which she dips for inspiration might be primitive in the sense that they were relegated to an unconscious realm where they were repressed and never allowed to develop. But it is because of this formative flaw that the artist, not content with stereotypical perceptions, returns to their unfulfilled state and finds in them freshness and imagination. Hence the artistic renunciation of the normative might be "a going backward, but a going back to look for something which could have real value for adult life if only it could be reached" (Milner, quoted in Fuller, 1980, p. 234).

Ernst Kris labeled the irruption of primary process into consciousness the inspirational stage of creativity (1952, p. 61). Previously repressed instincts and tightly bound primitive processes are let loose. They make the artist feel as if overtaken by an unknown force or hit by a sudden flash of insight—the "aha" experience. They inspire her with a novel perspective that comes from within. Van Gogh saw an ordinary sunflower but in his painting of the sunflower he bypassed logical perceptions and was inspired by the brilliance and creativity of an inner perception.[1]

> God guard me from those thoughts men think
> In the mind alone,
> He that sings a lasting song
> Thinks in marrow bone. (Yeats, 1966)

Primary process freed from constraints is experienced as arising from a mysterious, unknown part of the artist: "The creator is driven; he is in an exceptional state. Thoughts or images tend to flow, things appear in his mind of which he never seemed to have known" (Kris, 1952, p. 35). Sometimes inspiration seems to "come like a foreign guest," as Goethe said.

> "Muses, who make man's mind widen with knowledge,
> And his tongue speak from heaven." (Hesiod)

RELIGIOUS ILLUMINATION

Inspiration that arises in religious experience is called illumination. The artist's sudden flash of insight is to the religious person an experience of being grasped by God or having truth unveiled. Illumination has its roots in the purgative stage of religious experience. By cracking the crust of the false self that had kept hidden beneath it the true self and its vital openness to experience, the person dies to the old and becomes receptive to the new.

> A death blow is a life blow to some
> Who, till they died, did not alive become,
> Who, had they lived, had died, but when
> They died, vitality begun.
> (Emily Dickinson, quoted in Phillips, 1977, p. 43)

Once the "doors of perception" are cleansed, the inner psychological processes that were kept in the dark, especially in the dark night of the soul, are illuminated. Whereas ego functioning had based its perceptions and interpretations on the accumulation of previously stored input (automatization), the direct and immediate experience of God represents the illuminative restoration of primary process.

Some light can be shed on this experience by comparing it with the free association that takes place in psychoanalysis. Free association begins with a withdrawal from the mundane concerns that distract a person from the task of concentrating on inner psychological processes. Deautomatization of rigid ego processes similarly gives the person greater access to the spontaneous world of her inner unconscious. Rather than setting constraints on or fitting what arises out of the unconscious into preconceived mental categories, the person learns to focus uncritically on its reactivated feelings and thoughts.

Meditation likewise helps a person to become like a mirror: to reflect everything she sees without discrimination. By being a mirror to inner and outer stimuli, the person suspends the cognitive processes that automatically store stimuli and interpret it through previously stored categories. She learns neither to be disturbed by sensations and images nor to analyze them, but to "watch them flow by like a cloud." Hence rather than selecting only particular thoughts or feelings that enter her mind and rejecting what does not fit in a narrow range of perception, she becomes more receptive and attentive—both to a wider range of external stimuli and to an equally vast inner range of nonautomatic psychological processes. Even Freud stated that while he "safely doubted" that the meditative practices of mystics could "put one in the possession of ultimate truth, from which all good flows," he acknowledged its deautomatizing ability to break through rigid cognitive structures and recover unconscious processes:

> Certain practises of the mystics may succeed in upsetting the normal relations between the different regions of the mind, so that, for example, the perceptual system becomes able to grasp relations in the deeper layers of the ego and in the id which would otherwise be inaccessible to it . . . we must admit that the therapeutic efforts of psychoanalysis have chosen much the same method of approach. (1955b, p. 11)

The mystic, like the artist, dismantles the stereotypical filter of ego and experiences life openly and intensely. She stops analyzing truth or beauty. Rather than keeping them objectively at a discernible distance, she directly grasps their meaning in an act of what Hegel called "immediate knowledge" (quoted in Abrams, 1971, p. 232). She sees life with a clarity that comes from an inner perspective; she experiences it, as she experiences God, from deep within herself, from the immediacy and inspiration of the creative primary process. Coleridge wrote in his "Apologia Pro Vita Sua":

> The poet in his lone yet genial hour
> Gives to his eyes a magnificent power.
> Or rather he emancipates his eyes
> From the black shapeless accident of size—

In unctuous cones of kindling coal,
Or snake upwreathing from the pipes trim bole,
    His gifted ken can see
    Phantoms of sublimity.

Dharmakaya is an example of piercing normative perception and direct experience of life. It is the Buddhist state of a person who by having "emptied himself" has allowed the inner *dharma* or truth to guide him. Christians who die to self subsequently are inspired or directed by the Holy Spirit. Taoism speaks of the *chi*, an inner energy that when free of ego manipulation stimulates a more integrated relationship with life.

Yoga similarly aims to activate the *prana*, an energy that seems to be of the same stuff as primary process. It is an inner drive whose life force was lost in the overemphasis on rational cognitive processes (*vighana*). Yoga discipline helps the mind to relax in order to allow the *prana* or *shakti* energy to be released from where it is stored within the *kundalini*. So too the earlier described *Tat tvam asi*, or Thou art That, represents people's ability to embody the divine energy or at least to participate in it, if only they can get past their resistance to it. In any case, according to Goethe, "Man cannot stay long in the conscious state: he must time and again go back to the unconscious, for here is the root of his being."

> Art is a kind of innate drive that seizes a human being and makes him its instrument. The artist is not a person endowed with free will who seeks his own ends, but one who allows art to realize its purpose through him. (Jung, 1969, p. 221)

JUNG AND REGRESSIVE PRIMARY PROCESS

Jung's description of regression as a necessary loss of self and the liberation of psychic energy shows similarity to the release of *prana* or of the illuminative movement of the Holy Spirit. Regression of this type is based on Jung's idea of libido. Libido is the psychological flow of energy that arises out of the drive to reconcile opposites (enantiodromia). Libido emanates from the tension that exists between the conscious and the unconscious, or sleep and waking. It is experienced in a progressive fashion when it balances the various tensions in a way that adapts harmoniously to the demands of the external environment. When, however, the conscious mind becomes the dominant force—as it does in the shaping of the persona—it draws most of the libido away from the inner self. The exclusive investment of psychic energy in the persona might make the latter appear to be successful and in control but, as this work has examined, it also makes the person defensive and alienated.

Regression is required in order to return libido from the seemingly mature persona to the inner self. The withdrawal of libidinal energy from the conscious mind restores it to the broader source of psychic energy that had been hidden beneath (and usurped by) the dominance of the persona: "I regard the loss of balance as purposive, since it replaces a defective consciousness by the automatic and instinctual activity of the unconscious" (Jung, 1953b, p. 110).

INTUITION AS AN EXAMPLE OF CREATIVE PRIMARY PROCESS

The reactivation of primary process brings a new and vital source of energy to consciousness. With the attenuation of normal ego functioning in the purgative stage of religious experience, primary process activity is amplified. The result is an enlarged scope of awareness. Perceptual skills once confined to "realistic" external stimuli are replaced with an inner perception directed by uninhibited impulses and primitive processes. Religions traditionally have referred to this internal perception as seeing with the heart, inner vision, direct grasp of reality, immediate apprehension of God, and so forth.

For example, most people learn to relate to the environment through logic and control. However, when attention is withdrawn from ego functioning and refocused on unconscious processes, a person's normally logical approach to resolving tasks is replaced with an intuitive approach. That is, she gains greater trust in inner unconscious processes. Instead of indirectly experiencing life through the .filter of rational cognitive processes, she learns to "grasp" a situation, to "know" something or someone. Her experience is closer to that of a musician or a lover.

Intuitive experiences also allow a person to appreciate the whole, the totality. They enable her to see life from a wider and less constricted angle, to appreciate the oneness of things or their interrelatedness, rather than dissecting the parts that constitute the whole. In the end, she discovers that primitive processes such as intuition are no less effective—and sometimes are more effective—in resolving problems and grasping truth than are secondary functions. Hartmann suggested that even in scientific thinking—the "undisputed domain of rational thought"—a person could adaptively regress to irrational and intuitive thinking and find that "far from being a handicap, [it] actually can be helpful" (1958b, pp. 17, 18).

When Jesus said that people must be born again, Nicodemus asked incredulously how a person could return to the womb (Jn 3:3). Jesus' teaching demonstrates the illogical working of primary process thinking, which seeks immediate results and pierces logical structures—regardless of apparent contradictions—in order to bring about direct apprehension. Hence Nicodemus' logical and controlled mind not only could not comprehend an intuitive message such as that of Jesus, but defended against it—especially against the inner world of spontaneity, openness, and fears or unresolved conflicts it might resurrect (unresolved feelings of maternal attachment and hence of being born again, for example).

The Zen koan is another example of recovering primary process and utilizing it to broaden one's life beyond constricted logical reasoning. The koan is a puzzle that is intentionally irrational or apparently nonsensical. Because the koan cannot be cognitively comprehended according to preconceived notions of reality, the Zen initiate—after struggling with logical reasoning and confidently assuming she will be able to resolve the conundrum—finally has to abandon ineffective secondary functions. "The koan is neither a riddle nor a witty remark. It has a most definite objective, the arousing of doubt and pushing it to its furthest limits" (Suzuki, 1960, p. 53). With the abandonment of rigid cognitive processes, the person regressively returns to primary process thinking to answer the koan. She sinks into an unconscious realm—a nondual realm where logical cognitive processes and the distinction between self and not-self do not exist—and by experiencing the koan as an indistinguishable part of herself she intuitively apprehends its meaning.[2]

In the unconscious realm of primary process the religious person, like the artist, discovers that contradictory thoughts—being born again or one hand clapping—can coexist.

> Einstein had concluded that a person falling from the roof of a
> house was both in motion and at rest at the same time. The
> hypothesis was illogical and contradictory in structure, but it
> possesses a superior logic and solution. . . . In an apparent de-
> fiance of logic or of physical possibilities, the creative person
> consciously formulates the simultaneous apparition of antitheti-
> cal elements and develops these into integrative entities and cre-
> ativity. (Rothenberg, 1979, p. 52)

The mystic and artist learn to accept, and even to find creativity in,
the contradictions between primary process immediacy and the ordered control of reality.[3] Contradictions that previously threatened
to destroy unity (assertiveness vitiated passivity, for example, while
reality opposed fantasy) can be reconciled—especially that of unity
and separateness. Before examining healthy symbiotic regression in
the next chapter, I offer a brief note to suggest that another regressive recovery of primary process, that of hallucination, can also be
adaptive.

Hallucinations are the regressive recovery of primitive cognitive processes. They substitute images that express wish-fulfilling
thinking for reality. Yet hallucinations are not always pathological.

Michelangelo, for example, was able to gaze at a block of marble
and actually see his sculpture *David*. Mozart was said to be able to
hear a whole symphony in his head before he composed it. And
Wagner wrote the opera *Das Rheingold* from an auditory hypnagogic
image. These images or hallucinations directed the artists through
their creative task, and religious visions can do the same.

The psychiatrist Arieti suggested that religious visions, like
those of the artist, can serve as guides (1959, p. 277). Jung (1963)
suggested that the same thing takes place when the hero engages
psychological "helpers" to assist him in overcoming obstacles in his
journey. So too dreams, by being "the royal road to the unconscious," can produce images that guide a person through inner psychological processes that are normally inaccessible to consciousness.

Religious visions that are confused with reality result in psychosis. When instead they are beneficial guides—projected images of
one's psychological needs that help a person become aware of otherwise hidden unconscious needs—the result can be psychological
growth. When Jesus was in the garden of Gethsemani, for example,
abandoned and alone, he hallucinated an angel to take away his suffer-

ing. Had Jesus clung to the hallucination the result would have been psychosis. Instead he found sufficient comfort in his vision to regain the equilibrium that was lost in his fear of abandonment. At that point the hallucination disappeared—as the hallucinated maternal breast disappears when the infant learns to achieve gratification on her own—and Jesus was stimulated by the experience to return confidently to his quest.[4]

8

Regressive Restoration and Reparation of Symbiotic Unity

INTRODUCTION

As we discussed, the undisturbed libidinal bond between infant and mother is a form of symbiosis. Freud suggested that oceanic experience is a regressive return to this paradisiacal state. He did not, however, dismiss as pathological other regressive experiences that similarly suspend separateness and restore unconscious unity, and even saw in one a metaphor for the creative potential of symbiotic regression:

> We cannot do justice to the characteristics of the mind by linear outlines like those in a drawing or in primitive painting, but rather by areas of color melting into one another as they are presented by modern artists. After making the separation we must allow what we have separated to merge together once more. (Freud, 1939, p. 79)

Although Freud's depiction of religious experience allows no such regenerative symbiotic regression, I suggest that it is possible. Jung thought so. He agreed with Freud's assessment of the regressive nature of oceanic experience[1] but took it one step further:

> There lie at the root of the regressive longing, which Freud conceived as "infantile fixation" and "incestuous wish," a specific value and a specific need which are made explicit in myths. (Jung, 1966, p. 119)

What is the specific value and need that can transform the regressed state of religious experience into a healthy and even enlightening experience? That is, what makes the symbiotic experience of Nir-

128

vana or communion with God a healthy regression in service of the ego?

Several notable psychologists have described the healthy loss of self and submersion into unity. Maslow's "peak experiences," for example, raised oceanic experiences to new heights of desirability (1964, p. 164), and Harvard psychologist Kohlberg's hypothesized seventh stage of moral development transcends rational development: "A contemplative experience of a non-egoistic or non-dualistic unity" (1973, p. 501). Erich Neumann described it as "an encounter that occurs between ego and non-ego in which the contradiction of world, ego and self are suspended (1968, p. 380). Norman O. Brown rapturously described the dissolution of individuality and return to undifferentiated bliss:

> Dionysis, the mad God, breaks down the boundaries; releases the prisoners; abolishes repression; and abolishes the "principium individuationis," substituting for it the unity of man and the unity of man with nature. (1968, p. 161)

A regenerative restoration of unbounded symbiotic unity is most incisively observable in the arts.[2]

> The oceanic experience of fusion, of a "return to the womb," represents the minimum content of all art; Freud saw in it only the basic religious experience. But it seems now that it belongs to all creativity. (Ehrenzweig, 1967, p. 121)

The similarities are striking between mystics who write about unity with the God they behold and artists who "in the stage of inspiration becomes [sic] one with their work" (Kris, 1952, p. 61). Compare these with tenets of Buddhism or statements of Eckhart on shedding the dualistic distinctions between seer and seen, knower and known, and the artist's experience of beauty perceived and being a perceiver of beauty.[3]

> For the uniquely distinguishing feature of aesthetic experience is exactly the fact that no such distinction of self and object exists in it. . . . The two are so integrated that each disappears. (Dewey, 1934b, p. 249)

There occurred, at least sometimes, a fusion into a never-before known wholeness; not only were the object and oneself no longer felt to be separate but neither were thoughts and sensations and feelings and actions. (Milner, 1950, p. 142)

Notice the similarity between the earlier description of mystics who experience a loss of self in an illuminative state of consciousness and Milner's account of losing herself in the creative act:

The ordinary sense of self had temporarily disappeared, there had been a kind of blanking out of ordinary consciousness; even the awareness of the blanking out had gone, so that it was only afterwards, when I returned to ordinary self-consciousness, that I remembered that there had been this phase of complete lack of self-consciousness. (1958, p. 154)

Observe also the similarity between the accounts of people discussed previously who, when they ceased reflecting on God, focused so intently on their experience that they seemed to merge selflessly into it, and the psychoanalyst Schafer's succinct description of the creative individual's merger "in the representation of oneself as thinker and thought" (1968, p. 99).

Religious or creative individuals become so selflessly absorbed in their experience ("attention which is so full that the 'I' disappears"—Weil, 1952, p. 172), that they do not, at the moment, think about the experience. They do not interpret how they feel about it and especially do not try to make rational sense of a temporary loss of separate consciousness as they become absorbed in the experience. Instead, by becoming single-mindedly attentive to it, they (1) eliminate all distinctions, (2) halt automatic cognitive processes of thinking about and analyzing the experience (deautomatization), and (3) (without this automatic cognitive process), lose the distinction between self as thinker or experiencer and that which is thought about or experienced.[4]

To gain pleasure, one suspends representations of oneself reading. In being gratified by reading, we merge with the source of gratification as once feeding child and nurturing mother formed a unit . . . [this] involves a sense of the boundaries blurring between self and other, a feeling of merger which derives ultimately

from a recreation of the same symbiotic at-oneness with the
mother. (Holland, 1973, p. 85)

The symbiotic unity elicited when a person surrenders self and
becomes one with God, as the artist's experience of unity with his
work, can be creative and lead to enhanced psychological growth
rather than being the pathological regression described in the first
section. In what follows I examine what can take place in the regressed symbiotic oceanic state—from the reenactment of basic trust
to the reparation of underlying conflicts—that reverses regression
and transforms religious experience into a regression in service of
the ego. The first of these adaptive regressions taking place in the
unitive state is the experience of a temporary escape from—a moratorium on—anxieties of life that might otherwise be overwhelming.

MORATORIUM

A person attacked by a rabid dog probably does not take time to
wonder if climbing a tree is a regressive act of running from a conflict. Once safely in the tree, he might ask himself if he could have
defended against the danger without having fled. The security of his
escape gives him the luxury to reassess his actions; it also allows him
to "catch his breath," to recollect his thoughts and feelings so as to
decide the best way to respond to his situation. Fleeing, as a result,
might have been a "stepping back" in order to avoid the unmanageable situation but it might also have provided the security that allows
him to "step forward" in a more confident way.

> Where external dangers are concerned, the individual can help
> himself for some time by flight and by avoiding the situation of
> danger, until he is strong enough later to remove the threat by
> actively altering reality. (Freud, 1920a, p. 237)

Although Freud acknowledged that an escape from stress can be
beneficial,[5] he warned that the cost is too high in terms of lost ego
strengths and a return to childishness. For example, sometimes the
protection provided by the "tree" makes a person prefer to stay securely ensconced in it rather than confront the feared situation. Or, less
dramatically, the person might thereafter go through life constantly
needing to know where safe "trees" are located in the event danger

should arise again. In these situations, the regressive flight from danger is neither momentary nor in the service of growth. It instead reactivates unconscious defenses that transform what should have been temporary safety into a permanent reality (psychoses) or a security blanket by means of which life's vagaries are escaped (neurosis).

When responsibilities and expectations appear overwhelming, a perfect tree of safety is the experience of communion with God. Purgation of self and merger into an omnipotent deity regressively get rid of anxiety but do not necessarily result in irrevocable attachment to security. They do not have to result in habitual behavior of taking refuge in God each time anxiety arises (thereby avoiding the need to develop internal strengths to manage the anxiety). Instead, the person neither stays in nor remains pathologically attached to the regressed state: Moses comes down from the mountain, Jesus departs the desert, and Buddha arises from the shade of the boddhi tree. Each found in a hidden place a *temporary* refuge from the distractions and temptations of the world.

Unitive experience might begin as a flight from the world but it can become a critically important safe harbor or what Erikson labeled a "moratorium" (1958, p. 44). A psychological moratorium is a time of distancing oneself from certain anxieties that otherwise might prove overwhelming. In a world that sometimes feels so chaotic as to "take one's breath away" and so demanding as to "make me crazy," a moratorium is the time taken away from the world in order to catch one's breath and to become even-headed—pausing until one feels capable of managing the anxiety-arousing situation.

The experience of Nirvana or communion with God regressively restores an anxiety-free symbiotic unity that instead of being pathological can offer a moratorium from the sometimes overwhelming vagaries of life.

> We may find restitution following crises by undergoing transitory regression to very early ego states in which we re-establish contact with the world about us through feeling, initially, wholly at one with it, as we once felt in infancy. (Searles, 1960, p. 107)

Take, for example, a person who manages the stress he feels about an upcoming exam by praying to God for help. Turning to God for help is clearly regressive in that it (1) substitutes childish thinking for rational thought and (2) diminishes reliance on one's own strengths by (3) inducing a symbiotic relationship with God in which the person magically partakes in divine knowledge. This regressive act of praying, however, can also be a moratorium on stress. The anxiety of taking the exam makes the person nervous and thereby impedes his performance. With the elimination of anxiety, due to the moratorium in which the deity is invoked in prayer (or a religious ritual such as the sign of the cross made before a difficult shot in some sport), the person becomes less anxious and more clear-headed. His regressive prayer diminishes self-reliance and restores a symbiotic relationship but also makes him more calm and therefore better able to perform.[6] Meditation (another form of prayer) has been demonstrated to have a healthful effect by restoring calm to the respiratory system and reducing physiological/psychological stress in general, thereby inducing greater equanimity with which to approach life's exigencies (Murphy, 1989).

A more dramatic example of moratorium is the appeal of new religious movements to adolescents. Adolescence is a time of emotional upheaval, instigated by the pubescent appearance of confusing sexual drives coupled with feelings of rebellion toward those in authority (return of aggressive drives). Religious communities offer refuge from the uncertainties and feelings of inadequacy encountered during adolescence. Their disciplined environment, strict rules, and authoritarian leadership provide an escape from the emotional and physical confusion that to some young people appears intolerable. They surrender the autonomy and aggression needed to master the developmental tasks of adolescence, and lose themselves —along with their anxiety—in the reactivation of early forms of drive expression (passivity and dependence).

The security religious organizations offer can be destructive, leading to permanent dependency, but can also be a moratorium from developmental issues that at the time feel unmanageable.

> Young persons often indicate in rather pathetic ways the feeling that only by merging with a "leader" can they be saved, the leader being an adult who is able and willing to offer himself as a safe

object for experimental surrender and as a guide in the relearning
of the very first steps toward an intimate mutuality and a legiti-
mate repudiation. (Erikson, 1968, p. 168)

A moratorium on seemingly overwhelming tasks and uncontrollable
inner drives helps, as Winnicott wrote, "to defend against a specific
environmental failure by a freezing of the failure situation" (1955, p.
18). By becoming celibate in a cult, for example, or in a seminary
(Fauteux, 1990), an individual avoids the pressures society places on
his sexuality until such time as he is prepared to deal with sexuality
according to his own psychological/biological time schedule. "A
strategic retreat [from adolescent anxiety] is the surest road to vic-
tory" (Blos, 1967, p. 172). When the person is able to manage these
drives on his own, the function of the community to provide a moratorium on sexual anxiety will cease to exist, and its appeal will probably diminish.[7]

Moratoriums that offer temporary refuge can be found in religious experiences throughout adulthood. "Separation/individuation
is never finished; it remains always active; new phases of the life
cycle see new derivatives of the earliest processes still at work"
(Mahler, 1975, p. 3). Purgation of the false self, for example, provides a moratorium on pressures that began in infancy, and continue
into adulthood, to be ruggedly independent and rigidly in control. In
a world that focuses attention on doing things, on being logical and
staying one step ahead of alienation, the regressive surrender of self
and submersion into an anxiety-free unity occurs with an almost
tangible sigh of relief. It produces feelings of being saved or delivered from the anxiety induced in a society obsessed with superficial
pursuits. It creates a redemptive moratorium in which the person
feels as if he can catch his breath instead of always having to accomplish and to do; can relax and become comfortable with himself because he no longer has to prove his worth; and can feel recollected
and free of the many pressures that seemed to pull him in different
directions. "The dissolution of the persona in the collective psyche
positively invites one to wed oneself with the abyss and blot out all
memory in its embrace" (Jung, 1976, p. 119).

The Trappist monk Thomas Merton is a twentieth-century example of an individual whose experience of God began with taking
refuge from the anxieties of the world. His prolific writings are

replete with references to a world that emphasizes external pursuits and that rewards conformity with shallow feelings of success accompanied by inner feelings of alienation. Merton was an individual of vast intelligence and personal strength, and yet he too felt distracted by this materialistic world, alienated by its fraudulent values, and pulled apart by its unrelenting demands. Feeling he could not "know himself" or directly experience God in this world, he rejected the world and secluded himself in a Trappist monastery.

Monastic existence was to provide the fertile ground out of which Merton experienced a transformative encounter with God. But before this experience took place—and necessary to preparing the way for it—the monastery was a refuge from the pressures and anxieties of the world. In the Japanese edition to his *Thoughts in Solitude* (1981), Merton wrote that in hindsight he could see how his entrance into the monastery was an escapist flight from the world and its demands. It was a necessary flight. Had he stayed in the world he probably would have been distracted by its pressures and preoccupied defending himself against its seductive image of success. Had he not died to the world he would have never been able to refocus attention inward, to the inner reality that would have remained a stranger to him.

The monastic moratorium helped Merton escape an alienating society but the escape was only temporary. It was also only a preparatory step for a transformative submersion into communion with God. Erik Erikson discovered in Martin Luther's monasticism a similar adaptive moratorium and, as we will see later, a similar transformation.

> The monastery offers methods of making a meditative descent into the inner shafts of mental existence, from which the aspirant emerges with the gold of faith or with gems of wisdom. These shafts, however, are psychological as well as meditative; they lead not only into the depths of adult inner experience, but also downward into our more primitive layers, and backward into our infantile beginnings. (1958, p. 109)

INCUBATION

Moratorium most notably takes place in the dark-night experience when the individual, exhausted by his efforts to extricate himself from the dark night, sinks into a primitive state of passivity. The experience is reminiscent of an event between infant and mother. When the infant feels anxious and desperately cries for attention but that attention is not forthcoming, he finally gives up crying and falls asleep. The psychiatrist H. S. Sullivan called this resignation a feeling "of the occasional inadequacy and powerlessness" of behavior that normally produces the desired object, such as the crying that produced the mother's breast (1953, p. 70). He labeled the act of giving up "apathy." Adults repeat this process "more or less frequently throughout life" (ibid.), as when their normal efforts to achieve satisfaction are not only as futile as the infant's unheard cry but also make them feel powerless.

The dark night is a situation in which an adult gives up repeated ego attempts to overcome anxiety and resigns himself, as in infancy, to its futility. There are certain times when according to all norms a person should meet a situation with unequivocal strength but also times when such efforts are not only futile but can exacerbate anxiety. In these latter times, such as during the dark night, continued striving to overcome the anxious situation intensifies the feelings of helplessness, resulting in even greater despair. Before the helplessness and despair of trying to cling to God drive the person to such extremes as suicide or insanity, however, he gives up in exhaustion. Just as the infant finally gives up crying and apathetically falls asleep —in order to "prevent a serious complicating effect" from feelings of powerlessness (Sullivan, 1953, p. 70)—so too the adult, exhausted and drained of energy, gives up and lets go of the last remnant of the futile ego to experience God.

> After the suffering . . . his brain was exhausted, and at last he became calm, and sitting down he came to himself: and turning to God, and abandoning himself to His will, he said, "If it cannot be otherwise, fiat volutas tuo." (Underhill, referring to the mystic Suso's struggle in the dark night, 1911, p. 398)

The mystic becomes exhausted with his efforts and abandons any expectation of having his needs met. He gives up completely, renouncing all hope—even hope in God.

I said to my soul, be still, and wait without hope
For hope would be hope for the wrong thing; wait without love
For love would be love of the wrong thing; there is yet faith
But the faith and the love and the hope are all in the waiting.
Wait without thought, for you are not yet ready for thought:
So the darkness shall be the light, and the stillness the dancing.
(Eliot, 1943, p. 28)

In this passive state, the mystic does nothing but wait. The passivity might be a defense against aggression, as described, but in it, in the patient waiting, Kris found the roots of inspiration (1952, p. 317) and James the illumination that "often comes about not by doing, but by simply relaxing and throwing the burden down" (1961, p. 389).[8]

Waiting in the dark night is the waiting period of creativity after a person realizes the futility of struggling to solve a problem through analytical means.[9]

> To permit oneself to be determined by the intrinsic nature of the matter-in-hand here and now necessarily implies relaxing, waiting, receiving. The common effort to master, to dominate, and to control are antithetical to a true coming-to-terms with the material (or the problem, or the person, etc.). (Maslow, 1967, p. 52)

When one has struggled to solve a problem and given up in exhaustion, passivity is the resulting state of "sleeping on it." Then the inspiration to solve it comes effortlessly. Having let the problem sink into the "back of his mind" (into unconscious primary process), he stops planning, and by surrendering plans is liberated from the defensive self and becomes receptive to what is inspirational within.

> The thinker who relies on insight, having employed every known technical or dialectical device to the sciences or art involved and being yet fundamentally baffled, is forced in sheer desperation and defense of emotional balance to relax his effort for a time. The problem meanwhile is not altogether forgotten, but seems to sink back upon more profound levels of mind for gestation. (Hutchinson, 1949, p. 36)

These more profound levels of mind take over from one's consciousness the task of solving the problem. They attempt to solve it intuitively or to grasp its meaning directly. This inner approach to problem solving arises out of the incubation stage of creativity. The Oxford dictionary describes incubation as the "practise of sleeping in a temple or sacred place for oracular purposes." It is the "fallow period" that occurs after one gives up the struggle to solve a problem (Rhodes, 1961, p. 308).

The dark-night surrender of ego activity plunges the person into the passivity wherein unconscious processes that were dormant beneath consciousness are stirred up. We find an instance of it in Baudelaire:

> Pour us your poison that it may renew
> Our strength. Fire burns our brains. Now let us leap—
> Heaven or hell, what matter—into the deep,
> At the bottom of the Unknown to find the new.

The purgation of the ego and its resistance to inner unconscious processes allows one to disengage attention focused on so-called higher secondary functions, and to refocus attention directly into the repressed unconscious. He becomes open to and feels stirring within him—"sleeping in the temple or sacred place"—previously repressed feelings of communion and openness.

The Greek myth of Eros and Psyche reveals this experience. The libidinal bond of Eros and Psyche's love is destroyed when Psyche, having been warned not to look directly at Eros, does so and loses him. Psyche's need to look at Eros represents the interference of the ego, and especially its doubts or fears. The resulting dark-night despair of losing unity is rectified when Psyche learns to resolve certain tasks with the help of ants and eagles. That is, these creatures represent her unconscious, while being aided by them represents her becoming open to what her unconscious can teach her, open to seeing life from the illuminative light of her unconscious, which could only happen in the darkness of having surrendered the light of ego control and reason. "In this dark time/the eyes begin to see" (Roethke, 1966, p. 239).

The dark-night surrender of self allows unconscious processes, represented by God's infused grace, to come to power.[10] "In this state of contemplation which the soul enters when it forsakes meditation for the state of the proficient, it is God who is now working in the soul," says John of the Cross. The person becomes comfortable with and learns to trust this inner illuminated realm; he does not try, as he did before, to dominate it, to turn its craziness into logic or its chaos into control. He experiences what Keats called "negative capability": the capacity to risk "being in uncertainties, mysteries, and doubts without any irritable reaching after fact and reason" (quoted in Bion, 1973, p. 115). And he does not try to "help" the experience, as an artist does not try to force the inspiration or a gardener interfere with the opening buds of a rose, for helping will once again be the intrusion of ego.[11]

> When the new center of personal energy has been subconsciously incubated so long as to be just ready to open into a flower, "hands off" is the only word for us, it must burst forth unaided. (James, 1961, p. 172)

The replacement of rational self with vibrant unconscious processes marks the return to the true self. With the demise of the false self in the purifying fire of the dark night, the true self for which the person has unconsciously been longing or waiting is illuminated.[12] The inspiration that irrupts from the divine incubation manifests the return of pure instinct, need, openness, imagination, connection, and other aspects of the true self that existed prior to the defensive development of the false self.

> The infant is able to do the equivalence of what in adulthood would be called relaxing. The infant is able to become unintegrated, to flounder, to be in a state in which there is no orientation, to be able to exist for a time without being a reactor to an external impingement or an active person with a direction of intention or movement. . . . In the course of time there arises a sensation or an impulse. In this setting the sensation or impulse will feel real and be truly a personal experience. (Winnicott, 1958, p. 418)

RELIGIOUS EXPERIENCE AND "BASIC TRUST"

If, as this work has presented, religious experience is a stepping back from the world's alienating effects and a sinking into (and incubation of) unconscious processes, then, if the experience is to be in the service of growth, it must induce the internal change that makes one better prepared to step creatively forward out of the regressed state. A person who leaves the regressed state only because the danger that sent him there has subsided—as when the rabid dog has departed and he can come down from the safety of the tree—steps forward after stepping backward without any internal transformation. When that is the case, religious experience is a successful adaptation to danger but does not confront the inner fears and unresolved conflicts that unconsciously motivated the experience. Freud added a caveat to his idea that a person can adaptively flee external dangers:

> But one cannot flee from oneself; flight is no help against internal dangers. And for that reason the defense mechanisms of the ego are condemned to falsify one's internal perception and to give only an imperfect and distorted picture of one's id. (1920a, p. 237)

Unitive experience does falsify internal perceptions (hallucinations) and does distort one's id (magical gratification of drives when distinctions between inner and outer disappear). The self from which a person cannot literally run can, psychologically, disappear in the regressive submersion into this unitive state. But what happens to the self that dissolves in this regressed state? What happens when the self is divested of its autonomy and anxiety and blissfully merges into the symbiotic relationship with Mother/God? Does the person remain passively fixated within an inner world of unconscious processes, forever content with cathartically released instincts and fantasized falsification of perception? Frequently that is the case. But sometimes the regressively restored symbiotic unity—resurrected in therapy, art, and communion with God or Nirvana—can be the foundation from which new and healthy psychological growth takes place.

> Throughout life a person may temporarily suspend the distinction between self and others and thus momentarily experience a state of mind similar to the early unity with mother. . . . To merge in order to remerge may be part of the fundamental pro-

cess of psychological growth on all developmental levels. Such operations may result in nothing more remarkable than normally creative adaptations to circumstance. At the least it affords what William James called "return from the solitude of individuation," refreshed to meet the moment. At the most, it may result in transcending the limitations of earlier stages . . . to simplify, unify anew and recreate an expanded reality. (Rose, 1972, p. 185)

Unitive experience restores the symbiotic state in which a perfectly loving mother makes the infant feel secure enough and nurtured enough to develop what Erikson (1963) called "basic trust." Basic trust is the pervasive sense of well-being the consistently loving mother instills in the infant. It becomes the critical factor in the epigenetic unfolding of the life cycle as perceived by Erikson. Each stage of development has particular tasks that must be mastered in order to gain the security to confront the next stage and its attendant tasks. Basic trust is the earliest and most formative stage. It produces the feelings of acceptance and security that make gradual separation from the mother possible.

> Even under the most favorable circumstance, this stage seems to introduce into psychic life (and become prototypical for) a sense of inner division and universal nostalgia for a paradise forfeited. It is against this powerful combination of a sense of having been deprived, of having been divided, and of having been abandoned, that basic trust must maintain itself throughout life. (Erikson, 1963, p. 250)

Basic trust makes possible the infant's task of forging a separate identity. Basic trust is lost, however, in the pressure to deny communion feelings identified with the mother and to forge ahead in the individuation process. The basic task of religious experience, therefore, is to "reaffirm the first relationship" in order to overcome the "mistrustful remembrance" since having lost it (Erikson, 1958, p. 119). With purgation of the autonomy and aggression that developed to defend against this inner feeling of mistrust (and against the inner longing to return to maternal unity) comes a reactivation of basic trust in the mother and in the communion feelings once identified with that relationship. Surrendering a separate self and splitting off aggression "reactivate past internal object relations as a source of internal support in times of crisis, loss of external support, or of loneliness" (Kernberg, 1970 p. 270).[13]

The experience of Nirvana or communion with God represents the return of "internal objects" that make the person feel what it was like in infancy to be accepted and loved for who one is and not for what one does or accomplishes. The person feels affirmed, as he did when his parents loved him for no other reason than that he existed, and feels content without having to prove his worth through possessions or power. For the first time since childhood, he does not feel the need to be independent and constantly in control in order to subdue the abandonment anxiety first experienced in the loss of symbiotic paradise. Instead, he is able to reclaim basic trust in the openness, libidinal bonding, and other expressions of communion that once were the foundation of his self and now can be so again.

> Religion, it seems, is the oldest and has been the most lasting institution to serve the ritual restoration of a sense of trust in the form of faith while offering a tangible formula for a sense of evil against which it promises to arm and defend man. (Erikson, 1968, p. 106)

An incisive example of how religious experience revives basic trust in communion feelings was presented by Erikson in his study of Martin Luther (1958). Luther, like the monk Thomas Merton, "died" to the world and immersed himself in a monastic environment. The monastery was a womblike existence that served as a moratorium on the expectations of the world. Luther, again like Merton, was a man of vast intelligence and resolve. Erikson suggested that this strength came from the early relationship with his father. He developed a strong personal identity—even a rigid, anally retentive identity—in response to the pressure of his father (and of society) to disidentify himself from his mother and to become independent and in control. As a result, he became assertive but failed to integrate the early basic trust he experienced in feelings of openness and communion with his mother. He was logical and competitive but could not express feelings of spontaneity and receptivity. " 'I did not know the Christ child any more,' (*non novi puellum*) Luther said later, in characterizing the sadness of his youth: he had lost his childhood" (Erikson, 1958).

Luther developed in the monastery a deeply trusting relationship with a mentor. In that secure environment and relationship he felt comfortable surrendering the rigid control and detachment that defined his identity. Jung described such an experience in therapy: "It almost seems as though these patients had only been waiting to find a trustworthy person in order to give up and collapse" (1970, p. 110). Through the trustworthy relationship with his mentor Luther was able, first, to abandon his defensive ego and "morbid conscience" (Erikson, 1958, p. 119). Second, he was able to open himself to a God whose love and acceptance represented the reactivation of the communion feelings he sacrificed in becoming overidentified with defensive autonomy and control. He discovered "the relevance of mother and child in addition to father and son" (ibid., p. 119). Third, in the restored basic trust of that experience Luther was able to confront the defensive overidentification with the agentic qualities of his father so as to repair the loss of basic trust in communion feelings.

> I have implied that the original faith which Luther tried to restore goes back to the basic trust of early infancy inspired by Luther's mother and then threatened by Luther's father. (Erikson, 1958, p. 265)

NEW BEGINNING

The experience of Nirvana or communion with God represents recovery of the original unitive state and so has been referred to as being "born again," reexperiencing "original mind," reclaiming paradise, or being absorbed into the "Great Mother" (Neumann, 1954). By whatever name, the experience restores a basic trust that is "the only firm foundation for renewed progress" (Erikson, 1959, p. 133).

The recovery of basic trust allows for renewed progression *if* its recovery is not "merely to be a repetition of early experiences" (Erikson, 1983, p. 427). That is, recovery of basic trust must not

simply be a momentary enjoyment of communion feelings and primitive processes, only to leave them behind—as once Adam and Eve
left behind Eden and the infant repressed communion feelings. Nor
does it involve a person's clinging to them, as if Adam and Eve would
not assert themselves (for fear of losing paradise) or when an infant
remains autistically attached to symbiosis.[14] Rather, recovery of basic
trust is a renewed progression because it provides the firm foundation on which a person can repair the original developmental failure
and reconvene psychological formation from the fixated place at
which a more integrated identity was derailed.[15] The person might
have "become a child again, and is reborn, so to speak" as Menninger
said of people who regress in therapy, but "then he grows up again,
grows up better than he did before" (1958, p. 49).

Growing up better than the original experience requires coura-
geous acknowledgement of the conflicts and fears that first caused
the defensive development of the false self. This acknowledgement
can take place in the experience of an all-loving God who lets the
person once again feel what it was like to possess unequivocal trust.
A deity whose trustworthiness does not waiver restores the image of
a mother who could always be trusted. Such a mother provided what
Winnicott (1965) called a "holding environment." She is so loving
and protective that even when frustrations and conflicts arise, as they
inevitably do, the child continues to trust in her love and protection.
Pain does not mean the mother's absence nor does anger threaten to
destroy her benign image (as previously feared). The maternal holding environment thereby provides a continued reassurance in the
midst of conflicts, a reassurance that critically allows the child to be
able to tolerate—and therefore to experience—previously denied
feelings or fears ("optimal frustration," Winnicott, 1971, p. 238).

The basic trust restored in the experience of God makes the
person feel, as in the holding environment of infancy, that when
frustrations and unanticipated problems arise he can express the anxiety or previously forbidden feelings, and God will not vanish. The
holding environment of the all-good God frees the person to acknowledge what previously he escaped by means of the dark-night
moratorium placed on them. He feels secure enough in a God who
does not depart when he becomes frustrated or angry—and who
instead continues to "hold" him protectively—that he can express

these painful feelings. Even though he feels a certain amount of anxiety, the anxiety does not make him feel that he is being punished for or deserted because of these feelings (optimal frustration). Winnicott stated that splitting off pernicious impulses was a defense that froze the failed developmental situation, but that its freezing was meant to be only temporary:

> Along with this goes an unconscious assumption (which can become a conscious one) that opportunities will occur at a later date for a renewed experience in which the failure situation will be able to be unfrozen and re-experienced, with the individual in a regressed state, in an environment that is making adequate adaptation possible. (1955, p. 18)

The experience of a God who does not love the person any less for possessing once-forbidden feelings diminishes the unconscious pressure to maintain their repression. But this regressed unitive state enables the person to confront the revived conflicts and needs that first led to the repression of communion feelings (and that unconsciously motivated religious experience). A similar process that sheds light on how the unitive experience recreates a holding environment in which a person confronts and repairs developmental failures is the transference relationship in therapy.

THE SAFE ENVIRONMENT OF RELIGIOUS EXPERIENCE AND TRANSFERENCE

Freud (1955a) labeled "transference" the phenomenon he encountered in patients who made unconscious connections between him and their parents. They perceived in him the fantasized parental objects of their childhood wishes, and related to him like the son or daughter they unconsciously remember being, or wished to be.[16]

Transference begins in a therapeutic relationship that establishes the safe environment—the authority and benevolence of the therapist, for example, and the regular and dependable hours—whereby a person begins to feel sufficiently secure to relax normative ego control. (Winnicott even called it the "holding environment" of analysis—1965, p. 248). Through the relationship forged with the therapist, along with techniques such as free association, the individual overcomes the defenses that resist dismantlement. In the process he redirects the energy or attention invested in normative ego functions into inner psychological processes such as recovering unconscious conflicts and forming the transference relationship that facilitates recovery. "The libido (whether wholly or in part) has entered on a regressive course and has revived the subject's infantile imagos" (Freud, 1912, p. 182).

Transference facilitates the revival of these infantile imagoes. The diminishment of ego control ruptures the clear boundaries that once existed between the person and therapist, and subsequently restores—in the form of unconscious libidinal attachment and trust in the therapist—the earlier maternal imagoes or what Heinz Kohut called the "self-object" (1984, p. 149).[17] Before this early symbiotic-like relationship can be reactivated, however, the therapist must guide the person through his resistance to it. For in the process of surrendering ego control and returning to early infantile imagoes, the person also recreates in the relationship with the therapist early unconscious fears, such as abandonment anxiety and unresolved traumas (negative transference). Through interpretation of the resistance, and an increasing trust in the therapist, the person finally surrenders resistance and repeats in the therapeutic relationship the libidinal attachment, fantasies, and bonding originally experienced in the early relationship with the mother (positive transference).

Transference of the archaic self-object onto the therapist makes transference the replacement of one neurotic symptom—that for which the person comes to therapy seeking relief—with another: the unconscious attachment to and expression of childhood feelings toward the therapist (transference neurosis). By ridding the person of the neurotic symptoms that motivated him to attend therapy, the transference neurosis eventually makes the person feel secure enough to express toward the therapist the earlier repressed impulses or unresolved conflicts that press unconsciously for expression toward significant figures from the past. In this way the transference relationship becomes a "therapeutically mobilized regression": it creates "the relative security" or "therapeutic symbiosis" that allows the person to feel safe enough to express the unfulfilled needs and hidden conflicts that were repressed when infancy was left behind[18] (Kohut, 1984, pp. 114, 115; Searles, 1979, p. 172).

Transference forms a symbiotic therapeutic relationship in order to expand the person's psychological boundaries to include direct access to repressed feelings and hidden needs. Because the patient experiences in the transference relationship that the therapist—representing the "good mother" in infancy—will not judge, condemn, and especially not abandon him for expressing the secret feelings or unresolved conflicts he previously resisted, he is able to acknowledge them.

Heinz Kohut suggested that the transference elicitation of self-object can take place in areas outside of therapy.

> When the adult experiences the self-sustaining effect of a maturely chosen self-object, the self-object experiences of all the preceding stages of his life reverberate unconsciously. When we feel uplifted by our admiration for a great cultural ideal, for example, the old uplifting experience of being picked up by our strong and admired mother and having been allowed to merge with her greatness, calmness and security may be said to form the unconscious undertones of the joy we are experiencing as adults. (1984, p. 49)

The unitive experience of God can be one expression of these transference relationships that merge the person back into the secure maternal symbiosis. As discussed throughout this book, purgative stages of religious experience commence with the various disciplines that, although more ascetical than the subtle sensory deprivation of a therapist's couch or ego-relaxing free association, aim to rid the ego of its defensive resistance to unconscious processes. Erikson even referred to the therapist on the other side of the couch as possessing the "asceticism of the expendable face" (1958, p. 151). Freud himself acknowledged the similarities:

> Certain practises of the mystics may succeed in unsettling the normal relations between the different regions of the mind, so that, for example, the perceptual systems become able to grasp relations in the deeper layer of the ego and in the id which would

otherwise be inaccessible to it . . . we must admit that the therapeutic efforts of psychoanalyses have chosen much the same
method of approach. (1955b, p. 11)

The purgative stage of religious experience creates the secure
environment—via the spiritual authority of God or a revered tradition—that, as in the safe environment of dependable hours and the
venerable authority of the therapist, makes the person feel trusting
enough in God to surrender control. Having relinquished resistance
to God, the person merges into a nondual relationship that elicits
unconscious feelings of libidinal attachment toward the mother.
These feelings of communion continue until the dark night in which,
having stripped himself of control, he experiences an underlying
dread of being out of control, or abandoned, and clings desperately to
God with the last remnants of control (negative transference).

God, or a spiritual teacher, like the therapist, guides the person
through this trenchant resistance to surrendering himself to the experience. He thereby is able to recognize the defensive nature of self
and to surrender final fragments of resistance while merging into a
libidinally secure unity with God (positive transference).

The surrender of self and submersion into God forges a transference symbiotic unity. "The mystic's merger with God, like that of
the trusting merger with the therapist, takes place in the restoration
of the self-object" (Kohut, 1971, p. 37). A divinized self-object replaces neurotic symptoms (fear of individuality or of sex, for example) with neurotic transference of childhood feelings toward God
(expressed in selfless unity and pregential celibate sexuality, respectively). The transference relationship with God[19] becomes a type of
"therapeutic symbiosis" that expands psychological boundaries so as
to make the person feel secure enough in the libidinally bonded relationship, first, to begin to acknowledge previously repressed conflicts and impulses; second, to feel he is not judged or abandoned for
acknowledging them; and third, to confront the anxieties and fears
he had been fleeing.

THE SAFE ENVIRONMENT OF THE ARTIST

Therapeutic transference takes place in part because of the therapist's neutrality. The therapist keeps his personality out of the rela-

tionship, offering instead a type of blank screen onto which the person projects infantile imagoes and through which he feels safe expressing repressed impulses or conflicts. God provides a similar blank screen onto which a person projects the symbiotic maternal imago and through which he feels safe expressing forbidden feelings and forgotten fears. Such a God can be more incisively understood when compared with the painter's canvas, or the sculptor's piece of clay, which are also a type of blank screen shaped according to the unconscious processes the artist expresses on it. Kohut (1985) even called artistry "creative transference."

The artist momentarily dips into a potentially creative unconscious where he, like the person in therapy or in religious experience, discovers not only an untapped realm of positive libidinal feelings but also dark-night types of unresolved conflicts and primitive impulses. "The painter passes through stages of fullness and emptiness. That is the whole secret of art" (Pablo Picasso, quoted in Johnston, 1986, p. 72). Rather than being overwhelmed by disconcerting feelings or being compelled to re-repress them, the artist, first, finds in the previously discussed incubational unconscious a secure place to allow hidden conflicts or needs to be reactivated. It is a type of " 'womb' in which repressed and dedifferentiated images are safely contained, melted down, and reshaped for re-entry into consciousness" (Ehrenzweig, 1967, p. 121). The artist then finds in his artwork—his canvas, acting, music, and so forth—another type of safe environment or "aesthetic illusion" in which to express these processes incubating in his unconscious.

Aesthetic illusion is the sense of unity that exists between the artist and his work. The bond between artist and art turns art into a safe environment for expressing the unconscious feelings that otherwise could not be expressed. Instead of acting directly on hostile impulses or being overwhelmed by repressed traumata that arise in the inspirational dip into the unconscious, the artist is able to "play" with them, to struggle with and work them out. He accomplishes this by bringing them safely to life on a canvas. By displacing repressed feelings or drives onto a canvas where they do not cause destruction, and where they are experienced simultaneously as "out there" and as an extension of himself (aesthetic illusion), the artist is able to lift hidden feelings and impulses safely out of his unconscious. By bringing repressed feelings out of the darkness of the netherworld and onto the "light" of his canvas, the artist is able to test his previously inaccessible unconscious feelings against what is "real"—that is, to find if his inner conflicts and needs can be made acceptable or manageable.[20]

The experience of communion with God can also be an aesthetic illusion. Communion with God becomes a safe extension of self. The restored symbiotic state makes the person feel secure enough to liberate primitive instincts, unresolved conflicts, grandiose fantasies and fears. Without this aesthetic illusion of communion the person feels starkly alone with his fears and forbidden impulses. On his own he seems to be traumatized or at best inadequate to manage them, but when he experiences them as belonging to the experience of communion with God, he no longer feels alone.

Furthermore, previously feared feelings and instincts can be expressed when the all-loving deity with whom one feels united, like the canvas for the artist, neither judges nor is destroyed by them. As explained above, the God of the holding environment remains present and loving regardless of the anger or frustration a person expresses (which was not true of the dark-night experience of anger or frustration). Because the person aims those potentially destructive or bewildering feelings not directly at himself, but at the God with whom communion makes him experience those feelings as not being entirely his own, he can "play" with and express them in the safety of divine aesthetic illusion. In this way he learns more about these repressed feelings and is able to test them—to see in his relationship with God if they are acceptable or manageable—without having to act directly on what could be their overwhelming intensity.

The situation of St. Anthony of the Desert and his vision of naked women is an example of this aesthetic illusion. St. Anthony could not directly acknowledge lascivious instincts because their presence would have been anathema to his saintly quest; hence they were repressed. Like the effect of the canvas in liberating hidden feelings from within the artist, however, St. Anthony's hallucination allowed him to express the lustful feelings he thought he had vanquished. He was able to express them on the blank screen of his vision, where, because they were experienced as "out there," he did not have to experience them entirely as his own. This vision of naked women became the canvas on which he could struggle with instincts without having to act on them directly. The struggle thereby allowed St. Anthony to examine his sexuality and potentially to work through what he learned rather than to repress and to be forever plagued by unconscious sexual longings. As Underhill said, the mystic's visions can be "sources of helpful energy and courage" (1911, p. 321).

ACKNOWLEDGEMENT OF REPRESSED FEELINGS AND WITHDRAWAL OF THEIR PROJECTIONS

The safe environment of communion with God can make people secure enough to reexperience some of the fears and unacceptable feelings they had projected onto the world and which they thought were left behind with their rejection of that world. "Each person has something specific to accept . . . let us just say that the thing we have to accept is whatever we want to escape" (Jung, 1976, p. 321). Upon feeling safe enough to acknowledge the "thing" they tried to escape—the fears, hidden conflicts, or forbidden feelings—people can no longer blame the chaos and sexual allure of the world for them. *Maybe* the world is so seductive that they would succumb to its pleasures if they did not reject it; so possessive they would not be able to resist its fraudulent values and hence must withdraw from it; so hostile they have no choice but to dominate or else to become passive; so materialistic they would become greedy if they did not take a vow of poverty. Maybe this and more is true, but it is also true that while the world deserves criticism for its overemphasis on sexuality and materialism, much of the sex and greed that is criticized is the sex and greed that has been repressed and projected onto the world. And when these feelings are experienced in the world, they are experienced as evil because they elicit people's own deep insecurities and fears about dealing with them.

What is evil and what makes people feel sinful is not sex and aggression but their fear and repression of sexual and aggressive impulses, and the resulting unconscious clinging to—and subsequent conscious repulsion toward—the sex and aggression projected onto the world. A Zen saying states: "Before I was enlightened I saw trees as trees and mountains as mountains. Once on the path to enlightenment, I saw beyond trees and beyond mountains. Now that I am enlightened, I see trees as trees and mountains as mountains". The enlightened person does not see the world for the superficial qualities projected onto it, nor see beyond it to an all-good euphoria that real trees and mountains do not provide. Instead he withdraws fears and idealized wishes from the world onto which he had projected them and sees the world with a clarity that previously was clouded by those repressed inner needs.[21] His religious experience might have begun with the renunciation of the world as evil but when in the holding environment of that experience he feels secure enough to acknowledge the hidden needs he projected onto the world, he realizes that he, and not the world, is the source of the feelings that made him feel alienated or sinful. Hence Thomas Merton wrote about walking in the city of Louisville and realizing that the people and the world he had spurned were not different from himself: "It was like waking from a dream of separateness, of spurious self-isolation in a special world, the world of renunciation and supposed holiness" (1968, p. 156).[22] The withdrawal of feelings projected onto the world thereby allows people like Merton to become better acquainted with the inner feelings they once denied and with a world that no longer bears the burden of those feelings.

> We have no reason to mistrust our world, for it is not against us. Has its terrors, they are our terrors; has its abysses, these abysses belong to us; are dangers at hand, we must try to love them. (May, 1969, p. 69)

CONFRONTING "BASIC FAULT"

To be a healthy regression in service of the ego, the experience of the safe environment of a monastery or a unitive state must not only recover a person's underlying conflicts but lead to their confrontation and resolution.

The recovery of hidden fears and forbidden impulses through religious experience does not mean that a person secure enough to express these feelings is mature enough to manage them. A person's recovery of repressed instincts might be no more than cathartic, without effecting any real psychological change. The reactivated conflicts and fears might make a person feel guilty about having "given in" to sinful desires, and even overwhelmed by—or less dramatically obsessed with—the feelings he anxiously experiences as his own.

> As he abandons all prejudice, he forfeits the mechanism of projection: his danger becomes introspection and "introjection," an over-concern with the evil in himself. One may say that he becomes prejudiced against himself. Some measure of this must be tolerated by men of good will. Men of good will must learn to fear accurately and to cope judiciously with the anxiety aroused by a renunciation of prejudice. (Erikson, 1963, p. 417)

Men and women of good will not only withdraw projections and thereby learn more about themselves in religious experience. Self-awareness is valuable but if it does not lead to the confidence to manage the inner processes that have been resurrected, then the experience is no better than a therapeutic encounter that provides insights into the conflicts it helps uncover without helping confront them. Transference is not therapeutic simply because it regressively induces enough security to recover and gain insight into hidden conflicts. Their restoration is a step in therapy but it is not therapeutic until the person learns in the transference relationship to confront them.[23]

The unconscious libidinal attachment forged in the transference relationship creates the security not only to acknowledge hidden conflicts but to reexperience and work through them. The latter, however, is a difficult task. Confronting and resolving unconscious forces is met with greater resistance than surrendering oneself to the therapeutic transference that induced them. But that is the task of therapy, made possible through the transference relationship.

A similar transference relationship in religious experience eventually makes a person secure enough to confront—rather than to remain permanently dependent on the spiritual guide/God to resolve for her—the conflicts and needs restored in that relationship. These various and unresolved conflicts originally caused a rift in the psychological structure of the self, a sense of impairment or defectiveness described by the psychoanalyst Balint (1979) as "basic fault." Developmental deficiencies are not healed; rather, a type of scar forms over them. For some this scar is the seemingly irreversible result of maternal deprivation or narcissistic injury. For most, the scar or basic fault forms through an overemphasis on autonomy and control, an overemphasis through which people learn to hide—not heal—the inner conflicts of leaving behind communion feelings in the formation of a separate identity. A superficial strength and a false sense of self build over the scar but the scar remains, and is susceptible to resurfacing under certain circumstances—such as when anxiety over an experience of separation or feelings of inadequacy make it visible.

> An old, partially unresolved sense of self identity and of body boundaries, or old conflicts over separation and separateness, can be reactivated (or can remain peripherally or even centrally active) at any and all stages of life. (Mahler, 1975, p. 3)

Religious experience restores the communion structures that existed prior to the anxious development of a separate self and hence prior to the fears, conflicts, and basic fault that formed out of the infant's earliest unitive state. Reactivation of this preconflictual unity instills the symbiotic security from which a person learns to confront previously hidden aspects of his basic fault. The archaic sense of wholeness that Martin Luther experienced in the transference relationship with his spiritual mentor not only awakened basic trust but led subsequently to his feeling secure enough to confront the early basic fault created through overidentification with his father and the loss of trust in the true self. He, like others, was able in the safe environment of a relationship with God or a spiritual teacher to reexperience the original trauma, to go through once again the grief of losing basic trust in communion feelings, and finally to heal the psychological scars that had been covered over by the defensive false self. Nietzsche wrote in *Ecce Homo,* "I am, to express it in the form of a riddle, already dead as my father, while as my mother I am still living and living old."

Another kind of religious experience that regressively restores unconscious processes in order to resolve them is the ritual trance state, one example being that of the Sioux Indians as studied by Erikson (1968). The trance state can regressively restore early psychological wounds or forbidden impulses so that one can reexperience them and end the developmental arrest caused by them. The ritualistically induced Sioux trance state creates an altered state of consciousness that restores maternal unity and provides the opportunity to reexperience the early aggressive feelings one learned to associate negatively with the loss of that unity (as when the infant bites the mother's breast during suckling and hence associates aggression with withdrawal of the mother's nurturance). The ritual induces a trance state that prepares the young brave for admission to adult expressions of aggression by subjecting him to the painful deprivation and bodily mortification that "manfully atones for the sin which cost him the paradise of habitual closeness to the mother's breast" (Erikson, 1968, p. 19).[24]

The Sioux trance state is a defensive response to the extreme pain of the ritual. Its altered state of consciousness is the biological effect of the brain's shutting down its receptivity to corporal pain, as well as a regressive return to primitive psychological states in which no pain exists. The regressive return engendered by this trance allows the young brave, by means of the ecstatic safe environment of the trance, to reexperience primitive conflicts that bound him to the defensive image of aggression and that required emancipation if he were to express aggression in an adult manner. Hence the trance state, which traditionally has been described by psychologists as proof of mental imbalance, can be the reparative regression described by some anthropologists as a return to the unconscious in order to bring out of it solutions to personal (or tribal) problems (Kraus, 1972, p. 27).

Another example of a reparative altered state is Jesus' experience in the desert. A special relationship formed between Jesus and God when, after having been baptized as God's specially anointed, he withdrew to the desert where he communed with God. This was not an escapist experience, however. Jesus learned to confront in that withdrawn state the inner feelings of grandiosity and omnipotence that the divine baptism must have elicited (as represented in the devil's seductive offer of power and glory, and in Jesus' working through it by overcoming temptation [Lk 4:1–14]).

A less dramatic example of redemptive reparation is prayer. An everyday example of how prayer can elicit unconscious processes that lead to confrontation of unresolved tasks is the often recited

Psalm 23: "Though I walk through the valley of death I fear no evil, for You are with me." The valley of death represents a person's fear of mortality, or of any dreadful situation that elicits underlying feelings of abandonment or separation anxiety. While most people possess some trepidation about death, the person who can turn to a God who "walks" with him through the valley of death has less reason to be afraid. His belief that the divine walks through death with him can even completely overcome fear: "Death where is your sting?"

The regressive nature of Psalm 23 is evident. It is an ego-regressive refusal to deal maturely with death, an instinctual regression to being led about passively by an omnipotent figure, and a symbiotic regression in which the person and God walk as one through an anxiety-free world. Yet after having walked safely with God the person might discover—through the transference relationship with God—that the fears he had toward death, toward abandonment or separation, were not as terrifying as he had imagined. He might unconsciously have replaced a neurotic fear of death with a neurotic attachment to God, but the sense of God walking beside him can help him remember walking with parents who made him feel safe enough to walk on his own. His belief that his parents would catch him if he fell reinforced his basic trust in them. It gave the child what Bowlby (1973) called the "secure base" from which to feel supported in confronting his fears and taking the risk of walking. "Only if someone has her arms around the infant at this time [separation] can the I AM moment be endured, or rather, perhaps risked" (Winnicott, 1965, p. 148).

The experience of a God who walks through the valley of a person's fears has the potential to make the person feel safe enough to confront the trepidation that originally made him fear walking on his own and so seek refuge in God. Just as walking alongside protective parents allows the child to learn to walk and let go of fear, so the adult's experience of a secure base of walking with God allows him to ask himself "Why was I afraid?" He is able to answer, in the safe environment of the valley in which a deity walks with him, that he feared being abandoned, or being hurt or left alone. These fears could not be expressed earlier, for their expression would dispel the illusion of a tranquil and anxiety-free relationship with God, but in the safe environment of walking with God he knows God will continue walking with him even if he has doubts or conflicts from having been hurt in the past. In the regressive walking with God he becomes secure enough to confront the unresolved conflicts that inhibited progress earlier.[25]

> Far from establishing one in unassailable narcissistic security, the way of prayer brings us face to face with the shame and indignity of the false self that seeks to live for itself alone and to enjoy the "consolation of prayer" for its own sake. (Merton, 1969, p. 24)

The transference relationship that forms in religious experience—whether within prayerful supplication or the monastic experience of people like Luther and Merton—can regressively recover unconscious structures, not in order to stay in them but to gain the security to repair the underlying basic fault that drove the person to God for refuge. A religious experience of this type is a regression in service of the ego—a detour toward maturation of self via a temporary retreat from reality and a return to early unconscious structures, offering an opportunity to repair what was not resolved and a chance to redirect personal identity away from the early fixated past and transform it by bringing it back more meaningfully to the present. This is not escapist regression but a "withdrawal from the external world and return to it with improved mastery" (Hartmann, 1945, p. 57).

9

Elaboration of Religious Experience

INTRODUCTION

Religious experience is not a regression in the service of the ego simply because it illuminates what previously was in the dark. Recovery of unconscious processes can lead as easily to escaping fears as to repairing the basic fault that resulted from those fears. A final stage of religious experience distinguishes a restoration of unconscious processes that is in the service of the ego from one that is a psychological defense. This final stage is characterized by the "emergence" out of the regressed unitive state, and by what the person then does with what was experienced. And what she does, or fails to do, will be the lens through which what transpired in the regressed state will be seen as pathological or progressive.

> We all relive earlier and earliest stages of our existence in dreams, in artistic experience, and in religious experience, only to emerge refreshed and invigorated. (Erikson, 1964, p. 69)

REGRESSION AND ELABORATION IN CREATIVITY

An invigorating emergence out of the regressed unitive state is distinguished, in art, by its being transitory and creatively expressed. Regression in service of the ego is temporary (Kris, 1952, p. 253). It is of limited duration. Its "dip" into repressed primary process thinking is what inspires the artist, but she does not remain permanently attached to the inspiration. It is only one stage in the creative process.

An artistic submersion into unconscious processes is a retreat from the distractions or stereotypical perceptions of the world, a retreat that if creative will let the artist return—armed with the new perceptions and insights of the inspirational experience—fuller and richer than she was before. "Man can find no better retreat from the world than art, and man can find no stronger link with the world than art" (Goethe, quoted in Stierlin, 1976, p. 56). Kris labeled the experience of emerging out of the unconscious and "giving color" to that which it inspired "creative elaboration" (1952, p. 60).

Elaboration is the final stage of creativity. It is the act of expressing, of communicating to others and giving shape to that which inspired the artist.[1] The intense feelings and archaic images that arise from the artist's dip into the unconscious are inspirational but are not in themselves creative. They are an assortment of repressed instincts and unbounded sensations. Art is not the reactivation of this inner unconscious nor its derivative flash of insight; art is "the experience of expressing one's emotions" (Collingwood, 1938, p. 275). Michelangelo's vision of a face in a particular piece of marble was inspirational; what he did with the marble to draw the vision out of it was creative. As exciting and dramatic as recovering the inspirational unconscious might be, it is only a stage in the creative process and does not become a creative experience until the artist paints it or the poet puts it into words.

> When the artist has something to report from the nether world. . . . When he has received from the depths a creative conception, or at least feels a stirring of a creative impulse. . . . Then he must reverse his orientation and, so to speak, return to earth. There, using tools and material, he must seek to embody his conception in objective form. He must show us what he has found in the world below and above natural consciousness. (Abell, 1957, p. 331)

EMERGENCE OUT OF UNITIVE EXPERIENCE

The elaboration stage is as critical in turning religious experience into a healthy regression as it is in leading artistic regression out of its inspirational state. Jesus, Buddha, Moses, and in more recent times mystics such as Merton, at one point in their lives departed the world and its apparently alienating effects and retreated to a secluded environment. Although "dying to themselves" and experiencing

God represented a regressive recovery of symbiotic communion feelings, this was not pathological because, like creativity, the experience was characterized first by its transitory nature.

William James's suggestion that one of the four salient qualities of mystical experience was its transitory nature (1961, p. 375) predated Kris's psychological inquiry into the temporary state of regression in creativity. More recently, Maslow expressed the same idea when he described peak experience as "transitory self-actualization": "If this is going into another world, then there is always a coming back to the ordinary world" (1971, pp. 48, 159).

For example, as tempting as it was, Jesus did not succumb to the wish to cling to the magical omnipotence encountered in the desert (represented in the devil's seductive offers of power and glory—Lk 4:1–14). Buddha did not remain permanently pacified beneath the boddhi tree, though he too was tempted (again represented by the devil, or mara, who suggested that he should stay beneath the boddhi tree because it would be a waste of time to teach his experience to those who would not understand it). So too Moses did not stay transfixed in the burning intensity of his mountaintop encounter with God, Merton did not remain ensconced in the silence of his solitude, and others did not become attached to the ecstatic realm of an altered state of consciousness.

As with the artist and her regressive dip into the unconscious, these individuals' abandonment of the world and retreat into primitive psychological structures was temporary. "Grant me a break from myself/but let me come back" says Robert Frost in "Swinging on Birches." Their retreat was a time to rid themselves of self-centered thinking and to wrestle with demons and to wait patiently in the dark night for the experience of God. In the end, Jesus emerged from the desert, Buddha rose from beneath the boddhi tree, Moses came down from the mountain, Merton spoke of his silence, and others returned from the immediate gratification of "living happily ever after" in a paradisiacal altered state of consciousness.

The experience on the mountain or in a monastery might have been illuminative but it was only one stage in the process of experiencing God/Nirvana. Buddha and Jesus did not confuse their experience with the fulfillment of the spiritual practices that guided them toward enlightenment. A common misconception of mystical unity is that it is achieved when a person experiences selfless communion with God. But like the experience of artistic creativity (which has also been misconstrued as the inspirational return to unconscious processes), the heights of unitive experience are not reached as long as the person stays in the desert or in the illuminative altered state of mind.

Just as an artist might equate the intensity of inspiration with creativity, so too a religious individual might associate euphoria, miracles, or "meeting Buddha on the road" with Nirvana or God while failing to do something with that experience to bring it into its fullness. What was meant to be a temporary regression turns into a permanent fixation.

> Since normal experiences of ecstasy do not aim at destruction but are founded on fantasy of libidinal union between the self and object world, they result in a transitory sense of self expansion and the feeling that the self and world are rich. Such experiences of merging, which may briefly retransform the images of the self and the object world into a fantasy unit vested with libidinal forces, permits an immediate re-establishment of the boundaries between them. By contrast, pathological regressive fusions caused by severe aggression may result in an irreparable breakdown of these boundaries and hence of the self and object representation. (Jacobson, 1964, p. 65)

When the emotional high of religious experience subsides or the burning bush expires—as inevitably they do—the person who clings to the regressive aspects of her experience will feel bereft of God. If she does not do something with or elaborate on her experience, she feels close to God only when the bush is burning or when she is enraptured with celestial visions. As Merton said, this might once have brought the person into direct contact with God but now it is "a retreat into the realm of images and analogies which no longer serve for a mature spiritual life" (1969, p. 77). Such a pseudo-enlightening experience represents the inauthenticity or at least the premature closure of the experience, as St. Theresa suggested: "If anyone told me that after reaching this state of union he had enjoyed continued rest and joy, I should say that he had not reached it at all" (quoted in Duerlinger, 1984, p. 68).

The regressive urge to remain permanently attached to symbiotic security is understandable. Emergence from the unitive state—

whether that of the infant's symbiotic relationship with the mother or the adult's communion with God—is not undertaken without stress, and especially not without separation anxiety—the fear that leaving the unitive state will forfeit the love and security therein experienced. The loss of the "all-good symbiotic mother, who at one time was part of the self in a blissful state of well-being," is a depressing prospect (Mahler, 1972, p. 338).[2] The fear of venturing beyond the secure symbiosis and into the unknown, or of being alone and losing the love object, makes staying in the symbiotic relationship seductively enticing.[3]

The devil that tempted Jesus with glory, for example, represented the projection of Jesus' inner struggle with regressive wishes to cling to the magical omnipotence of his desert experience. Buddha's attempt to convince himself of the preferability of staying beneath the boddhi tree rationalized his reluctance to emerge out of the euphoric and into the mundane, or out of the security of the known and into the risks of the unknown. So too Goethe's Faust sold his soul to Mephistopheles and was warned that he could return to the present (presumably having resolved the unconscious conflicts that motivated the regressive pact) only if he did not succumb to the temptation to utter "Linger, thou art fair." Campbell elaborated on this:

> The first problem of the returning hero is to accept as real, after an experience of the soul-satisfying vision of fulfillment, the passing joys and sorrows, banalities and noisy obscenities of life. Why re-enter such a world? Why attempt to make plausible, or even interesting, to men and women consumed with passion, the experience of transcendental bliss? As dreams that were momentous by night may seem simply silly in the light of day, so the poet and the prophet can discover themselves playing the idiot before a jury of sober eyes. The easy thing is to commit the whole community to the devil and retire again into the heavenly rock-dwelling, close the door, and make it fast. (1950, p. 218)

When adults do leave the unitive state and return to the world, or to normative consciousness, the depression they feel over the loss of paradise is reinforced. After Jesus died, for example, his disciples —on the road to Emmaus and in the upper room—became forlorn and bereft of hope. They became depressed, as artists sometimes experience depression after their creative work is completed. Artistic inspiration or divine illumination restored a sense of unity with the lost libidinal object, only to lose it again when the painting is finished or one emerges out of the desert and returns to normal consciousness. Mothers often experience "postpartum blues," a feeling of depression over the loss of biological unity with the fetus, shortly after giving birth. The neonate, the artwork, the unitive experience, is no longer inside one's body or mind, no longer the perfect fantasy of what has been and could have been; instead it becomes part of the real world with its real limitations.

The resistance to emerging out of the unitive state and returning to the real world must be overcome eventually. A person who stays in the cocoon of that experience forfeits further growth and stagnates. What Mahler said of the first encounter of symbiosis is true in the adult's regressive recovery of that experience in the unitive state, and that is that at some point "the primary stage of unity and identity with mother ceases to be constructive for the evolution of an ego and an object world" (1975, p. 10).[4] The experience of communion with God recreates the holding environment or basic trust that instills what Mahler called an "optimal symbiosis": a libidinally bonded unity that, as in infancy, makes the person secure enough to explore separateness without fear of being abandoned, thereby allowing for a "smooth differentiation and expansion beyond the symbiotic order" (1975, p. 17). That is, healthy unitive experience, like healthy maternal unity, stimulates growth and the emergence into reality rather than fixation and the avoidance of reality. The adult who does not emerge out of unity is unattached due not to the unity but to a flawed unity.

Winnicott said, "The basis of the capacity to be alone is the experience of being alone in the presence of someone" (1965, p. 33). The child feels safe being alone—that is, reaching out of symbiotic union and exploring the world beyond its merged psychological boundaries—because her first experience of being alone is with a mother who continues to be present and to love her even as she forms an identity of her own (rather than being made to feel that by becoming separate she loses mother's love and presence). The religious individual emerges out of the symbiotic unitive state because her experience of God makes her feel that she is still loved and supported even as she returns to the world from which she fled. Hence she is able to be alone with her fears, to walk alone through the valley of death, because her first experience of it is being alone in the presence of a God who walks with her. Because that God does not abandon her when she feels secure enough to confront her fears and to walk on her own, she is able to overcome the pressure to remain securely attached to walking with God. For her, at that point, walking on her own two feet—with all the demands and risks it involves—becomes religious experience.[5]

The disciples on the road to Emmaus or in the upper room had a vision of Jesus after his death—a regressively restored precognitive hallucination that defended against the depressive loss of their identification—but instead of clinging to it they found in that experience the courage to help them mourn their loss. They recreated Jesus in their vision and by keeping him alive they prevented their fragmented lives from totally collapsing until they were prepared to get on with their lives.[6]

Aldous Huxley explains it thus:

> To discover the Kingdom of God exclusively within oneself is easier than to discover it, not only there, but also in the outer world of minds and things and living creatures. It is easier because the heights within reveal themselves to those who are ready to exclude from their purview all that lies without. And though this exclusion may be a painful and mortificatory process, the fact remains that it is less arduous than the process of inclusion, by which we come to know the fullness as well as the heights of spiritual life. Where there is exclusive concentration on the heights within, temptations and distractions are avoided and there is a general denial and suppression. But when the hope is to know God inclusively—to realize the divine ground in the world as well as in the soul, temptations and distractions must not be avoided, but submitted to and used as opportunities for advance; there must be no suppression of outward turning activities, but a transformation of them so that they become sacramental. Mortification becomes more searching and more subtle; there is need of unsleeping awareness and, on the levels of thought, feelings and conduct, the constant exercise of something like an artist's tact and taste. (Quoted in Phillips, 1977, p. 375)

Evelyn Underhill suggested that the return from unity to the world is "the rare and final stage in the evolution of the great mystics" (1911, p. 266). More than a mere emergence out of the regressed unitive state, the return to the world is marked by the individual's expression or communication of that which was experienced. As sublime and illuminative as the experience might have been, a time came when people like Jesus and Buddha had to emerge out of *and* express what they experienced. This is the final elaboration stage of creativity as defined by Kris.

The religious individual, like the artist, has withdrawn emotional involvement in the world and invested it in internal pursuits. With the resolution of the conflicts and fears resurrected in the unitive experience, the individual reinvests herself in the world through the expression of what she experienced. Jesus not only left the desert but elaborated on what he experienced in his gospel message. Buddha emerged from beneath the boddhi tree and expressed what he experienced through his *dharma,* and Moses came down from the mountain and expressed the intensity of his experience with the ten commandments. Zen Buddhism's "ten ox pictures" represents the search for Nirvana as beginning with a meditative retreat from the world but ending when, having achieved Nirvana, the person "returns to the marketplace" in order to share that experience.

> The man of deep enlightenment gives out no "smell" of enlightenment, no aura of "saintliness"; if he did his spiritual attainment would be rejected as still deficient. Nor does he hold himself aloof from the evils of the world. He immerses himself in them whenever necessary to emancipate men from their falling, but without being sullied by them himself. (Kapleau, 1967, p. 313)

Joseph Campbell similarly said that the hero, after his adventures and conquests,

> still must return with his life-transmuting trophy. The hero shall now begin the labor of bringing the runes of wisdom, the Golden Fleece, or his sleeping princess back into the kingdom of humanity, where the boon may redound to the renewing of the community, the nation, the planet, or the ten thousand worlds. (1950, p. 193)

RECOVERED PRIMARY PROCESS LEADS TO PSYCHOSIS AS WELL AS TO ILLUMINATION

The task of elaborating religious experience seems simple: What began as a regressive loss of self and a subsequent submersion into symbiotic unity is reversed and leads back to reality when the individual begins to express what she experienced. Something has to take place, however, in the regressed state, that makes a person do something creative with what was experienced. Otherwise, the unconscious processes recovered in that experience not only can seduce the person to stay attached to their regressed realm of paradisiacal pleasures but can overwhelm the person with the fury of the unconscious forces they unleash.

This work has presented the regressive recovery of primary process as a creative function of religious experience, since a person cannot achieve greater psychological fullness until the repressed structures that thwarted growth are awakened. "He gives way to the regressive longing and deliberately exposes himself to the dangers of being devoured by the monster of the maternal abyss" (Jung, 1953b, p. 180). However, a person might find that the maternal abyss is too seductive or voracious and *does* devour her. That is, when the ego that once maintained control over unconscious drives is surrendered or "died to," primary process and the instincts that were frozen in their orally voracious state ascend to consciousness, and they ascend with such unneutralized force that the person experiences them as beyond control. She is flooded with unbearable emotions and overwhelmed by insatiable appetites. A nonexistent or passive ego makes her feel controlled by thoughts instead of in control of them, and dominated by impulses instead of having them under her authority.

Kris, for instance, observed that regression in the creative process makes available unconscious processes that—because they are unneutralized and unrelenting—can result in "the psychotic condition in which the ego is overwhelmed by the primary processes" (1952, p. 60). So too the "wish for reunion with the love object," as Mahler has stated, brings "fear of reengulfment by it" (1975, p. 37). Even Jung, who described a more positive unconscious, acknowledged how a frightening and psychotic state can develop "if the unconscious simply rides roughshod over the conscious mind" (1970, p. 110).[7] That is why Jung, in an apparent contradiction to his openness to numerous approaches to experiencing the unconscious, warned Westerners against utilizing Eastern meditation practices: They "abolish the normative checks imposed by the conscious mind and thus give unlimited scope to the play of the unconscious 'dominants' " (1969, p. 520).

As in the parable of the man who feverishly swept his house clean only to have its emptiness inhabited by demons, the religious individual can "sweep" herself clean of her ego, can become celibate to be free of lust and obedient in order to lose willfulness, only to find that instead of the enlightenment she expected she experiences a frightening resurgence of demonic impulses. The experience is akin to an individual's submersion into unconscious processes that are so bizarre and uncontrollable as to lead to psychosis. Psychosis results when a person surrenders ego control and instead of emerging out of the regressed state becomes lost within it. She is unable to find her way out of the swirling whirlpools of drives and conflicts that she feels powerless to manage; she becomes absorbed in, exceedingly fascinated by, this inner realm, to the point of excluding all else. The result is a forfeiture of everyday functioning, with a gross impairment or severe deterioration in reality testing.

The religious individual, like the psychotic, can become submerged in an unconscious darkness so unregenerative as to offer little hope for return to light. Having died to her ego, she appears to be in danger not only of being overwhelmed by uncontrollable instincts but, again like the psychotic, of not being able to distinguish between self and not-self (communion with God), between stimuli that arise from inside and those from outside (hallucinations), and between thoughts and actions or wishes and deeds (prayers). Further, she might fluctuate between euphoria and depression, irrational thinking and primitive logic, impulsiveness and masochism, or fantasy and reality.[8] Hence the difference between the psychotic and the "mystic turned upside down" is often difficult to discern.

> It is evident that from the point of view of their psychological mechanisms, the classic mysticism and these lower mysticisms (diseased) spring from the same mental level. (James, 1961, p. 417)

The recovery of a seemingly insatiable unconscious, of uncontrolable primitive instincts and magical mentation, does not have to lead to psychosis. While *Three Christs of Ypsalanti* (Rokeach, 1964) clearly portrays men who regressively experienced a psychotic identification with Jesus, people can have religious experiences that restore primitive unconscious processes, even those bordering on madness, without degenerating into psychosis. Plato observed that "there are two types of madness, one resulting from human ailments, the other from a divine disturbance of our own conventions of conduct." There is also a madness by choice, as when "conventions of conduct" (i.e., the false self) create feelings of superficiality and inner emptiness that cause a person to opt for a more creative expression of self. According to Hamlet:

> I am, and by my fancy. If my reason
> Will there to be obedient, I have reason;
> If not, my sense better pleased with madness,
> Do bid it welcome.

More recently, psychiatrists like Jung, Perry, and Laing have proposed that the same regressive experience that leads to madness can lead to growth. "Madness need not be all breakdown. It may also be breakthrough. It is potentially liberation and renewal as well as enslavement and existential death" (Laing, 1967, p. 133). A tenuous link exists between human madness and divine madness, with the regressive excursion into the former being capable of developing into the latter. The same forbidden drives or inner emptiness that elicit demons and uncontrollable sensations can induce growth. According to the *Tao Te Ching*:

> Yield and you need not break:
> Bent you can straighten,
> Emptied you can hold,
> Turn you can mend.
> (*Tao Te Ching*)

Even if a person feels overwhelmed by regressive experience, by the resurgence of repressed instincts and unresolved needs, she does not have to remain permanently overwhelmed. A. T. Boisen's religious experience, for example, involved a psychotic breakdown, a regressive return to what he called his "bottomless depth." He believed, however, that his experience created an "openness" to "a reparative confrontation." "It was necessary for me to pass through the purgative forces of horrifying psychosis before I could set forth in my promised land of creative activity" (1936, p. 279; 1960, p. 208).[9]

Why does one individual who regresses into a bewildering

realm of uncontrollable drives and primitive affect experience a creative breakthrough, while the seemingly same descent into unconscious processes causes another to be overwhelmed by them? Why does one person maturely manage a resurgence of sexual feelings thought to have been successfully renounced while another castrates himself in a similar situation?[10] Both have had experiences that exposed them to the dark caves of the inner self and that forced them to do battle with the dragons of the unconscious, as Jung said in reference to the hero, but while one was devoured by the dragon of maternal abyss, the hero masters it (1953b, p. 180). Or in the metaphor of the oceanic experience into which a person submerges, Joseph Campbell suggested that

> the schizophrenic patient is actually experiencing inadvertently that same beatific ocean deep which the yogi and saint are striving to enjoy: except that, whereas they are swimming in it, he is drowning. (1979, p. 200)

Drowning in the ocean of the unconscious is due to feeling overwhelmed by the regressive return of tumultuous repressed drives and hidden fears. Swimming in the same experience is the result of not being overwhelmed by, and instead, of doing something creative with, the ocean of the unconscious. That is, the person *elaborates* on the experience.

ELABORATION OF RELIGIOUS EXPERIENCE GIVES CRITICAL SHAPE TO UNBOUNDED PRIMARY PROCESS

Recovered primary process and primitive instincts are not overwhelming when acting on them provides the structure they require to become manageable and meaningful. Creativity once again provides insight into how this is accomplished. Creative inspiration generally is experienced when primitive processes erupt from an incubational unconscious and produce novel insights. Their resplendent recovery is the energy that fuels the creative process but that energy requires the artist's particular aesthetic discipline—possibly driven by years of study and practice—in order, first, to prevent their raw instinctual intensity from being overwhelming, and, second, to turn untamed instinctual energy into socially meaningful and creative expression.[11]

In regard to the first, the psychoanalyst Klein (1937) suggested that the artist's unbounded primitive impulses—especially aggression—are safely channeled into the "container" of aesthetic form. A particular work of art provides the tangible structure within which intolerable or chaotically unmanageable primary process thinking can be expressed, and eventually mastered. It can be expressed because the aesthetic form provides a structure in which it is made creatively stable and tolerable. Normally repressed fears or pernicious passions can be expressed on a canvas, for instance, because the canvas provides a type of playground on which the artist can experiment with these feelings (without having to acknowledge them as her own).

Once the unconscious processes that inspired her are safely expressed, the artist is able to master them. By "playing with" unbounded primary process through the disciplines of her particular art form, the artist eventually gains control over—rather than feels controlled by—these intense and sometimes chaotic inner processes. Unstable precognitive processes (such as William Blake's visions) are thus stabilized on a canvas, while unmanageable instincts (such as in Van Gogh's volatile unconscious) are brought under control.[12]

Painting or sculpture becomes for artists a type of salvation from their hypervulnerability to inner conflict. When they paint, they creatively are able to bind, or constrain, the impulses and psychic conflicts that, outside of their art, sometimes seem overwhelming. The work of art thereby lifts the inspirational experience out of the artist's precarious unconscious. It provides the guide or form in which she can "grab hold of" the inspirational forces that appear to have "grabbed hold of her."

> The artist finds the way back to reality from his world of fantasy by making use of special gifts to mold his fantasies into truths of a new kind which are valued by men as precious reflections of reality. (Freud, 1911b, p. 223)

More than control, however, the artist's expression of unconscious processes also gives shape to their hitherto unformed nature. If the exhilarating freedom of inspirational and unconstrained primary process is to become more than a mere cathartic explosion of emotions or release from tension, the artist must consciously use her creative discipline to direct this development. She has to work with the unconscious processes that irrupt into consciousness; she has to struggle for the right word or the best color. In doing so, she provides direction and shape to the unconscious processes that inspire creativity but that are also directionless and boundless. "The great work of art is marked by an intensity of impulse, matched and dominated by an even greater intensity of discipline" (Gombrich, 1963, p. 22). Or as Dewey succinctly said, "Unconsciousness gives spontaneity and freshness; consciousness, conviction and control" (1910, p. 217).

Just as the potter's wheel gives shape to the artist's inspiration, so too the gospel, *dharma,* or ten commandments, as well as monastic labor and spiritual writings, are the disciplined crafts that give shape and structure to religious experience. The poet Caudwell's thoughts on the writer's discipline apply equally to the religious individual's discipline:

> In order that he shall be able to give expression to the inspiration that visits him he must work constantly, keeping himself in readiness, preparing his faculties, sharpening his vision and his understanding. (1951, p. 64)

The religious individual did not suddenly immerse herself in an inner realm of demonic drives and fears. Her ascetical undertakings and spiritual practices—which Kris called in artistic creativity a valuable and "purposeful" regression (1952, p. 257)—developed over time to prepare the person for the ecstatically archaic processes that irrupt in religious experience. The spiritual as well as artistic disciplines that once were expressions of ego regression now become vehicles for the creative communication of the unconscious processes they regressively restore. The skills that once were necessary to "shut off the world" and liberate unconscious processes become vital to expressing those inspiring unconscious processes in a creative way, as the philosopher Santayana said:

> All discipline is mere repression until . . . the discipline embodied in human impulses becomes the starting point for a creative moment of the imagination, that firm basis for ideal constructions in society, religion and art. (Quoted in Dewey, 1934b)

A pianist gives recognizable form to inspirational processes through the same disciplined skills that made her feel free enough to become open to that inspiration. Spiritual disciplines similarly can "lift" religious experience out of its regressed precognitive altered state of consciousness by giving it the structure that guides and masters the primary process it evokes. Meditation's focused attention, for example, helps a person suspend normative ego functions and subsequently allows potentially unwieldy unconscious material to rise to consciousness. This differs from the psychotic encounter of such a surge in unconscious material in that the meditator learns to develop an attentive awareness to what transpires in the experience. When, during meditation, her stilled mind is suddenly disturbed with an infusion of unconscious processes, she learns not to be overwhelmed by them and instead to let them float by.

Jung wrote about a mystical experience that recovered vivid images and powerful drives. He thought these regressed unconscious processes were at best incomprehensible and at worst overwhelming:

> An incessant stream of fantasies had been released, and I did my best not to lose my head but to find some way to understand these strange things. . . . There was no doubt in my mind that I must find the meaning of what I was experiencing in these fantasies. (1970, p. 200)

The yoga discipline Jung was practicing at the time provided the structure that allowed him to surrender himself to those processes rather than feel frightened by them. "I abandoned this restraint upon emotions and allowed the images and inner voice to speak afresh" (1970, p. 200).[13]

The shaman's discipline is another example of how the unconscious processes evoked in religious experience are given structure. His deliberate entrance into an altered state of consciousness regressively restores primitive processes. These unconscious processes often appear to produce psychotic behavior but also can be seen as shaped into creative expressions of the experience. The psychoanalyst Boyer (1964) made extensive studies of shamans and concluded that this ability to make constructive use of what was experienced in the regressed trance state was what distinguished the healthy shaman from the pseudo-shaman. Rather than fixate within the regressed experience, the shaman emerges out of it with the disciplined skills to share what was revealed, and to share it for the good of the community. Not only does his concrete sharing of the revived unconscious processes enable him to gain control over them; it also provides a means of control for those with whom he shares that experience. "The shaman provides the sick woman with a language by means of which unexpressed and otherwise unexpressable psychic states can be immediately expressed" (Eliade, 1964, p. 193).[14]

The shaman's work gives shape to precognitive trance experiences in a way similar to artists like Michelangelo giving concrete shape to their visions through sculpting that vision. Both take what was experienced beyond space and time ("eternal now") and through the mystic's teaching or the musician's chords make their experience temporal and spatial.

> A symphony, as Mozart reposited, can be simultaneously present, with all its details and relationships, in the timeless moment of conception, only later to unfold successively in the temporal dimension as a stream of note-pictures, graphic symbols lined up in space. (Neumann, 1989, p. 242)

The timeless experience of Nirvana or unity with God, like that of Mozart's music or of an intuitive grasp of Truth, eventually must flow out of that precognitive transtemporal moment into a concrete reality populated with the particular "notes" and "stanzas" that combine to make the music, art, or religious message that expresses what was experienced in the timeless moment. Neumann continued, "The 'I will' comes into being in the creative 'I am' and brings forth a world out of the point-of-nothingness of space and timelessness" (1989, p. 244).[15]

Jesus' gospel, not unlike the music of the composer or the message of the shaman, gave shape and structure to the unconscious processes that had been reactivated in his desert experience. Rather than remaining obsessively enticed by the magical omnipotence evoked in the desert, or childishly hoarding symbiotic feelings of unbounded love to himself, Jesus elaborated what he experienced by sharing it with others. His gospel was a type of "container," similar to that described earlier in reference to the artist, that gave mature direction to the primitive primary process restored in the regressed desert of his unconscious.

The sermon on the mount, for example, provided a concrete way for Jesus to work out, to gain control over and to develop, the unbounded sensations and unconventional ideas elicited in his experience of God. The concrete ways in which his message taught others to love, and in which he himself loved others, shaped and reshaped the experience of feeling unreservedly loved by God. His gospel became the way he worked at the various feelings and thoughts he experienced until he felt he "got it right." An archaic image of libidinal bonding thereby was transformed into a mature expression of intimacy,[16] just as aggressive feelings that once were repressed from that libidinal unity and projected onto a devil were realistically expressed in angry feelings and messages of justice.[17] As Coleridge wrote about the effect of the poet's words to master inspirational processes and thereby to become the "Gods of love which tame the chaos" (1895, p. 96), so too Jesus' gospel was his way of finding the words and behavior to communicate, and thereby to tame or develop, the often chaotic unconscious processes that arose in the illuminative experience of God.[18]

Buddha is another example of an individual whose elaboration of religious experience gave mature shape to the unconscious processes it elicited. Rather than remain permanently ensconced in an archaically blissful symbiotic Nirvana, he emerged out of and gave shape to that experience by expressing it through the "right action" and "right thinking" of his Eight-Fold Path.

Moses' ten commandments gave literal concrete shape to what otherwise could have remained a cathartic explosion of emotions derived from isolation and physical deprivation. And Merton used words to enflesh or give voice to preverbal experiences that otherwise would remain mute. He worked at putting words together to explain his experience rather than expressing himself in a wish-fulfilling reliance on a God who knows all thoughts before they are voiced or through an effortless glossalalia that does not have to put words together coherently in order to express feelings. Emily Dickinson wrote: "A word is dead/When it is said,/Some say./I say it just/Begins to live/That day." Archibald Macleish quoted a Chinese poet to express a similar process in poetry: "We poets struggle with Non-being to force it to yield Being. We knock upon silence for an answering music." Macleish then elaborated:

> The "Being" which the poem is to contain derives from "Non-being," not from the poet. And the "music" which the poem is to own comes not from us who make the poem but from the silence;

comes in answer to our knock. The verbs are eloquent: "struggle," "force," "knock." The poet's labor is to struggle with the meaninglessness and silence of the world until he can force it to mean; until he can make the silence answer and the Non-being be. (1961, p. 9)

Shakespeare said it even more poetically in *A Midsummer Night's Dream:*

The poet's eye, in a fine frenzy rolling, doth glance from heaven to earth, from earth to heaven; and as imagination bodies forth the form of things unknown, the poet's pen turns them to shapes, and gives to airy nothing a local inhabitation and a name.

Furthermore, Merton's writings and the gospel of Jesus not only provide the structure in which to express their experience but provide a vital tradition in which others' experience of God is given structure. That tradition places the experience in its larger historical context. To have that experience—and especially the fears and confusion it elicits—explained in recognizable terms such as rebirth, beatific vision, dark night, and so forth, is to be provided a purposeful structure that takes away some of the doubts and anxieties of the experience (unlike the situation of the psychotic, who has no tradition within which to interpret her experience). The individual has less reason to fear forbidden feelings—and hence less reason to resist unconscious processes—when her tradition explains them.

Pahnke (1970) discovered the importance of tradition in his studies on the difference between mind-altering drugs and mystical experience. Hallucinogenic drugs such as LSD provide a quick way to cleanse the windows of everyday perception and to reveal inner psychological processes. These drugs have a physical and psychological effect in the reduction of ego control and the recovery of an inspirational unconscious similar to that of religious practices such as fasting and chanting. Both can elicit exhilarating "highs" as well as overwhelming anxiety and fears. Pahnke discovered that when drugs taken for the expressed purpose of experiencing God were taken in a neutral as opposed to a friendly environment, and the people involved were not told what to expect or encouraged to develop trust in anyone (and so had only themselves to rely on), their experience was often of a psychotic nature.

A religious experience, on the other hand, that provides the person a supportive environment and guidance, and the trusted figures[19] and venerable tradition on which she can rely for support, helps prevent unconscious processes elicited in that experience from being overwhelming. Hence the Buddhist experiences unsolicited longings or fears but rather than encounter them in a vacuum, she experiences them under the structured guidance of the Eight-Fold Path. So too the Christian's experience of God takes place in the context of the beatitudes or—in the case of someone like a Benedictine monk—through the guiding discipline of "The Rule." The result can be the difference between sinking beneath the murky and often tumultuous waves of the oceanic unconscious and developing the disciplined skills to swim through it.[20]

Finally, the elaboration of what was experienced in the desert or under the boddhi tree helps facilitate the person's conquest of the temptation to remain attached to the secure regressed state. The artist experiences this when, after leaving the intensity of the inspirational experience and feeling she has lost the restored good object, she paints what she experienced—sometimes over and over again—thereby gaining greater mastery over it. What arose in the incubational state is kept alive by the working through (and embodying) of it in the artwork (a process that also results in the artist's being able to "let go" of the need to cling to the love object—Klein, 1937).[21]

So too the religious individual's elaboration of the unitive experience helps him emerge from an altered state of consciousness. He lets go of the lost libidinal object (symbiotic mother, represented in God) when, like the artist, he expresses the experience of it in his work. The ongoing effort to express and to work out the unconscious processes elicited in his experience makes the experience tangible and helps keep it alive, which makes letting go of the regressively recovered libidinal object (and the return to reality) less anxious.

Jesus was able to overcome his temptation to cling to the unbounded love and omnipotent power of the desert through the active love and teachings that kept that experience alive.[22] Buddha's *dharma* similarly enfleshed what he experienced beneath the boddhi tree and so made emerging from that blissful state possible, as the ten commandments, expressing what Moses experienced, helped him come down from mountain after the divine fire faded. Through acting on what was experienced these individuals were able to relinguish an unconscious clinging to the experience and to get on with their lives.[23]

FREEDOM IN STRUCTURE

The communication of religious experience, as valuable as it is, is not meant to be confused with the experience itself. Merton's words, for example, described his experience; they elaborated on the feelings it evoked, on what it meant to him. But they did not say "this is the experience," as if words replaced the experience or marked its termination and their ascent. Buddha was afraid of communicating the *dharma* for this reason. He feared that others, who had not had his experience, would misunderstand his words and even mistake them for the experience. Taoist warnings remind us that the Tao that can be spoken is not the Tao, and Zen offers the saying that when you ask someone where the moon is, you should not confuse the pointing finger with the moon. Even in art, "we are trying to talk about a process which stops being that process as soon as we talk about it" (Milner, 1958, p. 161).

Sometimes the best way to describe an experience is to say that it is beyond description, which is no less true of other intense emotional experiences, like love. Yet the religious person still needs to do her best to describe, to elaborate on, and to share the feelings of her experience. Even if expressed in symbols or poetry that at best can only allude to the experience, the experience is elucidated (from *elucidare:* to bring out of darkness and into the light of day).

The Tao that cannot be spoken, the silence that defies speech, must be communicated but the shape given to them must not alter their substance. The spatial qualities of the communication must not destroy the timelessness of the experience, nor the logical explanation of the experience dilute its mystery. So too the detached analysis of or reflection on the experience must not jeopardize its immediacy. And the expression of what is intensely personal—which thereby makes it social—must not vitiate its personal nature.

When the form that gives expression to content replaces content, the form, as it sometimes does in art, may become lifeless. In the attempt to express the inexpressible, the latter is destroyed, deadened, reified. The discipline, whether in art or religion, is superimposed on the experience rather than permitting an animated expression of the experience. (Dewey [1934b] called it "excessive baggage.")

Form, however, realistically imposes some control over the experience it expresses. Just as the confines of an artist's frame enforce certain constraints on unbounded inspirational processes, so too words, which attempt to shape the experience that took place in monastic silence, inevitably constrict that experience. Words have limitations and so cannot do justice to an experience that transcends limitations. That is why Buddha feared explaining his experience and the Tao spoken is not the Tao. But the shaping of the aesthetic or religious experience, if truly creative, does not impose form on the formless or word upon the silence. According to William Blake:

> He who binds to himself a joy,
> Does the wing-ed life destroy,
> He who kisses the joy as it flies
> Lives in eternities sun-rise.

Michelangelo did not force on a block of marble the shape that reflected his vision. The sculpted work of art became an extension of his vision; it brought the vision into greater focus without losing its vitality. So too the poet's words or rhymes provide form for an inspirational sensation that, without that form, would never be brought out of the realm of inner sensation or fantasy and into the realm of reality. Their limitations and boundaries keep the person from slipping back into the unconscious formlessness of the former. And rather than being oppressed by them, by the impossibility of colors or movement to fully express the intensity of that which inspired, the artist is creative with them. She becomes imaginative in her struggle against boundaries or tension.[24] "In general I would say that limitation makes for power: the strength of the genie comes of his being confined in a bottle" (Richard Wilbur, quoted in Ciardi, 1950).

People such as Thomas Merton similarly found in the literate communication of their religious experience the words that creatively shaped their experience. Their words or teachings took what was illuminated in an unconscious or unbounded altered state and expressed that experience in a way that did not diminish or constrict it, but gave a new freedom to their experience. Merton's disciplined writings, or Buddha's *dharma,* like the painter's skill, made possible the expression of the raw instincts and unbounded inspirational energy that otherwise might have been a euphoric albeit directionless explosion of repressed feelings.

MAKING SENSE OF THE EXPERIENCE

Words that bring boundaries to an unbounded experience also bring greater comprehension to an oftentimes incomprehensible experience. That which is illuminative and unitive frequently is also irrational and even frightening. By expressing that experience, as best one can, highly introspective and often bewildering feelings or thoughts are shaped into tangible and recognizable expressions. An intuitive experience that was not exactly scientific is made more precise and has given to its immeasurability a certain measurement. In the process of making that intensely subjective experience objective, the religious individual makes conscious what was unconscious (just as the artist makes visible what was invisible). Her elaborative expression of an experience that arose from the depths of her unconscious—whether perceived to be inspired by inner psychological dynamics or by God—not only makes others aware of her experience but makes the person herself more aware of the unconscious processes that inspired the experience.

When people like Merton or Jesus, for example, expressed in words what they experienced in silence or in the desert, they made accessible to conscious reason that which percolated and incubated and eventually became unified in their unconscious. They not only experienced unity, which Eckhart said is the goal of the mystic, "they then must 'return', which is to say, they must have a knowledge of God and be conscious of their knowledge" (Eckhart, quoted in Blackney, 1941, p. 80). Or as Jung suggested, the conscious representation of the unconscious creative process elicits a "Schopenhauerian mirror in which the unconscious becomes aware of its own face" (1963, p. 117).

The gospel of Jesus was not only a means of giving shape to unformed illuminative contents but a way of wrestling with (as the artist does on her canvas) what must have been to some extent its perplexing contents. His words and ministry crystalized, and clarified—for himself as well as for others, the sometimes incomprehensible images and intangible sensations experienced in the desert. The love he preached helped bring together and make sense of the unbounded libidinal feelings that were unquestioned in the magical atmosphere of the desert (feelings that when expressed outside that altered state often seem narcissistic or irrational).

Jesus' gospel made sense of his experience, as did Moses' ten commandments and Buddha's *dharma*, because, like the artist's canvas, it provided the concrete means to think logically about an experience that took place on a noncognitive unconscious level. What Milner said about the artist's experience applies equally to religious experience: "Life goes on at such a pace that unless these experiences can be incarnated in some external form, they are inevitably lost to the reflective life" (1958, p. 154).

Reflecting on an experience also affords the person some critical distance from the experience. It encourages her to question that which previously she immediately and maybe even impulsively indulged. Its noetic quality made the truthfulness of the experience evident, and as a result unquestioningly accepted. When, instead, the person elaborates on her experience she no longer is immersed in it. "Inspirational creativity," Kris suggested, "is manifested in the artist's stepping back to observe the effect" (1952, p. 253). Like an artist, the religious individual can stand back and analyze her experience; she can critically look at her work and acknowledge that the blues are too bright or the love too sentimental.

The act of standing back and recognizing that certain colors or expressions do not truly grasp the meaning of what was experienced affords the individual the opportunity to rework her painting or to struggle further with the meaning of her experience. The use of a lighter shade of blue or a new perspective on God's love refines and reworks what was experienced, allowing the person more perfectly to "grab hold of" and further be inspired by it. Her work of art or religious expression thereby not only represents new insights into reality but reveals new insights into herself and into her normally untapped creative/illuminative unconscious. This is what Maritain meant when he talked of poetry as a "sign": "both a direct sign of the secrets perceived in things . . . and a reversed sign of the subjective universe of the poet, of his substantial self obscurely revealed" (1966, p. 91). More specifically, he said,

> The object created by the poet is like the glory of the poet, and it
> is in this glory, through which he manifests himself to the world,
> that he manifests himself also to himself and becomes conscious
> in signified act, but in an inevitable imperfect and unsatisfying
> way, with his original experience. (Maritain, 1955, p. 85)

The concrete expression of religious experience provides the form not only for reflecting on that experience but for verifying it. Some psychologists have labeled the last stage of creativity "verification" (Koestler, 1964). Verification is the act of substantiating the inspirational visions or voices with that which is real. The gospel or the ten commandments, like aesthetic form to the artist, provide tangible means for the individual to verify that which took place in the fantasy and the primary process–dominated unconscious. The concrete expression of the experience serves as a type of feedback, challenging her to reexamine her inner experience, to test it for validity, meaningfulness, and, as Maritain said of poetic creativity, to determine whether it possesses "both a revelation of the subjectivity of the poet and of the reality that poetic knowledge has caused him to perceive" (1966, p. 91).

Verification of religious experience can also reveal that which in the experience is false or is the product of wish-fulfilling desires. Theresa of Avila (1957) was able to acknowledge when her visions were not only too bizarre to be essential to religious experience but were even detrimental to it. Buddhists safeguard against confusing inner psychological processes with reality by means of the simple command: "If you meet the Buddha on the road, kill him." And the psychoanalyst Kohut described how a young man was able to come to terms with the hallucinations he equated with divine visions "by eliciting the opinion of those whom he considered to be his mentors and spiritual guides, those traditional agents of realism and morality" (1985, p. 15).

Finally, the individual's concrete expression of her experience in a work of art or in a particular spiritual discipline not only inspires deeper self understanding but also makes that which inspired her acceptable to others. One of the salient factors in elaborating creative experience, as Kris noted, is that it is communicated. By partaking in common cultural forms such as language and symbols to share their experience, artists, as well as people like Jesus and Buddha, are able to keep an intensely personal experience from becoming solipsistically relevant only to themselves while incomprehensible to others. "It must be something that sooner or later, ordinary thinking will understand, accept and appreciate, otherwise the result would be bizarre, not creative" (Arieti, 1967, p. 121).[25]

The gospel and the *dharma* that communicate religious experience provide a type of cartography for others. They are maps that, by describing personal experience, reveal to others a potential direction to follow in discovering their own experience. But they are only maps. They are not the experience itself. Like the finger pointing to the moon they are not the moon, and like the artist's canvas they represent the expression of one's experience, but are not meant to interpret that experience for others.[26] People have to reflect on and ultimately understand for themselves the words and actions that shape these individuals' experience. What Jung said of the artist is true of the religious individual. "He has done his utmost by giving it form, and must leave the interpretation to others and to the future" (1966, p. 107). And what Freud said is the aim of the artist's work is also relevant to the religious person's elaboration of her experience, an elaboration that is not to repeat the experience but "to awaken in us the same emotional attitude, the same mental constellation as that which in him produced the impetus to create" (1914, p. 212).

Although communication of a religious experience does not interpret that experience for others, others' interpretation of it—like a viewer's interpretation of a particular work of art—can provide further feedback to the individual about her experience. She herself was able to glean from the concrete expression of her experience a certain amount of insight into that experience but by communicating it to others she is further able to gauge the relevance of her experience. Just as the actor depends on the audience to validate her skills, so too the religious individual needs others' assessment of her message to help determine its meaningfulness.[27] Others' responses can challenge her to rethink her experience or to test it for reality (or for hallucinatory lack of reality and solipsistic self-indulgence).

The locus of verification, however, remains within the experience. Even as the individual is responsive to feedback from others, the experience itself is the final and ultimate source of veridicality: the "self-validating, self-justifying moment which carries its own intrinsic value with it" (Maslow, 1964, p. 62). That self-justifying moment has to be expressed in order for the experience to be lifted out of its unconscious state yet its expression, like that of the artist, is not to solicit approval from others. If by expressing it the experience becomes relevant to others, so be it; if not, so be it. Hence communication of the experience, as the psychoanalyst Schafer suggested, is not always the necessary ingredient of creative process that Kris posited it to be (Schafer, 1958). An artist's painting or a dancer's dance does not have to communicate her experience to others and instead simply can be a form of self-expression.

> The artist evokes emotion and gives pleasure; he does not need to go beyond this to the translation of his imagery and to the language of the secondary processes. Art does not aim to cure; it arises out of conflict, not out of neurosis. (Beres, 1957, p. 421)

The artist's task to elaborate her experience does not mean that she "owes" the public a painting. Nor does the religious person "owe" the world an explanation of her experience. Few people have the writing skill of a Merton or a John of the Cross, nor the world-transforming vision of a Buddha or the social conscience of a St. Francis. Yet they too—if their experience is a creative regression in service of the ego—do not remain fixated in that which illuminated them. Instead, in their own way, they give shape and direction to their experience.

A person whose encounter of God takes place in the silence of a monastery, for example, might express that experience but not by writing about it or by rejoining society to live it. Rather, although this is incomprehensible to many (as numerous artists' works are incomprehensible to many), she expresses her experience through the way in which she works with and cares for others in the monastery. She elaborates her experience of God in the attentive way she lives—"When I eat I eat, when I sleep I sleep"—and in the nonmagical way she believes that her life of labor and prayer might be inspirational to others:

> A mystic who passes through all the phases of mystical introversion and attains to nothingness but returns from it in a creative state, that is, with a positive attitude toward the world, may be counted as a representative of this heroic mysticism. He may live

in mountain solitude or preach nothingness; provided he thinks he can thus exert a positive influence on the world, he is within the sphere of this mysticism. (Neumann, 1968, p. 397)

FROM PASSIVITY TO ACTIVITY IN ART

The expression of what took place on the mountain or in the altered state of consciousness marks a reversal from the backward direction of regression to a regression in service of the ego. The change of direction also marks a radical change in the essentially passive nature of the unitive experience. Religious experience began as a regressive renunciation of assertiveness and a selfless submersion into passive symbiotic unity.[28] This passivity comes to an end, and along with it the predominantly defensive nature of religious experience, when the person expresses what she experienced. Expression by itself is insufficient, however. What is required is a conscious acting on or doing something with the experience.

He has stepped out of the glowing darkness of chaos into the cool light of creation. But he does not possess it yet; he must first draw it truly out, he must make it into a reality for himself, he must find his own world by seeing, hearing, touching and shaping it. (Martin Buber, quoted in Johnston, 1986, p. 163)

An artist who paints what inspired her, without reflecting on or deliberately shaping it, does not consciously become involved in the creative process. She passively imitates on her canvas that which inspired her,[29] and does not actively elaborate what surges from within her. By forgoing an active struggle with or fashioning of that which inspired her, she remains a passive recipient of it. The particular discipline she employs to express what inspired her thereby does not help to form it, to bring it out of the unconscious by shaping and reshaping it. It is used instead for a cathartic release of unconscious conflicts or impulses. While the release of these inner dynamics can be exhilarating, their spontaneous irruption—even when expressed on a canvas or in a poem—is not in itself creative.[30]

Jackson Pollock contested the belief held by some that this abstract expressionism was an "accident" of the unconscious or an "illustration" of what was revealed. "The method of painting is the natural growth out of a need. I want to express my feelings rather than illustrate them" (quoted in Read, 1967, p. 45). Truly creative artists do not merely release their instincts; they work at and struggle with that which inspired them.[31] As George Bernard Shaw is said to have penned, genius is 10 percent inspiration and 90 percent perspiration.

A creative writer does not usually spout words or write whatever comes to mind and call that art. She writes what inspires her, but she also refines and polishes it, as some rare gem from her unconscious. Dancers similarly practice years to discipline inner inspirational energy into a recognizable and powerful expression of that energy. Philosophers and mathematicians work diligently to fashion logical and coherent formulas that "came" to them after having "slept on it." Mozart worked feverishly to put particular notes and chords to the complete symphonies that spontaneously reverberated in his imagination.[32] The poet's product—which might appear smooth and effortless—often is accomplished only after she struggles to find the *mot juste,* the one exact word that best expresses her idea. "Idly talk they who speak of poets as mere indulgers of fancy, imagination, superstitions, etc. They are the bridlers by delight, the purifiers" (Coleridge, 1895, p. 96).

The artist who initiates doing something with what the muses inspired ceases to be a selfless imitator of stimuli or a passive receptacle/conduit for unconscious processes. Her creative experience becomes what she does with that which was "given."[33] By making something of her revelatory experience she transforms her passive reception of inspirational processes into an active encounter with them: "participating in 'what the voice' has done" (Kris, 1952, p. 61).

The artist actively participates in the inspirational experience by getting her hands dirty. She takes the image that spontaneously came to her and dips her hand into the clay to shape it, or exhausts herself in the dance that directs its energy. Hence Michelangelo not only saw a vision in a piece of marble but participated in that vision by actively sculpting the marble until it produced the vision.

In the end, creativity not only takes from life that which is inspirational but through its active elaboration gives back to life something new. That is, creativity is innovative. It is bringing out of the inspirational unconscious and applying to life a new insight that enhances life. Thus we see in Picasso's paintings not only the keen observation of an image that was given to him from nature but a giving back to nature of his effort to do something creative with it. An equally perceptive artist said, "L'art c'est l'homme ajoute a la nature" (Art is man added to nature) (Van Gogh, 1958, p. 189).

FROM PASSIVITY TO ACTIVITY
IN RELIGIOUS EXPERIENCE

Religious experience—if it is reparative and regenerative—actively adds to life. It does not begin this way. Instead, its regressed unitive state or infused contemplation was one of being acted on, of being visited by God or having truth revealed. The person was only a vehicle for the message.

The essentially passive and defensive nature of religious experience comes to an end when, as in creative processes, the individual acts on the experience. She no longer passively waits for something to happen; what "acted upon" her in the desert or in the altered state of consciousness now is "acted on."[34] Rather than expecting magical gratification, the individual utilizes any number of spiritual disciplines to do something active with what was passively experienced. Doing something with the divinely illuminated unconscious requires no less than the 90 percent work that is involved in sculpting the 10 percent inspirational vision out of stone. Plotinus remarked about this process:

> And if you do not find yourself beautiful yet, act as the creator of a statue that is to be made beautiful: he cuts away here, he smooths there, he makes this line lighter, the other purer, until a lovely face has grown upon his work. So do you also: Cut away all that is excessive, straighten all that is crooked, bring light to all that is overcast. Labor to make all one glow of beauty and never cease chiselling your statue, until there shall shine out on you from it the godlike splendor of virtue, until you shall see the perfect goodness surely established in the stainless steel.

Jesus not only did not hoard the love he experienced from God for himself, nor merely express it by describing it, but acted on it through concrete works of intimacy and caring. As Kris said of the artist, his acting on what inspired him "repeats actively what had been passively experienced" (1952, p. 91). What was encountered by Jesus (or the artist) as a sense of "I have had an experience" is changed, by acting on it, into "I do something with the experience." What incubated in the unconscious of their experience—which was described earlier as necessitating a "hands-off" attitude in order not to get in its way but to let it gestate and come forth on its own—now is brought into maturity by doing something with it.[35]

So too Buddha emerged out of a tranquil Nirvana and worked diligently at the *dharma* of "right action" and "right living."[36] He also taught his disciples the need to "work out your salvation with diligence" (quoted in Foucher, 1963). Moses originally withdrew from his people and retreated into what the psychoanalyst Arlow (1951) labeled the "primitive orality" of waiting passively for God, but when God appeared Moses not only did not cling to the experience but acted on what he received in his return to his people. And Hindus counsel the aspirant to combat *tama*, or spiritual laziness, through *raja:* the willpower to act on what was experienced passively. In this way, the practices of religious experience are similar to those of creative experience:

> The practice of art is a discipline (yoga) beginning with attention (dharana), consummated in self-identification (samadhi) . . . with the object or theme of contemplation, and eventually in skill of cooperation (kausala). (Coomaraswamy, 1977, p. 90)

When people like Jesus and Buddha act on what they experienced in the desert or in an altered state of consciousness, they cease being solely passive vehicles for God's grace and Nirvana's insights. Acting on what they received makes them feel as if they are taking part in it. They "actively participate in the voice," as Kris was quoted in reference to the artist's elaboration of that which inspired. Evelyn Underhill said: "The awakened subject is not merely to perceive transcended life, but to participate therein" (1911, p. 195).

What once was inspirationally experienced as coming "through" the individual is experienced—by consciously doing something with it—as coming "out of" the individual. What once was "passed on" (e.g., truth) is now something that expresses the individual's personal involvement in the execution of what is passed on. In this way the person becomes a creator. As the artist becomes a creator when she acts on what inspired her, so too the religious individual becomes a creator alongside the grand creator: the God who created *ex nihilo* and by whose inspiration the person participates in shaping reality and even feels godlike in the ability to do so. Jesus himself quoted Isaiah: "Is it not written that you shall all be gods?" (Jn 10:34).

The religious individual becomes a creator when like Michelangelo she gets her hands dirty sculpting her inspirational experience. Hence the expression of what was illuminative is not automatic. An effortless and undisciplined expression of illuminative unconscious processes takes what was experienced and, in art, splashes it onto a canvas; the expectation in religious experience is that feelings such as love or communion will be made manifest without work or frustration. Such an experience makes a person nothing more than a passive receptacle or cathartic vehicle for releasing pent-up conflicts. As euphoric and inspirational as catharsis may be, it is neither art nor religious experience. Hamlet declared:

> My words fly up, my thoughts remain below:
> Words without thoughts never to heaven go.

Although religious experience *is* a regressive return to and cathartic freeing of unresolved needs, when it is only that it is what Neumann (1968) called "urobic mysticism" and William Blake the state of "Beulah"—an undisturbed peace and perfection that recaptures "The beloved infant in his mother's bosom incircled/With arms of love and pity and sweet compassion" (quoted in Abrams, 1971, p. 261). Wordsworth labeled the same state "Arcadia," and suggested that it was the result of "A wish to part/With all remembrance of a jarring world" (quoted in Abrams, 1971, p. 295).

When the bliss and security of unitive experience are not acted on, and instead are confused with a final product, the person becomes passively and permanently fixated in the regressed primitive state. She prefers the instant gratification of paradise and the effortless expression of wishes to the hard work of confronting the conflicts and acting on the basic trust that were also experienced. Merton described such a state as a spiritual disease in its total insistence on ideals and intention, in complete divorce from reality, from act, and from social commitment. Whatever one dreams, whatever one images: That is the beautiful, the godly, the true. (1973, p. 108)

Experiences of this type are manifested in the spiritual laziness and childish quiescence described by Christian mystics as "acidia" and by Hindus as "tamas." They are wonderfully warm and even ecstatic experiences, but without the conscious effort to act on them they become sterile and lifeless. They are decorative, even delightfully depictive of the experience, but also superficial. As the poet Auden said of art that is wonderful in its "primary imagination" but lacks the "secondary imagination" to express it, "its beauty soon becomes banal, its rhythms mechanical" (1962). Or as Confucius said, "If you have the wisdom to pursue the truth/But not the manhood to keep it,/You will find it/But lose it."

The anonymous writer was right when he or she penned, "Never to have seen the truth is better than to have seen it and not to have acted on it." Truth that is glimpsed but not acted on is nothing more than an evanescent glimpse that makes the person falsely believe she has to look no further. The experience is akin to a flash of lightning that illuminates a room, providing a momentary means of seeing what is therein. The illumination quickly disappears, just as the flash of insight into truth disappears, and unless the person does something with what she saw in that momentary illumination she will quickly forget its contents and will have learned nothing from her experience as she is once again immersed in the darkness.

Religious experience provides a glimpse into "truth," into the inner illuminative primary process and original sense of connectedness that had been relegated to the darkness of the unconscious. But when the person comes face to face with instinctual freedom and feelings of communion (true self) she must act on them. For the true self that is uncovered after the false self has been vanquished is not born into mature fullness. No Rousseauistic "noble savage" or "natural man" lies beneath the layers of encrusted and socialized self, waiting simply to be liberated in order to take the helm. The true self is the potential self, the unformed and open-to-experience self that, on recovery in religious experience, has to be acted on and developed.

To act on the true self, on the "Christ within" or Buddha Mind that represents this true self, is to bring the true self out of the realm of potentiality and into actuality. Religious experience might be the birth of this Christ within or true self but, as Underhill said, the "new person" is "destined to pass through many phases of development before its maturity is reached" (1911, p. 147). Without action on that which is born in religious experience the birth would be a stillbirth, just as Michelangelo's visions would have been stillbirths had he not actively sculpted them into life. Their automatic ascent into positions of power or personal identity would have been the product of wishful thinking, of the primitive unconscious need to gratify childish longings for a ready-made and perfect existence.

The manner in which a person learns (or fails to learn) to act on what was experienced in the unitive state determines the nature of her true self. That is, whether she does something constructive to develop the potentiality that is the true self or the Christ within determines if that which is ecstatically recovered in religious experience forms maturely or defensively. It determines if the experience results in fleeting inspiration or enduring wisdom, temporary insight into life or living that insight. For only by working at and giving shape to what was illuminated in religious experience does the person turn the formless experience of Being into a concrete and active part of life. Only after having purged the "doing" that first formed to defend against the original Being—thereby recovering Being (true self) and providing the opportunity to resolve the conflicts that repressed Being and forged the defensive doing—can the person do something creative with what she has experienced.

The individual who walked securely with God through the valley of death thus must act on that experience by taking the risk of stepping out on her own, just as the person whose unconscious incubated with the revelation of God must do something with what it illuminated. So too the Prodigal Son, who earlier was described as rejecting the false self and indulging instinctual desires until he discovered the true self ("he came to himself"), is greeted with a feast when he returns home—but in the end, if that experience is to be healthy, he must not remain contented in that feast and instead must act on the lesson he learned. Buddha declared "a beautiful thought or word which is not followed by a corresponding action, is like a bright hued flower that will bear no fruit." Or as Jesus more succinctly stated, "By their fruits you shall know them."

Finally, the active elaboration of religious experience changes life rather than reacts to life. What began in the desert or under the boddhi tree as a return to the oral incorporation of childhood—in which, like the child at the mother's breast, these individuals took in and consumed everything that God had to offer—is turned around when by acting on what was ingested these individuals had something to give back or contribute. Jesus and Buddha and others like them did not use their divine encounter to make life more manageable or more easily adaptable, but to offer new meaning to and transformative perspectives on reality. They took the illuminative experience, and the nondefensive openness they experienced within themselves, and by applying its diverse insights they offered something novel. As Van Gogh said of the artist, they added to and shaped life. In the stroke of a brush or the teaching of love they recreated reality. And although Bertolt Brecht was referring to the aesthetic world when he said that "art is not a mirror held up to reality but a hammer with which to shape it," such an image applies equally well to the "world-transforming mysticism" of the individual who returns from the altered state of consciousness with an active contribution to make (Neumann, 1989). Both images are brought together in Underhill's description of the true mystic as "an artist, a discoverer, a religious or social reformer, a national hero, a 'great active' among the saints" (1911, p. 414).

Conclusion

Religious experience is a regressive phenomenon. It begins with ascetical disciplines that consciously or unconsciously renounce ego functions. Loss of ego control subsequently allows primitive instincts and primary process thinking to return, often in the shape of visions and ecstasy. Finally, religious experience regressively restores the early symbiotic relationship with the mother, represented in submersion into an oceanic Nirvana or communion with God.

Religious experience, however, can also be a regression in service of the ego. As in therapy and in art, the regressive flight from reality and descent into unconscious processes can be reparative and regenerative. What began as a dying to self can be the critically important divestiture of a defensive ego and false self; the regressive return to unconscious processes can liberate drives and incubate a more creative perspective on life; and the restoration of symbiotic unity can revive the basic trust that becomes the foundation on which to act on the conflicts that originally derailed development.

A person's image of God profoundly changes when through that divine encounter he recovers and resolves the hidden conflicts that once regressively motivated it. The experience might have begun as a regression to libidinal feelings blissfully split off from volatile aggressive ones but, having eventually in that experience learned to express aggression, the person transforms the unresolved maternal relationship that once sheltered him from aggression and subsequently returns to adulthood no longer needing a paradisiacal unity to do the same. That is, the individual ceases to need a defensive relationship with God in which to find an idealized mother's vanquishment of frustration or an ecstatic indulgence of forbidden impulses.

Instead he has learned from a religious experience that restored inner longings and conflicts how to resolve those longings and conflicts, and by acting on them to develop the mature confidence to trust in himself.

What happens to God when a person repairs the conflicts that were unconsciously avoided through the experience of God? What happens when, in the safe environment of the unitive experience, the person recovers and becomes comfortable with the sexuality or autonomy he previously feared and found in God the means to escape? Does God still exist when a person learns he can walk through the valley of death on his own, or does the God from whom he learned to resolve his fear disappear with the disappearance of the fear?

> I have learned how to walk,
>   since then I have let myself run.
> I have learned how to fly:
>   since then I do not wish to be pushed in
>   order to get away.
> Now I am light; now I fly:
> Now I see beneath myself:
> Now a god dances though me.
> (Nietzsche, 1954, p. 152)

Freud, of course, would have answered that the God to whom one childishly turns for symbiotic security vanishes when the person learns to express mature forms of intimacy and assertiveness. That may be the case. The experience of God, as described throughout this book, represents the regressive return to unresolved conflicts and, in the "safe environment" of the unitive state, either the reinforcement of those conflicts' repression or else their reparation. With the latter, unconscious attachment to a symbiotic mother—and to the God representing her—has been meaningfully resolved. The person has grown up and no longer needs a God to defend him against the psychological past he has repaired.

A possibility exists, however, for a person not to abandon God even though he has healed the psychological scars. The child's original maternal attachment is left behind, but he continues to grow, even into adulthood, in a potentially expanding and nondefensive relationship with the mother. So too the adult can let go of the symbiotic need for a need-gratifying God and yet continue to grow in a potentially expanding and nondefensive relationship with God.

Rather than ceasing to exist, God, like the mother God represents, can become more real when shorn of the needs and feelings projected thereon. When the mother ceases to be omnipotent to the child, and instead sets limits, she becomes more real and less fantasized. In psychological terms, the mother becomes a "constant object"; she is real in herself, separate from and related to independently of the growing child's needs. The child "becomes increasingly able to respond to the 'whole mother', and realizes that one and the same person can both gratify and disturb" (Mahler, 1979, p. 119). A similar process takes place at the end of therapy when the individual, having resolved final transference issues, relates to the therapist for who he is and no longer for the unconscious needs projected onto him.

In much the same way a person's image of God—if it continues to exist once the transference issues that produced it are resolved—can mature and become more real with the psychological maturation of the individual. As the child's relationship with the mother emerges out of the fantasy of his mind and into reality, so too the experience of God emerges out of the desert or the mountaintop—and out of what those realms unconsciously represented—and moves into reality. Once one has worked through the hidden needs or conflicts that were experienced in those euphoric encounters, God no longer symbolizes immediate gratification of needs or isolation of aggression. God instead is experienced as being no less divine even when not gratifying unconscious needs, just as Nirvana is no less Nirvana even when it ceases to be a magical embodiment of paradise. The person's relationship with God thereby becomes real and enduring; it does not fluctuate according to whether needs are gratified or desires are frustrated (object constancy). The individual has learned to "unify the 'good' and 'bad' object" (Mahler, 1975, p. 110), and so the relationship with God is for who God is—loving and gratifying as well as challenging and frustrating—and not for what the unconscious once needed God to be.

The struggle toward psychological and spiritual growth continues long after the person's religious experience has resolved the basic fault that represented arrested growth. Just as a painter might paint the same experience over and over again in the attempt to master the underlying "lost object" that can never be perfectly mastered, so too people continue to work at understanding the depths of self that never can be fully comprehended. If a personal God is part of that process, then that God will not be a defensive means of hiding from the work that needs to be done but a part of facilitating it. Luther and Merton represent two individuals whose experience of God was a regressive return to unconscious processes and yet they, like others, having found in that experience the reparation of the conflicts that thwarted fuller psychological development, continued throughout their lives to work at themselves and their relationship with God.

An image of God that continues to illuminate deep recesses of a person's psyche is as real as the inspiration that does the same for an artist. Asking whether the illumination comes from a divine muse or an inner psychological process is less important than asking whether the experience leads to growth or to complacency. The artist does not query if the inspiration is merely the result of repressed unconscious conflicts, but expresses in his art that which inspired him. The image of God that might continue to exist for a person long after he has resolved unconscious conflicts similarly need not be questioned as to whether it is the product of unconscious processes or exists concretely in space and time. Either way, this divine image will be free of the unresolved conflicts that motivated religious experience and so rather than defensively thwart psychological growth will stimulate it. And just as an artist's canvas will change with the artist's greater self-awareness, so too the image of God will mature in proportion to the maturing of the individual—especially to his maturing in relationship to a God who began as a regression to unconscious processes and turned into a progressive reparation and regeneration. The psychoanalyst Loewald wrote,

> The mature individual, being able to reach back into his origins and roots of being, finds in himself the oneness from where he stems, and understands this as his freedom and his bond of love with God. The concept of God itself seems to change from that of a blindly omnipotent power to that of the transformation and incarnation of such power in individual freedom to love. (1953, p. 13)

In a similar way, Jung remarked:

> Nobody can know what the ultimate things are. We must, there-fore, take them as we experience them. And if such experiences help to make your life healthier, more beautiful, more complete and more satisfying to yourself and to those you love, you may safely say: This was the grace of God. (1938, p. 114)

Epilogue: Regression in Service of the Ego or Expansion of Ego?

Religious experience is a regression in service of the ego when what began as a renunciation of ego and leads to a restoration of unconscious processes is turned around with the reparation of those unconscious processes and the resumption of psychological development. A few psychologists, however, have suggested that regression in service of the ego does not correctly describe religious or even creative experience. People such as Schactel (1959) and Kubie (1961) in their investigation of creativity, and Hood (1976) in his studies of mysticism, suggest that what takes place in creative or religious experience is not a regressive constriction of ego but an expansion of ego.

Religious experience and creativity, according to this thinking, are straightforward progressive phenomena. They expose the old ego for its limitations and deliver it to a richer range of qualities—qualities that arise not from reactivating unconscious depths but from expanding normative ego strengths to include preconscious primary process.

The preconscious, like the unconscious, is not a normative state of consciousness. But unlike the inaccessible repressed unconscious, the preconscious is freely available to consciousness. It is comprised of feelings, thoughts, and needs that are not repressed but that, while not always available to consciousness, become available with some effort. The direct experience of God, like creativity, takes place according to this thinking when the work involved in expanding ego strengths uncovers these preconscious materials. Hence the ego that normally asserts control learns to relax, allowing for the recovery of preconscious material and its incorporation, when desirable, into consciousness. By expanding typical ego functions to include these underlying qualities, a person experiences God intuitively or directly.

The ability to relax control in order to tap preconscious processes and to utilize them to be creative or to experience God *is* expansive rather than regressive. It has been expressed by exceptional people like Jesus and Buddha, or Merton and Luther, who could be assertive and in control but also spontaneous and receptive. However, while this may be true, it is true only insofar as spontaneity and receptivity came about only after regression. Only after having "died to themselves" and to the world, after having retreated into the physical desert or monastery and into the psychological precognitive realm of visions and symbiotic bliss, and after having in that regressed state resolved the unresolved conflicts and repaired the basic fault, could these individuals be more spontaneous or enlightened.

If Buddha could have experienced Nirvana without first having renounced self and escaped to the security of the boddhi tree, if Merton and Luther could have become enlightened writers without having retreated to the safe environment of the monastery where they would be guided into confronting archaic parental representations, and if they and others like them were not motivated in their religious experience at least in part by these unconscious wishes; then their experience would have been an expansion of ego rather than regression of ego. But their experience of God was not a mere leaping out of themselves and engaging God or stretching their egos to include previously hidden preconscious qualities. It involved a regressive dying to self and resolution of primitive psychological mechanisms.[1]

The recovery and resolution of unconscious processes is what makes religious experience truly liberating and transformative. A simple expansion of the ego cannot confront and repair these various unconscious processes—just the opposite. The ego is part of the reason unconscious processes were repressed, and why communion feelings could be expressed only when the ego was purged, not expanded. The expansion of ego might appear to rectify some problems, but those problems are only symptomatic of the unconscious conflicts the ego cannot confront. The ego is in part defensive and will not willingly expand itself to include the communion feelings it staunchly keeps repressed. So too it tenaciously resists relaxing control, since the relaxation of autonomy and control elicits not only preconscious primary process but a pernicious resurgence of the primitive instincts that are kept repressed beneath ego control.

The ego attempts to make a person feel holy by rectifying some shortcomings and building better spiritual strengths. Pulling himself up on these spiritual steps makes the person appear to ascend closer to God. While the ego strengths extend upward, however, they do not extend downward to the liberating process of uncovering and repairing the deeply entrenched unconscious dynamics the ego resists.

No real change takes place in expanding ego control over spiritual traits, apart from feeling more spiritual. It is an enrichment of the ego without any substantive internal transformation, a reorganization of psychological defenses without confronting and overcoming them. A truly transformative conversion does not take place by adding on qualities, no matter how impressive, to the old self. "You cannot put new wine into old wine skins" (Lk 5:37). Real change is more than adding strengths, for such strengths simply build on the false self that needs to be repaired before a new or true self can unfold. Instead of exhuming the roots of the false self, an expansion of ego strengths solidifies them by making the person feel self-satisfied with the conquest of her sinfulness—a sinfulness that is only symptomatic of the false self and that by being overcome makes the person less inclined to confront the real disease.

Healthy religious experience begins with dying to self rather than expanding self. The latter represents "the faithful who try to remain children instead of becoming as children. . . . They do not gain their lives because they have not lost it" (Jung, 1970, p. 482). Because people have learned to identify their lives with the false self, with the rigid control and possessiveness that resist deeper longings and defend against inner conflicts, the only way the unconscious processes and unresolved conflicts that lie beneath it can be confronted is to lose or die to the self. Hence religious experience is more than adding on spiritual strengths and instead is the surrendering of self (and its rigid unconscious defenses) in order to repair the repressed processes that originally led to the development of the false self. If society does its best to make people into everything other then what they are, as e. e. cummings once said, then, according to T. S. Eliot:

In order to arrive at what you are not
  You must go through the way in which you are not.
And what you do not know is the only thing you know
And what you own is what you do not own
And where you are is where you are not.
(Eliot, 1943, p. 29)

The experience of oceanic unity, communion with God, Nirvana, or cosmic consciousness is regressive. It is not an expansion of self but a dying to self, and not a dip into preconscious material but a stepping back into previously repressed instincts and unconscious mental structures. In an ideal world a false self would never have developed in infancy, and hence no need would exist to have to die to self and to return to those processes that produced the false self. In this real world, however, basic fault, oedipal conflicts, symbiotic longings, and other unconscious dynamics do exist, and religious experience can be a regressive means either of furthering their repression or of dying to self and repairing them. In the end, religious experience will—if it does not remain fixated within the regressed state—result in an expansion of self. But it is an expansion of self that, if truly transformative, is not defensive. It is the result of psychological development that has been resumed by means of an experience that regressively returned to and repaired the place where it first derailed.

Turn your eyes inward, look into your own depths, learn first to know yourself. Then you will understand why you were bound to fall ill; and perhaps you will avoid falling ill in the future. (Freud, 1964b, p. 143)

In his "Intimations of Immortality" Wordsworth wrote:

Though nothing can bring back the hour
of splendor in the grass, of glory in the
flower;
We will grieve not, rather find
strength in what remains behind;
In the primal sympathy
which having been must ever be . . .

References

Abell, W. (1957). *The collective dream in art*. Cambridge: Harvard University Press.

Abrams, M. (1971). *Natural supernaturalism*. New York: Norton.

Alexander, F. (1956). Two types of regression. *Psychoanalytic Quarterly, 25,* 178–197.

Alexander, F. (1931). Buddhistic training as an artificial catatonia. *Psychoanalytic Review, 2,* 1929–1946.

Allison, J. (1968). Adaptive regression and intense religious experience. *Journal of Nervous and Mental Disease, 175,* 452–463.

Ansbacher, H. (Ed.). (1956). *The individual psychology of Alfred Adler*. New York: Basic Books.

Arberry, A. (1955). *Koran interpreted*. New York: Macmillan.

Arieti, S. (1976). *Creativity: The magic synthesis*. New York: Basic Books.

Arieti, S. (1964). The rise of creativity. *Contemporary Psychoanalysis, 1*(1), 51–68.

Arieti, S. (1961). The loss of reality. *Psychoanalytic Review, 48,* 3–27.

Arieti, S. (1959). Schizophrenia. In S. Arieti (Ed.), *American handbook of psychiatry*. New York: Basic Books.

Arlow, J. (1951). The consecration of the prophet. *Psychoanalytic Quarterly, 90*, 374–398.

Attar, F. (1978). *The conference of the birds*. New York: Samuel Weiser.

Auden, W. H. (1962). Making, knowing and judging. In *The Dyer's Hand*. London: Faber.

Augustine, St. (1961). *Confessions*. Harmondsworth, England: Penguin Books.

Aurobindo, S. (1939). *The life divine*. Calcutta: Arya Publishing House.

Bachrach, H. (1968). Adaptive regression, empathy and psychotherapy: Theory and research study. *Psychotherapy: Theory, Research and Practice, 5*(4), 203–209.

Bak, R. (1954). The schizophrenic defense against aggression. *International Journal of Psychoanalysis, 35*, 129–133.

Bakan, D. (1966). *The duality of human existence*. Chicago: Rand McNally.

Balint, M. (1979). *The basic fault*. New York: Brunner.

Balint, M. (1959). *Thrills and regression*. New York: International Universities Press.

Barron, F. (1972). The creative personality: Akin to madness. *Psychology Today, 6*, 42.

Barron, F. (1969). *Creative person and creative process*. New York: Holt and Rinehart.

Barron, F. (1968). *Creativity and personal freedom.* New York: Von Nostrand.

Beauvoir, S. de (1979). *The second sex.* New York: Vintage.

Berdyaev, N. (1962). *The meaning of the creative act.* New York: Collier.

Beres, D. (1957). Communication in psychoanalysis and in creative process. *Journal of American Psychoanalytic Association, 5,* 488–489.

Bettelheim, B. (1972). Regression as progress, 188–304 in P. Giovacchini (Ed.), *Techniques and theory in psychoanalytic therapy.* New York: Science House.

Bhagavad Gita. (1962) (J. Mascaro, Trans.). New York: Penguin.

Bion, W. (1973). Attention and integration. *International Journal of Psychiatry, 54,* 110–121.

Blackney, R. (1941). *Meister Eckhart.* San Francisco: Harper and Row.

Blake, W. (1975). *The marriage of heaven and hell.* New York: Oxford University Press.

Blake, W. (1969). *Complete Writings* (Geoffrey Keynes, Ed.). London: Oxford University Press.

Blos, P. (1967). The second individuation process. *Psychoanalytic Study of the Child, 22,* 162–186.

Boisen, A. (1960). *Out of the depths.* New York: Harper and Brothers.

Boisen, A. (1936). *The exploration of the inner world.* New York: Harper and Row.

Bowlby, J. (1978). *Attachment theory and its therapeutic implications.* Chicago: University of Chicago Press.

Bowlby, J. (1973). *Separation*. New York: Basic Books.

Boyer, G. (1964). Comparison of shamans and pseudoshamans. *Journal of Projective Techniques, 28,* 173–182.

Brown, N. O. (1968). *Love's body.* New York: Vintage Books.

Brown, N. O. (1959). *Life against death: The psychoanalytic meaning of history.* Middletown, CT: Wesleyan University Press.

Buddhist Scriptures. (1959) (E. Conze, Trans.). Harmondsworth: Penguin Classics.

Bush, M. (1969). Psychoanalysis and scientific creativity: With special reference to regression in the service of the ego. *Journal of the American Psychoanalytic Association, 17*(1), 136–190.

Campbell, J. (1979). Schizophrenia—the inward journal. In D. Coleman (Ed.), *Consciousness.* New York: Harper and Row.

Campbell, J. (1950). *The hero with a thousand faces.* Princeton: Princeton University Press.

Caudwell, H. (1951). *The creative impulse in writing and painting.* London: Macmillan.

Chatterjee, M. (1987). *Ghandi's religious thoughts.* Notre Dame: Notre Dame University Press.

Ciardi, J. (1950). *Mid-century American poets.* New York: Twayne.

Cloud of Unknowing. (1961) (C. Walters, Trans.). London: Penguin.

Coleridge, S. T. (1907). *Biographia literaria* (Vol. 1). Oxford: Oxford University Press.

Coleridge, S. T. (1895). *Anima poetae* (E. H. Hartley, Ed.). London: Heinemann.

Collingwood, R. (1938). *The principles of art*. Oxford: Oxford University Press.

Conway, F. (1978). *Snapping: America's epidemic of sudden personality change*. Philadelphia: Lippincott.

Coomaraswamy, A. (1977). Samuega: Aesthetic shock. In Roger Lipsey (Ed.), *Coomaraswamy* (3 vols.). Bollingen Series LXXXIX. Princeton: Princeton University Press.

Deikman, A. (1982). *The observing self*. Boston: Beacon Press.

Deikman, A. (1976). Bimodal consciousness and the mystic experience. In P. Lee (Ed.), *Symposium on consciousness*. New York: Viking Press.

Deikman, A. (1966). Deautomatization and the mystic experience. *Psychiatry, 29*, 324–338.

Deutsch, A. (1980). Tenacity of attachment to a cult leader: A psychiatric perspective. *American Journal of Psychiatry, 137*, 1569–1573.

Dewey, J. (1934a). *A common faith*. New Haven: Yale University Press.

Dewey, J. (1934b). *Art as experience*. New Haven: Yale University Press.

Dewey, J. (1910). *How we think*. Boston: D. C. Heath.

Dinnage, R. (1978). A bit of light. In Simon Grolnick (Ed.), *Between reality and fantasy*. New York: Aronson.

Dionysius. (1940). *The Mystical Theology*. (C. E. Rolt, Trans.). London: STCK.

Duerlinger, J. (1984). *Ultimate reality and spiritual discipline*. New York: Paragon House.

Ehrenzweig, A. (1967). *The hidden order of art*. Berkeley: University of California Press.

Ehrenzweig, A. (1953). *The psychoanalysis of artistic vision and hearing*. London: Routledge.

Eliade, M. (1967). *Myths, dreams and mysteries*. New York: Harper and Row.

Eliade, M. (1964). *Shamanism*. Princeton: Princeton University Press.

Eliot, T. S. (1943). *Four quartets*. New York: Harcourt.

Emerson, R. (1936). *Essays, Vol. II*. New York: Vantage.

Engler, J. (1984). Therapeutic aims in psychotherapy and meditation. *Journal of Transpersonal Psychology, 16,* 25–61.

Erikson, E. (1983). Concluding remarks: Infancy and the rest of life. In J. Call (Ed.), *Frontiers of infant psychiatry*. New York: Basic Books.

Erikson, E. (1969). *Gandhi's truth*. New York: Norton.

Erikson, E. (1968). *Identity, youth and crisis*. New York: Norton.

Erikson, E. (1964). *Insight and responsibility*. New York: Norton.

Erikson, E. (1963). *Childhood and society*. New York: Norton.

Erikson, E. (1959). The problem of ego identity. *Psychological Issues, 1,* 133.

Erikson, E. (1958). *Young man Luther*. New York: Norton.

Fairbairn, W. (1986). The repression and return of bad objects. In P. Buckley (Ed.), *Essential papers on object relations*. New York: New York University Press.

Fauteux, K. (1990). Religion's encouragement and inhibition of psychological maturity. *Journal of Religion and Health, 29:* 309–316.

Fauteux, K. (1987). Seeking enlightenment in the East: Self-fulfillment or regressive longing? *Journal of the American Academy of Psychoanalysis, 15*(2), 217–240.

Fauteux, K. (1981). Good/bad splitting in the religious experience. *American Journal of Psychoanalysis, 41,* 261–267.

Fischer, R. (1976). Transformations of consciousness—A cartography. *Confina Psychiatria, 19,* 1–23.

Fischer, R. (1972a). On creative, psychotic and ecstatic states. In J. White (Ed.), *The highest state of consciousness.* New York: Doubleday.

Fischer, R. (1972b). On separateness and oneness. *Confina Psychiatria, 15,* 165–194.

Fisher, D. (1976). Sigmund Freud and Romain Rolland. *American Imago, 33,* 1–59.

Fodor, N. (1949). *The search for the beloved.* New York: Hermitage Press.

Foucher, A. (1963). *The life of Buddha.* Middletown, CT: Wesleyan University Press.

Freud, A. (1965). *Normality and Pathology in Childhood.* London: Hogarth Press.

Freud, A. (1949). Aggression in emotional development, 489–497. In *The Writings of Anna Freud* edited by Dorothy Burlingham, (Vol. 4). New York: International Universities Press.

Freud, A. (1946). *The ego and the mechanism of defense.* New York: International Universities Press.

Freud, S. (1964a). A difficulty in psychoanalysis. *Standard edition* (hereinafter, *S.E.*) (Vol. 17). London: Hogarth Press.

Freud, S. (1964b). Outline of Psychoanalysis. *S.E.* (Vol. 23, pp. 142–207). London: Hogarth Press.

Freud, S. (1964c). Moses and monotheism. *S.E.* (Vol. 23, pp. 3–137). London: Hogarth Press.

Freud, S. (1963). The uncanny. *S.E.* (Vol. 17, pp. 217–252).

Freud, S. (1961a). *New introductory lectures on psychoanalysis.* New York: Norton.

Freud, S. (1961b). The dissolution of the oedipal complex. *S.E.* (Vol. 19, pp. 171–179). London: Hogarth Press.

Freud, S. (1961c). A religious experience. *S.E.* (Vol. 21, pp. 59–145). London: Hogarth Press.

Freud, S. (1961d). *Civilization and its discontents.* New York: Norton.

Freud, S. (1961e). The future of an illusion. *S.E.* (Vol. 21, pp. 3–56). London: Hogarth Press.

Freud, S. (1960). Group psychology and the analysis of the ego. *S.E.* (Vol. 13, pp. 65–199). London: Hogarth Press.

Freud, S. (1959). The ego and id. *S.E.* (Vol. 20, pp. 12–60). London, Hogarth Press.

Freud, S. (1957). On narcissism. *S.E.* (Vol. 14, pp. 73–102). London: Hogarth Press.

Freud, S. (1955a). The dynamics of transference. *S.E.* (Vol. 12, pp. 99–108). London: Hogarth Press.

Freud, S. (1955b). A difficulty in the path of psychoanalysis. *S.E.* (Vol. 17, pp. 5–182). London: Hogarth Press.

Freud, S. (1955c). Group psychology and the analysis of the ego. *S.E.* (Vol. 18, pp. 67–147). London: Hogarth Press.

Freud, S. (1950). *The interpretation of dreams.* New York: Modern Library.

Freud, S. (1940). An outline of psychoanalysis. *S.E.* (Vol. 23, pp. 179–208). London: Hogarth Press.

Freud, S. (1938). Splitting of the ego in the process of defense. *S.E.* (Vol. 23, pp. 275–278). London: Hogarth Press.

Freud, S. (1937). Analysis terminable and interminable. *S.E.* (Vol. 23, pp. 216–256). London: Hogarth Press.

Freud, S. (1928). Dostoevsky and parricide. *S.E.* (Vol. 21, pp. 177–196). London: Hogarth Press.

Freud, S. (1924a). Inhibitions, symptoms and anxiety. *S.E.* (Vol. 20). London: Hogarth Press.

Freud, S. (1923). Seventeenth century demenological neurosis. *S.E.* (Vol. 19, pp. 69–100). London: Hogarth Press.

Freud, S. (1920a). Beyond the pleasure principle. *S.E.* (Vol. 18, p. 366). London: Hogarth Press.

Freud, S. (1918). Question of lay analysis. *S.E.* (Vol. 20, pp. 177–250). London: Hogarth Press.

Freud, S. (1917). *Introductory lectures on psychoanalysis.* London: Allen and Unwin.

Freud, S. (1915a). Thoughts for the times on war and death. *S.E.* (Vol. 14). London: Hogarth Press.

Freud, S. (1915b). The unconscious. *S.E.* (Vol. 14, pp. 161–195). London: Hogarth Press.

Freud, S. (1915c). Instincts and their vicissitudes. *S.E.* (Vol. 14, pp. 109–140). London: Hogarth Press.

Freud, S. (1914). The Moses of Michelangelo. *S.E.* (Vol. 13, pp. 211–230). London: Hogarth Press.

Freud, S. (1912). The dynamics of transference. *S.E.* (Vol. 12, pp. 97–108). London: Hogarth Press.

Freud, S. (1911a). Psychoanalytic notes of an autobiographical account of a case of paranoia. *S.E.* (Vol. 12, pp. 1–80). London: Hogarth Press.

Freud, S. (1910). Five lectures on psychoanalysis. *S.E.* (Vol. 9, pp. 143–153). London: Hogarth Press.

Freud, S. (1907). Obsessive acts and religious practices. In *Collected Papers* ed. by Ernest Jones. (Vol. 2, pp. 25–35).

Freud, S. (1905). Three essays on sexuality. *S.E.* (Vol. 7, pp. 123–243). London: Hogarth Press.

Freud, S. (1904). On psychotherapy. *S.E.* (Vol. 7, pp. 257–270). London: Hogarth Press.

Fromm, E. (1960). *Zen Buddhism and psychoanalysis.* New York: Grove Press.

Fromm, E. (1959). The creative attitude. In H. Anderson (Ed.), *Creativity and its cultivation.* New York: Harper.

Fromm, E. (1956). *The art of loving.* New York: Harper and Row.

Fromm, E. (1955). *The sane society.* New York: Holt.

Fromm, E. (1941). *Escape from freedom.* New York: Farrar.

Fuller, P. (1980). *Art and psychoanalysis*. London: Writers Publishing.

Gandhi, M. (1968). *The selected works of Mahatma Gandhi*. Ahmedabed: Navajivan Press.

Gill, M., & Brennan, M. (1959). *Hypnosis and related states: Psychoanalytic studies in regression*. New York: International Universities Press.

Gilligan, C. (1982). *In a different voice*. Cambridge: Harvard University Press.

Giovacchini, P. (1972). Regressed states, timelessness and ego synthesis. *The Psychoanalytic Forum, 4*, 294–334.

Goleman, D. (1981). Buddhist and western psychology: Some commonalities and differences. *Journal of Transpersonal Psychology, 13*(2), 125–136.

Gombrich, E. (1963). *Meditation on a hobby horse and other essays on the theory of art*. London: Phaidon Press.

Gordon, L. (1970). Beyond the reality principle: Illusion or new reality? *American Imago, 27*, 160–182.

Gordon, W. (1961). *Synetics—The development of creative capacity*. New York: Collier.

Gottschalk, H. (1965). *Bertrand Russell: A life*. New York: Roy Publishers.

Grinker, R. (1945). *Men under stress*. Philadelphia: Blakiston.

Groddeck, G. (1937). *The unknown self*. London: Danile Co.

Grof, S. (1984). *Newsletter of the spiritual emergency network, 9*(3).

Hart, H. (1955). The meaning of passivity. *Psychiatric Quarterly, 29*.

Hartmann, H. (1964). *Essays on ego psychology.* New York: International Universities Press.

Hartmann, H. (1958a). Contribution to the metapsychology of schizophrenia. *Psychoanalytic study of the child, 13,* 127–146.

Hartmann, H. (1958b). *Ego psychology and the problem of adaptation.* New York: International Universities Press.

Hartmann, H. (1945). Notes on the theory of aggression, *Psychoanalytic study of the child, 1,* 11–30.

Hartmann, H. (1934). Psychoanalysis and concept of health. *International Journal of Psychoanalysis, 20,* 307–318.

Hegel, G. (1984). *The letters.* Bloomington: Indiana University Press.

Heidegger, M. (1977). Letter on humanism. In David Krell (Ed.), *Basic writings.* New York: Harper and Row.

Heidegger, M. (1966). *Discourse on thinking.* New York: Harper and Row.

Hillman, J. (1978). *The myth of analysis.* New York: Harper and Row.

Holland, N. (1973). *Poems in persons: An introduction to the psychoanalysis of literature.* New York: Norton.

Hood, R. (1976). Conceptual criticism of regressive explanations of mysticism. *Review of Religious Research, 17,* 179–188.

Horney, K. (1966). *New ways in psychoanalysis.* New York: Norton.

Hunt, H. (1984). A cognitive psychology of mystical and altered-state experience. *Perceptual and Motor Skills, 58*(2), 467–513.

Hutchinson, E. (1949). *How to think creatively.* New York: Abingdon.

Hutchinson, E. (1943). The phenomenon of insight in relation to religion. *Psychiatry, 6,* 347–358.

Huxley, A. (1954). *The doors of perception.* New York: Harper and Row.

Huxley, A. (1965). *The devils of Loudon.* New York: Harper and Row.

Jacobson, E. (1964). *The self and the object world.* New York: International Universities Press.

James, W. (1961). *The varieties of religious experience.* New York: Macmillan.

John of the Cross, St. (1983). *The ascent of Mt. Carmel.* Kent: Burns and Oates.

John of the Cross, St. (1959). *Dark night of the soul.* New York: Doubleday.

Johnston, C. (1986). *The creative imperative.* Berkeley: Celestial Books.

Joseph, E. (1965). *Regressive ego phenomena in psychoanalysis.* New York: International Universities Press.

Jung, C. (1984). *The Portable Jung* (J. Campbell, Ed.). New York: Viking Press.

Jung, C. (1976). *The vision seminars.* Zurich: Spring Publications.

Jung, C. (1970). *Psychological reflections.* Princeton: Princeton University Press.

Jung, C. (1966). *The spirit in men, art and literature.* Princeton: Bollinger Foundation.

Jung, C. (1963). Mysterium. In *The Collected Works of C. G. Jung* Ed. by Herbert Read (Vol. 14, pp. 128–162). New York: Pantheon.

Jung, C. (1953a). *Psychology and alchemy.* Bollingen Series XX. New York: Pantheon Books.

Jung, C. (1953b). Two essays on analytic psychology. In *The Collected Works of C. G. Jung* (Vol. 7). Princeton: Princeton University Press.

Jung, C. (1938). *Psychology and religion.* New Haven: Yale University Press.

Jung, C. (1969). Psychological commentary on the Tibetan book of the dead. In *The Collected Works of C. G. Jung* Ed. by Herbert Read (Vol. 2, pp. 202–228). Princeton: Princeton University Press.

Kapleau, P. (1967). *The three pillars of Zen.* Boston: Beacon Press.

Kegan, R. (1982). *The emerging self.* Cambridge: Harvard University Press.

Kernberg, O. (1979). *Object relations theory and clinical psychoanalysis.* New York: Aronson.

Kernberg, O. (1970). *Borderline conditions and pathological narcissism.* New York: Aronson.

Kernberg, O. (1966). Structural derivatives of object relationships. *International Journal of Psychoanalysis, 47,* 236–253.

Klein, M. (1957). *Envy and gratitude.* New York: Basic Books.

Klein, M. (1937). *Love, hate and reparation.* London: Hogarth Press.

Koestler, A. (1964). *The act of creation.* New York: Macmillan.

Koestler, A. (1959). *The sleepwalkers.* New York: Macmillan.

Kohlberg, L. (1973). Aging. *Gerontology, 13,* 497–501.

Kohut, H. (1985). *Self psychology and the humanities.* New York: Norton.

Kohut, H. (1984). *How does analysis cure?* Chicago: University of Chicago Press.

Kohut, H. (1977). *The restoration of the self.* New York: International Universities Press.

Kohut, H. (1971). *The analysis of the self.* New York: International Universities Press.

Kraus, R. (1972). A psychoanalytic interpretation of shamanism. *Psychoanalytic Review, 59*(1), 19–32.

Kris, E. (1952). *Psychoanalytic exploration in art.* New York: International Universities Press.

Kubie, L. (1961). *Neurotic distortion of the creative process.* New York: Farrar Straus.

Kuk, A. I. (1951). *Lights of holiness.* Jerusalem: Rav Kuk Institute.

LaBarre, W. (1970). *The ghost dance.* New York: Dell.

Laing, R. D. (1967). *The politics of experience.* New York: Ballantine Books.

Lewis, C. S. (1975). *Surprised by joy.* London: Colliers.

Lifton, R. J. (1963). *Thought reform and the psychology of totalism.* New York: Norton.

Lilly, J. (1956). Mental effects of reduction of ordinary levels of physical stimuli on healthy persons. *Psychological Reports, 5,* 1–28.

Loewald, H. (1981). Regression: Some general considerations. *Psychoanalytic Quarterly, 50,* 22–43.

Loewald, H. (1980). *Papers on Psychoanalysis.* New Haven, Yale University Press.

Loewald, H. (1953). Psychoanalysis and modern views on human existence and religious experience. *Journal of Pastoral Care, 7,* 1–15.

Macleish, A. (1961). *Poetry and experience.* Boston: Beacon Press.

Mahler, M. (1979). *Selected papers* (2 vols.). New York: Aronson.

Mahler, M. (1975). *The psychological birth of the human infant.* New York: Basic Books.

Mahler, M. (1973). The experience of separation-individuation. *Journal of the American Psychoanalytic Association, 21,* 255.

Mahler, M. (1968). *On human symbiosis and the vicissitudes of individuation.* New York: International Universities Press.

Mahler, M. (1952). On childhood psychosis and schizophrenia. *Psychoanalytic Study of the Child, 7,* 286–305.

Maritain, J. (1966). *Creative intuition in art and poetry.* New York: Meridian Books.

Maritain, J. (1955). *The situation of poetry.* New York: Philosophical Press.

Marx, K., & Engels, F. (1964). *On religion.* New York: Schocken.

Maslow, A. (1971). *The further reaches of human nature.* New York: Viking Press.

Maslow, A. (1968). Health as transcendence of environment. *Pastoral Psychology, 19,* 45–49.

Maslow, A. (1967). The creative attitude, *Explorations in creativity* Ed. by R. Mooney. New York: Harper and Row.

Maslow, A. (1964). *Religion, values and peak-experiences.* New York: Viking.

Maslow, A. (1962). *Toward a psychology of being.* New York: Van Nostrand.

Maslow, A. (1959). Creativity in self-actualizing people, *Creativity and its cultivation* Ed. by H. Anderson. New York: Harper and Row.

Maslow, A. (1958). Emotional blocks to creativity. *Journal of Individual Psychology, 14,* 51–56.

Masterson, J. (1981). *From borderline adolescent to functioning adult.* New York: Bruner.

May, R. (1969). *Love and will.* New York: Norton.

May, R. (1965). Creativity and encounter. *The creative imagination* Ed. by H. M. Ruitenbeck. Chicago: Quadrangle Books.

McKellar, P. (1957). *Imagination and thinking.* New York: Basic Books.

Meng, H. (1963). *Psychoanalysis and faith.* New York: Basic Books.

Menninger, K. (1963). *The vital balance.* New York: Viking.

Menninger, K. (1958). *Theory of psychoanalytic technique.* New York: Basic Books.

Merton, T. (1981). *Thoughts in solitude* (Japanese ed.). In R. Daggy (Ed.), *Introductions East and West: The foreign prefaces of Thomas Merton.* Greensboro, NC: Unicorn Press.

Merton, T. (1973). *Contemplation in a world of action.* New York: Doubleday.

Merton, T. (1969). *Contemplative prayer.* New York: Imago.

Merton, T. (1968a). The spiritual father in the desert tradition. *Cistercian Studies, 3,* 3–23.

Merton, T. (1968b). *Conjectures of a guilty bystander.* New York: Doubleday.

Merton, T. (1960a). *Disputed questions.* New York: New American Library.

Merton, T. (1960b). *Spiritual direction and meditation.* Minn., Collegeville Press.

Merton, T. (1949). First Christmas at Gethsemani. *Catholic World, 170,* 28–34.

Milgram, S. (1974). *Obedience to authority.* New York: Harper.

Milner, M. (1969). *The hands of the living God.* New York: International Universities Press.

Milner, M. (1958). *Psychoanalysis and art.* In *Psychoanalysis and contemporary thought.* London: Hogarth Press.

Milner, M. (1955). The role of illusion in symbol formation. In M. Kleine (Ed.), *New directions in psychoanalysis.* London: Tavistock.

Milner, M. (1950). *On not being able to paint.* London: Heinemann.

Modell, A. (1984). *Psychoanalysis in a new context.* New York: International Universities Press.

Morgan, B. (1941). *Martha Graham.* New York: Pearce.

Murphy, M. (1989). *The physical and psychological effects of meditation.* Esalen: San Rafael.

Nakamura, H. (1964). *Ways of thinking of Eastern people*. Honolulu: University of Hawaii Press.

Neumann, E. (1989). *The place of creation*. Princeton: Princeton University Press.

Neumann, E. (1968). Mystical man. In J. Campbell (Ed.), *The mystic vision*. Princeton: Princeton University Press.

Neumann, E. (1959). *Art and the creative unconscious*. Princeton: Princeton University Press.

Neumann, E. (1954). *The origins and history of consciousness*. Bollingen Series LXII. Princeton: Princeton University Press.

Nietzsche, F. (1982). *Daybreak*. Cambridge: Cambridge University Press.

Nietzsche, F. (1967). *The will to power*. New York: Random House.

Nietzsche, F. (1954). Thus spake Zarathustra. In W. Kaufman (Ed.), *The portable Nietzsche* pp. 18–108. New York: Viking Press.

Ornstein, R. (1977). *The psychology of consciousness*. New York: Harcourt.

Pahnke, W. (1970). Implications of LSD and experimental mysticism. *Journal of Psychedelic Drugs, 3*, 92–108.

Perry, J. (1976). *The roots of renewal in myth and madness*. San Francisco: Jossey-Bass.

Phillips, D. (1977). *The choice is always ours*. Chicago: Re-Quest Books.

Poincaré, H. (1952). Mathematical creation. In B. Ghiselin (Ed.), *The creative process*. New York: Harper and Row.

Prince, R. (1979). Religious experience and psychosis. *Journal of Altered States of Consciousness, 5,* 167–181.

Prince, R. (1966). Mystical states and the concept of regression. *Psychedelic Review, 8,* 59–75.

Rank, O. (1932). *Art and artist.* New York: Knopf.

Rapaport, D. (1967). *The collected works of David Rapaport.* New York: Basic Books.

Rapaport, D. (1958). The theory of ego autonomy. *Bulletin of Menninger Clinic, 22,* 13–35.

Read, H. (1967). *Art and alienation.* London: Camelot Press.

Rhodes, M. (1961). *An analysis of creativity. Phi Delta Kappan, 42*(7), 305–310.

Roethke, T. (1966). *The collected poems.* New York: Doubleday.

Rogers, C. (1964). Toward a modern approach to values. *The Journal of Abnormal and Social Psychology, 68*(2), 160–167.

Rogers, C. (1961). *On becoming a person.* Boston: Houghton Mifflin.

Rokeach, M. (1964). *The three Christs of Ypsalanti.* New York: Knopf.

Rose, G. (1972). Fusion states. In P. Giovacchini (Ed.), *Tactics and techniques in psychoanalytic therapy,* pp. 68–80. New York: Science House.

Rothenberg, A. (1979). *The emerging goddess: The creative process.* Chicago: University of Chicago Press.

Russel, B. (1957). *Why I am not a Christian.* New York: Simon & Schuster.

Sartre, J. (1957). *The transcendence of the ego.* New York: Noonday.

Schachtel, E. (1959). *Metamorphosis.* New York: Basic Books.

Schafer, R. (1968). *Aspects of internalization.* New York: International Universities Press.

Schafer, R. (1958). Regression in the service of the ego. In G. Linzey (Ed.), *Assessment of human motives,* pp. 224–246. New York: Rinehart.

Searles, H. (1979). *Countertransference.* New York: International Universities Press.

Searles, H. (1960). *The non-human environment.* New York: International Universities Press.

Searles, H. (1951). *Collected papers on schizophrenia and related subjects.* New York: International Universities Press.

Segal, A. (1952). Psychoanalytic approaches to the aesthetic. *International Journal of Psychoanalysis, 32,* 196–207.

Shattuck, R. (1963). *Proust's binoculars.* New York: Random.

Silverman, J. (1979). Shamans and acute schizophrenia. In D. Coleman (Ed.), *Consciousness,* pp. 184–198. New York: Harper and Row.

Silverman, L. H. (1982). *The search for oneness.* New York: International Universities Press.

Stern, D. (1985). *The interpersonal world of the infant.* New York: Basic Books.

Stierlin, H. (1976). Liberation and self-destruction in the creative process. *Psychiatry and the Humanities, 1,* 51–72.

Stravinsky, I. (1962). *An autobiography.* New York: Norton.

Streiker, L. (1984). *The gospel time bomb.* Buffalo: Prometheus Books.

Sullivan, H. (1953). *The interpersonal theory of psychiatry.* New York: Norton.

Suzuki, D. T. (1965). *Training of the Zen Buddhist monk.* New York: University Books.

Suzuki, D. T. (1960). The koan. In N. Ross (Ed.), *The World of Zen.* New York: Random.

Teresa of Avila, St. (1957). *The life of St. Teresa of Avila, by herself* (J. M. Cohen, Trans.). London: Penguin Books.

Teresa of Jesus. (1944). *Complete works* (E. A. Peers, Trans.). New York: Sheed and Ward.

Tillich, P. (1952). *The courage to be.* New Haven: Yale University Press.

Torrance, E. (1968). *The Minnesota studies of creative behavior.* Minneapolis: Graduate Research Fund.

Underhill, E. (1919). *Practical mysticism.* New York: Dutton.

Underhill, E. (1911). *Mysticism.* London: Methuen.

Upanishads. (1926). (F. Mueller, Trans.). Oxford: Oxford University Press.

Van Gogh, V. (1958). *The complete letters of Vincent Van Gogh.* New York: Little and Brown.

Weber, M. (1958). Science as a vocation. In H. Gerth (Ed.), *From Max Weber: Essays in sociology.* New York: Oxford University Press.

Weil, S. (1952). *Gravity and grace.* New York: Putnam.

Wells, F. L. (1935). Social maladjustments: Adaptive regressions. In C. Murchison (Ed.), *A handbook of social psychology*. Worcester: Clark University Press.

Wild, C. (1965). Creativity and adaptive regression. *Journal of Personality and Social Psychology*, 2(2), 161–169.

Winnicott, D. W. (1989). The concept of clinical regression compared with that of defense organization. In Clara Winnicott (Ed.), *Psychoanalytic exploration* (pp. 193–199). Cambridge: Harvard University Press.

Winnicott, D. W. (1971). *Playing and reality*. New York: Basic Books.

Winnicott, D. W. (1965). *The maturational processes and the facilitating environment*. London: Hogarth.

Winnicott, D. W. (1958). The capacity to be alone. *International Journal of Psychoanalysis*, 39, 416–420.

Winnicott, D. W. (1955). Metapsychological and clinical aspects of regression. *International Journal of Psychoanalysis*, 36, 16–26.

Wittgenstein, L. (1953). *Philosophical investigations*. New York: Macmillian.

Yeats, W. (1966). *The collected poems of William Yeats*. New York: Macmillian.

Zaehner, R. C. (1961). *Mysticism sacred and profane*. New York: Oxford University Press.

Zimmer, H. (1951). *Philosophies of India*. Princeton: Princeton University Press.

Notes

INTRODUCTION

1. In order to avoid sexist or noninclusive language, the pronouns *he* and *she* will be used in alternate chapters.

1. REGRESSION AND RELIGIOUS EXPERIENCE

1. While this work respects the difference of opinions among historians and theologians over whether the Buddhist's Nirvana or the Whirling Dervish's ecstasy is the same as the Christian's experience of communion with God, its focus is the psychological process that takes place in any experience—religious or secular, Buddhist or Christian—in which an individual surrenders a separate sense of self and submerges in an oceanic experience.

2. While I use the insights from Freud's three categories of regression in this analysis of religious experience, the explicit categories will not be used. Instead, regression in religious experience will be defined in categories more closely aligned with the stages of religious experience in which the regression takes place. Hence instead of formal and topographical regression, "dying to self" will be ego regression; reactivation of primary process and raw instincts, represented in visions and euphoria, will be instinctual regression; and unitive experience will be symbiotic regression.

2. EGO REGRESSION AND PURGATION

1. The word *islam* means submission, and the capital *I* in *Islam* is submission to Allah.

2. Self-chastisement can be for wishes or impulses themselves and not only for having acted on them, for they give rise to guilt feelings almost as strong as those produced by the actual sexual or aggressive behavior.

3. The resulting pain is masochistic when it elicits perverse pleasure, as

when physical pain pleasurably silences psychological pain. The pleasurable pain thereby becomes a sought-after goal in itself, rather than the liberation from constraints sought by the ascetical acts.

4. "The monk must make known to his elders every step he takes and every drop of water he drinks, to see if he is not doing wrong" (St. Anthony, quoted in Merton, 1968).

5. Social psychologist Conway called it "snapping," the alteration of cognitive processes that "severely affect the brain's ability to process information and may result in impaired awareness, irrationality, disorientation" (1978, p. 135).

6. The opposite is also true with the overstimulation of senses, which can result in a hyperexcited state.

7. The emphasis on purgation of self in order to experience God or the "Christ within" places so much attention on the self that the self ironically takes on a vitality of its own. "If the inner dispositions are right, we ask, what need of all the torment, this violation of the outer nature? It keeps the outer nature too important" (James, 1961, p. 131).

3. INSTINCTUAL REGRESSION AND RELIGIOUS EXPERIENCE

1. Rapaport expressed the corollary when he continued, "And since drives are the ultimate guarantees of autonomy from the environment, an excessive autonomy from the id must impair the autonomy from the environment" (1958, p. 18). A personal expression of drives manifests an individual's uniqueness. Too much autonomy toward or control over drives, diminishes the uniqueness of the person and has serious repercussions on her functioning as a unique person in society. Celibacy, as we will see, becomes an act of excessive autonomy from instincts and subsequently impairs personal relationships.

2. "Condensation" is the characteristic of primary process in which "the intensity of a whole train of thought is concentrated in a single ideational element" that does not represent the same space or time (Freud, 1911b, p. 195). God is that single ideational element in which the instinctual gratification that took place in the earlier space and time of an infantile relationship with mother is intensely concentrated.

3. William James suggested that ineffability is the most obvious of the four salient characteristics of mysticism (1961, p. 356).

4. The adult who attempts to communicate the experience often is reduced to the incoherent babbling of infancy, as in glossolalia or speaking in tongues.

5. A similar event can be found in the regression that takes place in group processes. "One of the gratifications which appears to be the common denominator among group activities seems to be the longing for regression to the time when words were not necessary for communication, where all experience was intimate, all activity play, and where delay of impulse discharge was not necessary" (Gordon, 1970, p. 166).

6. It is also indicative of the extant ego's continued attempt to cling to illusory control, and thereby perpetuate *samsara* or the cycle of bondage to this life.

7. As previously mentioned, nutritional deficiency and sleep deprivation can induce similar feelings of euphoria.

8. Sexual passion does not have to be acted on to elicit these anxious feelings—only thought about, or unconsciously aroused.

9. Later, drives will be bound by an ego that forms in part to manage frustration and to balance needs with expectations of reality. The child thereby will be able to tolerate the absence of need-gratifying objects, and, learning that reality is not always pleasurable, will be able to delay gratification of needs. Secondary functions develop as a result. Through thinking about experiences that bring pleasure, the child stores thoughts in her memory and, subsequently learning how to act on them, recreates on her own the actions that gratify needs (for example, feeding herself by imitating the mother's actions).

10. The hallucinated breast can even become more pleasing than the real breast. The physical breast is not always immediately available. The hallucinated breast—the recall of the pleasurable memories of being nurtured—is an image that is perfectly and immediately available (though it satisfies for only a short while, until the hunger reasserts itself).

11. Freud called visions "regressions" because they arise in a move "from the region of thought-structure to that of sensory perception," and "in the process thoughts are transformed into images" (Freud, 1905, p. 16; 1917, p. 227).

4. SYMBIOTIC REGRESSION: THE EXPERIENCE OF UNITY

1. Freud was not wrong when he found hidden hostility toward the oedipal father expressed in religious experience. The encounter with the divine involves various superego issues *but* when it is characterized by intense feelings of mystical oneness then that encounter involves developmental issues that precede the oedipal drama. Sexual feelings elicited in religious experience, for example, might be competitive genital feelings that arise out of the oedipal conflict. Yet when they express a sense of unity with

God, they represent pregenital sexual feelings of an earlier pervasively gratifying relationship with the mother.

2. Freud reserved his most critical analysis of religious experience to
describe the regressive restoration of the unitive state that preceded even
the earliest moments of symbiotic unity. He coined the phrase "nirvana
principle"—presumably appropriated from his perception of the nirvanic
oceanic experience—to describe the regressive return to the most primitive
of all states: nonexistence. The nirvana principle refers to the need to reduce all stimuli and action so as eventually to return to the anxiety-free state
of nothingness. Buddhism even calls Nirvana the experience of nothingness
or emptiness. Freud applied this idea to his controversial theory of the death
wish: the longing for the anxiety-free state that preceded life (thanatos).
People possess a life instinct (eros) yet the hunger for life makes them
anxiously aware of the many ways in which life can deprive them of the
gratification of this instinct. In response to the anxieties of life, people
experience an urge to return to an earlier state that is without tension and
anxiety. Hence the nirvanic experience of nothingness or selfless merger
into God are expressions of the unconscious longing for the passive death-
like state that escapes the inherent risks and responsibilities of life.

3. The psychologist Stern (1985) has questioned some of Mahler's ideas
concerning symbiosis. Through empirical studies (e.g., watching infants'
eye movements), Stern concluded that at an early age infants possess some
sense of differentiation between self and mother. He suggested that separation is inherent in the infant and awaits interaction with others, especially
with the mother, to develop. This is probably true but the separation, as well
as the resulting sense of self, still emerge out of a sense of unity—as imperfect as it might be—between infant and need-gratifying mother. So too the
adult unitive experience, which regressively restores this symbiotic state, is
not a perfect paradise in which absolutely no separation exists, but it does
revive the feelings of tranquillity, passivity, and unity that made the infant
feel symbiotically attached to the mother and that also defended against the
anxiety of separation. Hence symbiotic unity still seems the most incisive
way to describe unitive oceanic experience and the archaic infant-maternal
matrix it restores, although Kohut's "self-object" (1971) and the dual unity
of attachment theory (Bowlby, 1978) are not without merit, nor are Stern's
caveats ignored.

4. Freud would have agreed: "If we may assume that there are many
people in whose mental life the primary ego-feeling [oceanic] has persisted
to a greater or lesser degree, it would exist in them side by side with the
narrower and more sharply demarcated ego feeling of maturity" (Freud,
1960, p. 68).

5. Margaret Mahler concluded that the symbiotic state that occupied so

much of her research was the same as that referred to by Freud and Rolland when they "discussed in their dialogue the sense of boundlessness of the oceanic feeling" (1975, p. 44).

6. The submersion of self into a unitive state does not always involve God. It can be found in cultural images that express the longing for utopia, paradise, the Golden Age, or Shangri-la.

Knowest thou the land where the lemon blossoms into flower
Oranges glow like gold in a dark and leafy bower?
Where marble statues stand and at them silently gaze?
Why, poor child, tears are streaming down thy face!
(Goethe, quoted in Fodor, 1949, p. 209)

7. The euphoria that results is no longer the earlier described euphoria that derives from surrendering ego responsibility and indulging primitive instincts, but the euphoria of submersion into paradisiacal symbiotic unity.

8. Meditation is another example of a spiritual discipline in which suspension of ego functioning leads to a regressive indulgence in fantasy, out of which unsuspecting anxiety arises (to be discussed in more detail later). While not a state of sleep, meditation is comparable to sleep in that it involves a psycho/physiological slowing of metabolism or respiration, which can awaken anxiety, usually in the form of dreams or via meditation in the form of disturbing visions and free-floating anxiety that normally is kept quiet under the daytime activities of the ego.

9. Helplessness begins blissfully, as when the adult sacrifices ego functions that made him anxious and becomes reliant on God. But the regressive return to helplessness is double-edged. The infant originally felt blissfully helpless in the protective arms of mother—only to have the bliss broken when feelings of helplessness made him aware of the dreaded possibility of being dropped. The purgative loss of ego control and descent into a helpless reliance on God creates similar blissful feelings until the helplessness makes the individual dreadfully aware that he too might be dropped, abandoned in the abyss of nothingness.

10. Repetition of earlier attempts does provide some gratification. Freud called this action of the ego the "repetition compulsion," a regressive attempt to overcome frustration by repeating primitive means of dealing with it.

11. So too libidinal drives will be neutralized with aggression, a process that makes libidinal bonds less clinging and more an expression of intimacy and connectedness. This will be examined in a later chapter.

12. A person does not actually have to act on his aggressive instincts for them to destroy paradise; that is what makes them so dangerous. The individual has regressed in the unitive state to a primitive psychological structure that experiences the wish for gratification and the gratification of wish

as the same. Hence when the infant feels angry at the mother or, later, the child thinks hostile thoughts toward her for frustrating his needs ("I could kill her"), he becomes frightened—as if the aggressive thoughts were the same as deeds. A person with healthy ego boundaries experiences anger toward another but knows the anger that produces an urge to "kill" will not do so because psychological boundaries separate him—i.e., his wishes, feelings, thoughts, etc.—from the other. The person who renounces ego boundaries, on the other hand, and in the regressed state of communion with God encounters a resurgence of aggression, experiences anger toward God but, because the unitive state does not clearly distinguish between inner and outer, the intense wish to strike out at God is presumed to be felt as much by God as by himself. God knows the thoughts of the person even before he voices them; hence even the thought of anger threatens to destroy unity.

13. Passivity, as mentioned earlier, is one of the salient characteristics of mystical experience (James, 1961).

14. The philosopher Bertrand Russell's conversion to pacifism, for example, can probably be traced to unresolved maternal abandonment anxiety and the undoing of the aggression that in adulthood could reveal this underlying fear, and not to unresolved oedipal conflicts. Unresolved oedipal conflicts, however, certainly play a part in the experience, since they most likely become prominent as a result of earlier developmental issues with the mother that were not favorably settled (see Gottschalk, 1965). And although Gandhi's rejection of violence, embodied in his philosophy of *satyagraha,* derived in part from his early relationship with his father, much of it can probably be traced to pre-oedipal and oral issues; for example, the nonaggression of not talking (vow of silence), not eating (fasting), and his fear of losing the love of the British while rebelling against them (separation anxiety).

15. The psychoanalyst Searles suggested the experience of "oneness" with others is a defense against the hostility people actually feel toward them for the dependent feelings elicited in the relationship (1951, p. 132). So too the experience of unity with God defends in part against the hidden anger surrounding feelings of dependency on the all-good God.

16. Projection of aggression onto various groups or individuals does not imply they are not aggressive. Projection often has some basis in reality. What is significant for the purposes of analyzing projection is that the entity onto which aggression is projected is perceived as being aggressive at least in part because of the qualities projected out of self and onto it.

17. Other out-groups onto which a person projects aggression or hostility can be minorities, persons of the opposite sex, nonbelievers or foreigners.

18. Rationalization of aggression is necessary since the person is suppos-

edly free of all aggression. By distancing himself from the enemy by deper-
sonalizing and voiding him of any aspects of the all-good, he creates an
enemy so unlike himself that it lacks any human identity.

19. The person can defend himself against projected threats through less
direct though equally effective passive/aggressive behavior. For instance, a
male might project the aggression he associates with sexuality onto
women's sexuality, causing the "later conceptualization of all sexual relations as dangerous and infiltrated by aggression" (Kernberg, 1979, p. 60).
He then becomes celibate in the purgative stage of religious experience,
making his sexuality passive—a passivity, however, that indirectly expresses his hostility toward women and that defends him both against the
projected "dangerous" sexuality of women and against his own inner susceptibility to temptation. (See the earlier discussion on St. Anthony of the
Desert's vision of women, or consider Gandhi's passive/aggressive celibate
act of sleeping with "beautiful" women.)

20. The person preaches with such aggressive force because, in part, his
aggression is unneutralized.

21. The contentment he experiences in the unitive state is not an inner
security that makes a person calm in the midst of difficulties, but a calm that
is the absence of conflict.

5. REGRESSION AND ADAPTATION

1. Maslow (1971) went a step further, suggesting that growth not only
does not always arise out of conflict but that it can arise out of higher needs,
such as the need for truth or beauty.

2. Different terms have been applied to the stages of creativity, some
stretching out the process and others condensing it. Henri Poincaré's
(1952) is probably the most famous: investigation, impasse, illumination,
and verification. Incubation is also a critically important aspect of creativity.
The psychologist Torrance, who contributed significant research in the
study of creativity, summarized: "I have chosen to define creativity as a
process whereby one becomes aware of problems, difficulties . . . for which
he has no learned solution; searching for clues in the situation and in exist-
ing knowledge; formulating hypotheses or possible alternative solutions;
testing those hypotheses, modifying and retesting them; and communicating the result" (1968, p. 10).

3. Other psychologists have referred to this stage by different labels.
Kubie (1961) called it the "intelligo" phase of creativity, that which takes
the preconscious material that spontaneously irrupted into awareness ("cogito" phase) and deliberately fashions it so as to make it meaningful. McKellar (1957) called it the transformation of "A" thinking (autistic creativity)

into "R" thinking (reality-oriented). Rapaport suggested that elaboration gives structure and "relationship" to amorphous primary process, "turning the idiosyncratic 'inventive' product of the individual into the social communication of art or science" (1967, p. 720).

4. Kris (1952) referred to several factors in addition to elaboration that prevent recovered primary process from succumbing to the vagaries of pathological regression: Creative regressions are temporary and purposeful (p. 253). They are also voluntary, so that if too much anxiety arises, the person can stop the regression and reverse it rather than be "driven crazy" by unmanageable inner drives or fears. Kris also suggested that regression is only partial; that is, it does not affect the entire personality. An individual regresses to early infantile needs but does not become an infant (losing bodily functions, for example).

5. To demonstrate how this takes place, psychological theories other than those of Kris will be included in the analysis of regression in religious experience. For example, Erikson's suggestion that healthy regression evokes early childhood experiences of basic trust will be examined, as will Winnicott's description of how regressively restored unconscious processes can become "the resting state out of which a creative reaching out can take place" (1971, p. 55).

6. ADAPTATION IN EGO-REGRESSIVE "DYING TO SELF"

1. Boys and girls both learn to separate from the mother and to form distinct autonomous identities. Girls, especially in a male-dominated society, tend to retain more of these early attachment feelings than do boys, but they too learn to repress primary process, and in the push to replace the fantastical and irrational with the practical and logical they too become alienated from a rich inner world of imagination and creativity.

2. Note Carol Gilligan's (1982) assessment of Kohlberg's moral stages as overemphasizing agentic authority and allowing no room for attachment or care.

3. R. D. Laing called the false self the "egoic self" (1967, p. 70); Jung gave it the more familiar label "persona" and suggested that it was "designed on one hand to make a definite impression upon others, and on the other hand to conceal the true nature of the individual" (1953b, p. 190).

4. From a philosophical perspective, what once was the "lumen naturale" or natural light of inner human essence is dimmed if not completely darkened by the light of reason. The latter lifts the child out of the darkness of the unconscious and into the light of consciousness but, by shining the light exclusively on reason and control, the child eventually forgets wonderment and openness. Heidegger (1966) referred to losing the "core" of

Being when openness to object is replaced with desire for object. Where once the child was open and responsive to perceptions, he is socialized to analyze, to control, to make effective use of and hence to possess perceptions. His desire for objects causes him to lose his ability to respond to what he perceives in a nonmanipulative way. In the process he might become proficient at mastering all that he perceives but he forfeits being moved by and open to it (as well as being open to his own inner essence or "the dimensionality which Being is"), and thereby lives according to a narrowed or restricted vision (Heidegger, 1977, p. 213). "The Ego steals its light from the lumen naturale, and the Ego expands, not at the expense of primordial darkness . . . but at the cost of childhood's godlike, dimmed light of wonder" (Hillman, 1978, p. 45).

5. Maslow labeled the disciplined experience "voluntary surrender" (1958, p. 80); artist/psychoanalyst Milner called it "creative surrender" (1955); Kris described it a purposive regression aimed at getting rid of a rigid ego rather than something done out of weakness (1959, p. 251); and the psychoanalyst/art critic Ehrenzweig labeled it "surrender of ego" or more forcefully "heroic self-surrender of the creative mind" (1953, p. 123; 1967, p. 121).

6. The sociologist Max Weber recognized the importance of religious experience for maintaining the proper perspective on what is alienating and what is meaningful: "It is the fate of our times, with its characteristic rationalization and intellectualization, and above all disenchantment, that precisely the ultimate, most sublime values have withdrawn from public life either into the transcendental realm of mysticism or the brotherliness of direct personal relationships" (1958, p. 115).

7. The Church Father John Chrysostom suggested religious individuals' discipline should be practiced like that of athletes, "exercising themselves everyday in the palestra under a master and ruler."

8. Kris (1952) suggested that voluntary surrender of self in creativity is a salient factor in making the experience a regression in the service of the ego. So too the voluntary aspect of a person's surrendering resistance to a teacher (or to a therapist) is what distinguishes it from the experience in which a person's surrendering resistance is due to coercion or brainwashing.

9. A similar phenomenon takes place in art, referred to as *horrum vacuui*, whereby the artist meticulously fills in every space of a painting. So too is fasting a regression, a denial of basic needs, but can also be a disciplined means to overcome an oral compulsion to fill oneself.

10. Perhaps one reason for the criticism of cults is that their general practice of nonmaterialism and living according to a simpler life-style seems like an indictment of society's superfluous and superficial pursuits.

11. Jung even described the artist's experience as a "drastic purgation"

(1966, p. 119), and Berdyaev suggested that the artist "must give up the quiet havens of life, must renounce the building of his own house, the safe and assured ordering of his own personality.... The creative way of genius demands sacrifice ... no less sacrifice than that demanded by the way of sainthood" (1962, p. 161).

7. ILLUMINATION AND ADAPTIVE REGRESSION IN THE SERVICE OF THE EGO

1. Milner (1950) wrote of how she intentionally forfeited linear styles of painting in order to expose herself to this less ordered and more open psychological realm.

2. Intuitive apprehension of the experience often involves the regressive absorption of self into the timelessness of that experience. But this loss of self and of a sense of time evokes the immediacy of unconscious processes that can be creative, just as the artist's descent into the primary process timelessness of her inspirational absorption (Neumann, 1959, p. 150). As William Blake wrote:

To see the world in a grain of sand
And heaven in a wild flower,
Hold infinity in the palm of your hand
And eternity in an hour.

3. Jung (1966) and Koestler (1964) suggested that creativity comes from the tension between these two.

4. Hallucinations disappear after providing comfort in other areas of loss, such as in the death of loved ones. People sometimes "see" the departed person; this vision represents unfinished mourning, a longing for (and clinging to) a lost object that takes visual form. Hallucination of the dead is a way of resisting returning to reality, of denying the finality of loss. But hallucination can help the person by providing comfort, and even being a guide, telling the person how to do things in order to get through the crisis and get on with life. The Emmaus disciples' encounter of Jesus is such a hallucination. The source of their inspiration and even identification is dead, and seeing him is a hallucinatory clinging to that which they cannot let go. But after the image of Jesus comforts them, reassuring them of the meaning in their lives, it disappears and they renew their lives.

8. REGRESSIVE RESTORATION AND REPARATION OF SYMBIOTIC UNITY

1. "This piece of mysticism is innate in all better men as the 'longing for the mother', the nostalgia for the source from which we come" (Jung, 1977, p. 119).

2. Melanie Klein (1937) said art was the reparative recovery of oneness with the "lost libidinal object." Erich Fromm wrote about attaining union through "creative activity, be it that of the artist, or the artisan. In any kind of creative work the creating person unites himself with his material" (1956, p. 14).

3. Underhill suggested that the mystic's experience of the oneness of "seer and seen" is "the essential action of the artist" (1919, p. 26).

4. The psychoanalyst Deikmann's studies on meditation (1966) demonstrate this phenomenon. He showed how people's focused attention on an object caused a deautomatization of the cognitive structures that analyze objects. They abandoned normative observation, allowing themselves and the object to lose distinctiveness as they merged in an immediacy of perception not subject to automatized perception.

5. Beneficial escape from stress even can include the denial of reality, as in the case of patients whose denial of the seriousness of their operations makes them more optimistic and subsequently able to heal faster.

6. Of course the person who performs better on the exam might attribute it to the efficacy of prayer. He will not think to give credit to the stress-reducing effect of prayer's autohypnosis. But it is also possible that his better grade induces more confidence in himself. Having mastered the test, he might recognize and appreciate his own contribution to doing well and so might feel less insecure—with or without prayer—the next time he encounters a test.

7. He might choose to stay within the community, but the choice will now be based on realistic strengths and not on childish escapist urges or the manipulation some religious organizations employ to make candidates for the religious life stay.

8. Even Freud acknowledged that although passivity is a defense against aggression it is a defense that can lead to greater goals, as he discovered in his study of Michelangelo when he observed that Michelangelo depicted not the rage of Moses in destroying the tablets of stone but a man who was sublimely calm: "The giant frame with its tremendous physical power becomes only a concrete expression of the highest mental achievement that is possible in a man, that of struggling successfully against an inward passion for the sake of a cause to which he has devoted himself" (1939, p. 233).

9. Waiting of this type, however, is not an expression of laziness. It is the waiting of the bridegroom whom Jesus told to wait vigilantly for the arrival of the bride. It is an attentive waiting, much as the musician who abandons regular discipline in becoming more receptive to what "moves" him does so by virtue of having first developed the discipline to be attentive to the inspirational. "These efforts then have not been as sterile as one thinks; they have set going the unconscious machine and without them it

would not have moved and would have produced nothing." (Poincaré, 1952, p. 38).

10. The length of the waiting period before incubational unconscious processes become inspirational or illuminative varies from person to person. For the unconscious to reveal its "truths," to illuminate its or God's mysteries, certain depths that are relative to each individual have to be plumbed. They are relative to the tenacity with which a person resists illuminating those depths, as well as to the extent to which communion feelings and primary processes have been repressed. Coleridge's "Kubla Khan," for instance, came to him in a short reverie, while many of Yeats's inspirations came to him in a "flash." Nietzsche's *Thus Spake Zarathustra*, on the other hand, took eighteen months of gestation. Regressive waiting for divine illumination can be of a relatively short duration, as when St. Paul was blinded for three days by his Damascus encounter, or can require a long time as signified by the number forty to describe Jesus' days in the desert or Moses' sojourn in the wilderness. It can also take a lifetime of discipline and patience, as in the case of a monk who lives in a monastery.

11. Although he is not allowed to help the actual inspirational process, he later must act on it; this will be discussed in the last chapter.

12. The Prodigal Son, after having rejected the false self and indulged repressed longings and instincts, finally "comes to himself." The Ancient Mariner, who became alienated from himself and left his home (with a departing view of its "light house top and hill and kirk") finally finds himself in his return "home."

Oh! dreams of joy! is this indeed
The light house top I see
Is this the hill? Is this the kirk?
Is this mine own countree?

13. Hence while the splitting off of the aggressive image of God is a defense against the dreaded dark night, it is an adaptive defense that allows the "good internal object" to be resurrected and so to find the support that could not be found without it. "Man continues to create and recreate God as a place to put what is good in himself, and which he might spoil if he kept it in himself along with all the hate and destructiveness which is also to be found there" (Winnicott, 1965, p. 95).

14. Neumann (1968) called the latter type of religious experience "urobic mysticism."

15. From this perspective, the Christian concepts of purgatory and heaven, or the Eastern belief in the samsaric cycle of birth and death and rebirth, represent the regressive wish to be free of a separate self and to return to paradise. This can be a regressive wish to return to symbiosis because the original symbiosis had its creative potential devalued and the

wish to return to it is the wish to repair that developmental flaw (and so to be free of the emptiness its failure to develop forged—i.e., the false self).

16. Freud first thought that transference of childhood feelings out of the unconscious and onto the therapist hindered therapy. It was a regressive resistance to dealing directly with issues. He later realized that by projecting onto the therapist the authority, benevolence, trust, and admiration that had been given to parents in childhood, the patient was able to bring to therapy the unconscious feelings and unfulfilled needs that had to be recovered if psychological growth was to take place. Hence transference, and the analysis of the person's resistance to it, became one of the salient factors—"the most powerful ally"—in therapeutic treatment (1905, p. 117).

17. The self-object is the maternal image that is experienced by the infant as part of the infant's own self. Through what Kohut labeled "pathognomonic regression" (1984, p. 196), the adult therapeutically diminishes the ego control that resists transference and experiences the therapist as part of himself (self-object). He merges with the therapist, who represents the parental images and the unconscious childhood wishes projected onto him (mirroring transference), and, via the diffusion of psychological boundaries, partakes in the idealized strengths of the therapist (idealizing transference).

18. So too the psychologist Silverman's research on the therapeutic effect of the subliminal message "Mommy and I are one" revealed that the symbiotic message creates a safe therapeutic environment in which a person once again feels secure expressing repressed longings and fears (Silverman, 1982).

19. Freud suggested that Jesus' ability to accept people with their faults and especially to forgive their sins would require "a call for unlimited transference" (quoted in Meng, 1963, p. 126).

20. Those who observe his art might experience a similar evocation within themselves of the forbidden impulses or conflicts that are expressed in that work. The experience is most notable in theater, where a safe environment is created in which people can experience—without punishment or guilt—the resurgence of their own hidden impulses in response to observing the same impulses being acted out on the stage.

21. Maslow said that clarity of perception is a salient characteristic of the self-actualizing person (1976, p. 253).

22. Of course Merton probably could not have had this realization of the spurious isolation of the monastery without first having experienced in the holding environment of that monastery the safety to acknowledge the fears from which it offered him isolation.

23. Freud discovered this truth in his early experiments with hypnosis (1955a, p. 446). He originally used hypnosis to induce an artificial transference. It allowed a person temporarily to surrender defenses and return to

unconscious structures. But when hypnosis was concluded, Freud soon realized, restored unconscious conflicts were not consciously reexperienced and resolved. At best they provided insights into the person's unconscious, and often made a person dependent on the suggestive powers of hypnosis to maintain positive transference feelings. To effect real change, the transference relationship not only had to gain insight into unconscious conflicts but then had to lead to those unconscious conflicts' being reexperienced so as to provide the opportunity for their confrontation and resolution.

24. The disciplined practices of Christian mysticism also attempt to atone for and to confront, mythically, the pain of original sin, and psychologically, the anger or anxiety of the original trauma of separating from maternal paradise.

25. Of course the individual who no longer feels terrified because of God's walking with him might not confront his fears and instead either continue clinging to God and thereby never experience anxiety, or always rely on God to avoid the next stressful situation. "O Lord, I know that the way of man is not in himself; it is not in man that walks to direct his steps" (Jer 10:27).

9. ELABORATION OF RELIGIOUS EXPERIENCE

1. Other psychologists refer to the elaboration stage differently. Kubie (1961), for example, called it the intelligo phase of creativity that emerges out of the preconscious cogito, while McKellar (1957) described it as autistic "A" thinking that lies beneath reality oriented "R" thinking.

2. Klein (1937) labeled the infant's separating from mother the "depressive position" because the reality it introduced left the infant forlorn without the omnipotence of nondifferentiated maternal attachment. The infant discovers the "other" is not self and that she can be abandoned. The adult similarly is depressed over leaving the unitive experience not only because of the return to realistic limitations but because God is then experienced as not being self and so too can abandon or reject her.

3. "Even normally, the vanishing belief in his omnipotence will teach the child to prefer security to pleasure and therefore to accept a strong love object that gives him security" (Jacobson, 1964, p. 103).

4. The length of stay before the point in which the infant's symbiotic attachment becomes unhealthy is generally around eight to ten months. The length of stay in the regressive return to this early unitive state, whether in religious experience or in creativity, before it becomes pathological, varies (see the earlier discussion on incubation). A general rule might be that the

regressive stay should be no longer than necessary to repair the basic fault
and to allow unconscious processes to incubate.

5. Even the depression that often sets in when "walking" on one's own
separates the person from unity can facilitate the healthy emergence out of
unity. The depression an infant initially experiences when her fledgling
separateness makes her aware of the demise of symbiosis begins the process
of mourning the loss of the mother's perfection and subsequently of letting
go of the need to idealize her ("depressive position"—Klein, 1937). Letting
go of the idealized mother is at first depressing but the child who feels safe
enough to let go "becomes aware of mother's absence without omnipotent
possession" (Klein, 1937, p. 39). So too the religious individual lets go of
the regressed unitive state that represents the idealized mother in order to
mourn the loss of the idealized object and so to see it, and life in general,
without the omnipotent possessiveness that had defensively defined that
relationship (such as the pervasive tranquillity of the boddhi tree or the
magical powers of the desert). If the mystic does not let go of the unitive
state, just as if the infant does not let go of mother and the artist of the
inspiration, creativity or output will not be forthcoming. The disciples
would have remained stuck in the upper room, melancholically attached to
an image of Jesus rather than letting go of that image and being inspired to
do something creative with it.

6. In a similar way artists recreate their lost love object and keep it alive
on a canvas. Note the similarity of the psychoanalyst Segal's description of
creativity to that of the above-mentioned experience of the Emmaus disciples: "Creativity is really a recreation of a once loved and once whole, but
now lost and ruined object, a ruined internal world and self. It is when the
world within us is destroyed, when it is dead and loveless, when our loved
ones are in fragments, and when we ourselves are in helpless despair . . . it is
then that we must recreate our world anew, reassemble the pieces, infuse
life into dead fragments, recreate life" (1952, p. 199).

7. Maslow labeled this type of experience the Jonah syndrome, whereby
the individual is exposed to the inner "fear of being torn apart, of losing
control, of being shattered and disintegrated, even of being killed by the
experience" (1967, p. 163). R. D. Laing more graphically described its
recovered unconscious state with the image of "body half-dead, genitals
dissociated from heart, heart severed from head" (1967, p. 55).

8. Dying to self can also result in a depersonalization not unlike that of
the psychotic. Both seem to have lost a sense of self as unique, as real.
Mystics often write that they feel unreal about themselves, that the only
reality is God. They become distant from feelings or needs, aloof and alienated from a concrete sense of personhood. In his examination of mystics'
potential regression in the service of the ego, Prince (1966) suggested that

many develop the "imperceptivity" of infancy: They become unresponsive to auditory or tactile stimulation, and withdraw into an impervious autistic shell.

9. "There exists increasing evidence that many individuals who experience episodes of non-ordinary states of consciousness accompanied by various emotional, perceptual and psychosomatic manifestations, are undergoing an evolutionary crisis rather than suffering from a mental disease. If properly understood, and treated as different stages in a natural developmental process, these experiences, 'spiritual emergencies' or transpersonal crises, can result in emotional and psychosomatic health, creative problem-solving, personality transformation and conscious evolution" (Grof, 1984, p. 4).

10. The early Christian Father Origen, for example, took literally Jesus' "pluck out your eyes rather than be sinful with them" when he castrated himself in order to avoid sexual feelings.

11. Erich Neumann called it the *gesttaltwerdung:* "that is, the turning into form of what until then had been just formless energy" (1989, p. 41).

12. Kris made control the salient factor in regression that turns it into a regression in service of the ego as opposed to pathological regression: "Inspiration—in which the ego controls the primary process and puts it into service—needs to be contrasted with the opposite, the psychotic condition in which the ego is overwhelmed by the primary process" (1952, p. 60). The psychotic does not feel in control of tapped unconscious processes and so is frightened, even paralyzed, by the inner feelings and conflicts that reveal her to herself. The psychologist Wild performed several experimental studies that compared how creativity in art students made them feel about themselves with how creativity in schizophrenics made them feel (1965, p. 169). He concluded that a major difference between the two was that art students were excited about what their art had to tell them about themselves while schizophrenics were fearful of the introspective nature of their art. The psychotic might have been enchanted by what she experienced in the regressed inspirational stage of creativity, especially by the heightened awareness. But lacking the control of nonpsychotic art students, she was not able to manage what was experienced. She could remain hyperexcited by the experience or tremble in fear, but could not make the revealing experience an integral part of her identity. The artist, on the other hand, was able to organize—through her disciplined work—what was experienced within her unconscious into a self-identity, and thereby be inspired by the variety of drives and needs she experienced.

13. The ability to "play about with psychosis," to acknowledge unconscious forces and to entertain them in one's mind, constitutes creativity (Winnicott, 1965). In the process of surrendering oneself to unconscious

processes, Jung and others recognized that the hidden feelings and drives that once would have been overbearing and thus incapable of being acknowledged instead are acceptable and even exciting. Ehrenzweig suggested one reason for this was that the "sane artist" was able to find within himself a secure realm in which inspirational unconscious processes safely incubate, and so could "absorb the ego's temporary decompensation into the rhythm of creativity," while the psychotic artist experiences the loss of ego as fragmenting and finds "inside himself a hostile nothingness" (1967, p. 124).

14. The schizophrenic, on the other hand, usually drowns in unconscious processes. Society perceives her experience as an aberration to be cured rather than as a crisis that if the individual is guided through it, can become a gateway to self-understanding. The schizophrenic's experience usually is extremely private and isolated, taking place away from the supports of society and thereby causing her to feel less confident with unconscious processes. "The essential difference between the psychosocial environments of the schizophrenic and the shaman lies in the pervasiveness of the anxiety that complicates each of their lives. The emotional supports and the modes of collective solutions of the basic problems of existence available to the shaman greatly alleviate the strain of an otherwise excruciatingly painful existence. Such supports are all too often completely unavailable to the schizophrenic in our culture" (Silverman, 1979, p. 124).

15. Rank wrote about the "will to form" (1932, p. 273), and Tillich spoke of the "I" that comes into being out of the nothingness of religious experience: "The courage to be is rooted in the God who appears when God has disappeared in the anxiety of doubt" (1952, p. 190). I suggest that in the will to paint, in confronting the conflicts and expressing the unconscious processes that arose in the regressed state, the "courage to be" arises.

16. The failure to give structure to recovered unconscious processes, on the other hand, causes their surge into consciousness to be at best a cathartic explosion of emotions and at worst an act of self-destruction. The mythological figure Icarus represents the individual whose experience of unconstrained primary process—symbolized in his ability to fly—led not to creativity but to domination by those processes until they destroyed him. Intoxicated by the freedom to fly—i.e., having ecstatically lost his limited self to unbounded primary process—Icarus forgot to place constraints around his wishes, as his father Daedalus had warned, and kept flying higher until the sun melted his wings and he plunged to his death.

17. The anger and other assertive expressions of what he experienced are, if healthy, direct expressions of feelings or the desire to master a task rather than expressions of the need to dominate those onto whom repressed aggression is projected.

18. Chaotic unconscious processes resurrected in religious experience

are organized in their elaboration—an organization whose original absence contributed to spontaneity and inspiration but whose later presence became critical to creativity. That is, primitive processes are valuable in their undifferentiated openness, in their nonautomatized capacity to take in information without routinizing it into preconceived categories. But this early undifferentiated perception eventually must be able to do something with that which it has taken it. It must develop a cognitive capacity to record experiences, to organize and to make sense of it, which acting on that experience effectively accomplishes.

19. Spiritual directors, roshis, or gurus perform critically important functions within these traditions. They keep the spiritual sojourner from becoming lost or prematurely straying into areas too frightening. (They also can lead the individual into them, but that is another subject.) Laing (1967, p. 133) (previously quoted) stated that the regressive descent into the unconscious can lead to breakthrough as well as breakdown. He concluded that what decided one or the other is a *good* guide.

20. The same can be said of the person who in therapy regresses to a primitive unconscious and finds that the therapeutic alliance "saves him from being 'swallowed and lost' in his disorganization" (Giovacchini, 1972, p. 304).

21. Freud observed this phenomenon in the actions of a young child. During brief separations from mother, a child was observed by Freud rolling a spool with thread attached to it. When he rolled the spool away, he would express "o-o-o-o," and when he rolled it back he was visibly excited. Freud called the game "disappearance and return." He suggested that the child was able to overcome his anxiety about separating from his mother by turning the loss of the object—separation from his mother, represented by rolling the spool out of sight—into a repeated action of separation and return (1920a, p. 15).

22. The experience can also be kept alive by clinging to it, by institutionalizing it and ritualisticly replicating it. This, however, has the effect of deadening the experience. It solidifies the regressive reestablishment of the infantile quiescence that resulted when all needs are met and hence desire is lost in the pervasively peaceful/pleasurable state. Unitive experience can be kept alive, on the other hand, by living it, by acting on what was experienced and thereby transforming the desire that originally manifested itself in a defensive clinging to unity into a passionate desire to live the experience.

23. The same can be said of the person in a transference relationship who, by acting on what is experienced, is able to let go of that merged state and to return more confidently to reality. Hence the transference relationship between Freud and his mentor Fleiss (Kohut, 1971) ignited a creative

spark in Freud that led to fruition when Freud elaborated on that experience (and in the process relinquished his unconscious attachment to Fleiss).

24. Jung said that tension was a salient ingredient of creativity (quoted earlier), while Fromm said that a lack of tension "leads to marginal and superficial experiences, which exclude creativity" (1959, p. 52).

25. Because the psychotic's experience of unconscious processes, on the other hand, does not have the structure through which to act on or to make sense of it, it has no relevance to those outside his experience and remains meaningful only to his private idiosyncratic inner world. LaBarre described the prophet's success in being a prophet: "The more he expressed a real social need, the more he succeeded; but the more he expressed a mere narcissistic wish, the more he failed." For example, "Moses and Aaron handled snakes, and so did George Went Hensley. But Moses and Aaron also embodied larger social and ethical ends; the Southern snake handlers, absorbed in strictly personal sins, were a poor second in this feature" (1970, p. 613).

26. Numerous Christians, for example, have equated prayer with uttering the words "Our Father, who art. . . ." They do this because Jesus, when asked how to pray, said those words. Jesus, however, was teaching prayer as a reverential attitude, voiced in words that express that attitude, not prayer as the recitation of those particular words. Jesus' words were not the experience but were the finger pointing to the experience. Benjamin Franklin's aphorism is simple but appropriate: "What significance knowing the name if you know not the nature of things."

27. On a deeper level the artist might crave the audience's approval, in its approval of her work, and the religious individual might feel a need for some approval due to the uncertainties surrounding the "darker" or more precarious aspects of her experience.

28. The passivity and submissiveness of the unitive state was a defense against aggression; by suspending assertiveness and restoring primitive symbiosis the experience turned back the original developmental progression from primitive processes and passivity to adult secondary functioning and activity. Although this regressively restored symbiotic state has the potential to become a safe environment, free of stress and stereotypical thinking, within which repressed unconscious processes again could incubate, it too is essentially a passive state.

29. Imitative art, especially as found in the representational art of the Renaissance, did have its admirers, who looked on it as the attempt to duplicate precisely that which was perceived in nature, thereby instilling within the artist a clear appreciation of nature.

30. Not only is the inspirational irruption not in itself creative; it can be

psychotic. It is doing something with that which is inspirational that saved the artist from the latter experience: "All that distinguished me from a foolish madman was my quest to work through with my own powers what had deeply stirred me, to earn with my own merit what I had received," Goethe said.

31. Even the surrealists, who attempted to penetrate directly into the unconscious and to express what they experienced (and hence acknowledged their debt to Freud for his revealing the way into the unconscious), still gave shape to that unconscious via the frame of their canvas or celluloid strip.

32. Mozart's auditory hallucinations were "real" but their reality was not clearly defined until they took shape and form on the musical score. The psychotic, on the other hand, experiences an equally "real" vision or hallucination yet is unable to express it. She cannot give it shape or elaborate it. She instead makes her vision as real to her as the concrete works of art that express an inspirational vision are real to the artist. So too the mystic who, not unlike the psychotic, misinterprets visions for reality, makes her inner world of fantasy more real than the outside world. She is more comfortable with visions and ecstasy than with maintaining contact with external reality. What is real is what is in her mind and not what she does with what is in her mind, and so visions and euphoric feelings are as real to her as dreams are real to a psychotic or to a frightened child.

33. The artist is "given" inspiration while what she does with it is the "created" (Winnicott, 1975, p. 711).

34. The psychiatrist Deikman (1976) called the former the "receptive" and the latter the "active" aspects of bimodal consciousness. The receptive mode is rooted in the perceptual-sensory system of infancy, that of taking in stimuli, while the active mode does not commence until the later development of muscles that enable the infant to act on what was taken in. While the receptive mode is inspirational and the return to it in adulthood is critical to restoring inspiration, it must be acted on if it is to be constructive or creative.

35. The psychotic, on the other hand, does not have to do anything with what was incubating in her unconscious for it to be brought to life. Simply because she does not act on what was uncovered in the regressive descent into the unconscious does not keep her from thinking that her experience directly affects the world. Kris examined this type of thinking in his study of the difference between the way in which healthy artists perceive the effect of their work and the perception of psychotic artists (1952, p. 62). He suggested that a psychotic artist believes that what she expresses on her canvas actually changes people (just as the experience changed her). While

she substitutes magic for aesthetics, the healthy artist on the other hand knows that her painting does not directly change people. She recognizes that her work might influence people, or inspire them, but knows that it does not magically manipulate them (as in voodoo practices). So too healthy religious people might believe that praying in a monastery can indirectly influence others but they do not believe it directly changes their lives. To believe that sitting on a mountain or praying in a monastery, without having to do anything with that experience, will directly affect others is, like the psychotic's experience, a magical attempt to twist reality (usually to fit a self-fulfilling image). "Art has deteriorated from communication to sorcery" (Kris, 1952, p. 61).

36. W. Somerset Maugham said the same when he wrote in his *Writer's Notebook* that the value of art is not in beauty alone "but in right action. . . . Art, unless it leads to right action, is no more than the opium of an intelligentsia." And René Descartes wrote: "For it is not enough to have a good mind: one must use it well. The greatest goods are capable of the greatest vices as well as the greatest virtues; and those who walk slowly can, if they follow the right path, go much further than those who run rapidly in the wrong direction."

EPILOGUE

1. Kohut offered a similar view of the transference relationship: "We define therapeutic progress toward mental health not primarily by reference to expanded knowledge or increased ego autonomy, but by reference to the laying down of permanent self structure via optimal frustration" (1984, p. 153).

Index